God Knows What It's Like To Be A Teenager

Teen Life and the Psalms

by

Mark Marshall

139 Press

GOD KNOWS WHAT IT'S LIKE TO BE A TEENAGER

Copyright, Mark Marshall © 2001

All Bible quotations are taken from the New American Standard Version of the Bible. Permission granted from the Lockman Foundation.

Pulished by 139 Press
Need of the Times Publishers

ISBN 0-9647552-5-4
Library of Congress Card Catalog Number - Pending

Printed in U.S.A.

Acknowledgments

I want to thank all those who encouraged, helped, and prayed for me and this work. These include Keith Chancey, Rob Shiflet, Rick Mill, and Denny Mulder. Thanks to Tommy Nelson for his excellent teaching on Psalms and on the whole Bible, and for putting his name on the line for me. Jimmy McWhinney and Luke Zimmerman gave me the push I needed to be more of a team player.

Mack Tomlinson stretched the boundaries of his editing and publishing to include me. I am grateful to him -- and to Augie Zimmerman for referring me to Mack!

Jeff the Girl and the rest of Five Iron Frenzy are so cool. It would be so easy for her to say they're too busy to help me out. And with their crazy schedule, they are busy. But she was crazy enough to enthusiastically help me out and write the foreword.

MxPx, Jars of Clay, John Reuben, Keith Green and Moby have inspired me and countless people. I'm grateful to be able to use some of their words.

Thanks to Joshua Stevens (pen name. He's humble.) for sharing his poetry with me and now with the world.

I especially appreciate the many teens who helped me write this book and prayed for me. Among them are Luke Batey, Christy Bedford, Brian Haley, and Aaron Kirakofe (Semper fi!). Thanks to Nancy (Nansi14) for her help with Psalm 6, to Nicole M., Amy D., Linus, Miranda K., Lia B., Laura L., Megans, D.M. (for the "hippies" idea), and Augusta J. And special thanks to David Martin and his class.

What an awesome word from Allysa! Thanks to her and all the others who have sent encouraging emails.

With his graphics genius, Ryan helped me big time with both the book cover and web site. Timothy Sheaff put a lot of work and creativity into what the book looks like in between the covers.

Thanks to Markuss, Aaron, and Ben for being seen in all their punkishness by thousands. Oi!

Thanks to Senator for being Sent.

Because of space and my defective memory, I've probably left a lot of names out. But I've seen God use all sorts of people to encourage me, teach me, and, yeah, love me with His love. You all have an important role in who I am and in what this book is. God knows who you are, and I thank you.

Above all, I thank my Lord, Who inspired me and strengthened me through this whole project. I'm especially grateful for the Psalms. Without them, this work and my sanity would not be possible.

Mark Marshall
Denton, Texas
Spring, 2001

Foreword

Throughout history, music has been an important means of communicating the values, beliefs, dreams and hopes of a culture. But does our mainstream picture of music offer even a glimpse of what it is like to be a teenager today? By turning on Mtv, VH1 or BET, one can see how the reality of life is masked over by video image dreams and fears of a new culture. The complexity of teens is distorted as well.

Still, today's music speaks to teens' emotions and hopes. Entertainers of all genres hold the teenage population in their hands, branding them into groups based on what style of music they listen to. The hardcore kids, the punks, the emo kids etc... Millions of teens recruit themselves into these groups based on what style of music they prefer and what particular type of mood they like to evoke from that music.

People in biblical times weren't that much different. Their identities and deepest thoughts were intertwined with their songs. Music spoke for the masses and was used to evoke one to a spiritual harmony with the God of the Old Testament.Throughout the Bible, lyrics speak of God's goodness, His promises and amazing feats. Music also allowed a young man named David to voice his fears to a generation that at times loved and followed him, only to despise him later.

Every care-free spirit found in ska, every ethereal mood found in techno, or overwhelming somber reflection from emo can be traced in the Psalms. From 1 to 150, David and other's Psalms depict an accurate picture of God working in a person's life. Not always predictable or manageable, but drenched in the emotion and chaos of the day's events.

God Knows What It's Like to be a Teenager addresses the vision of the Psalms. God chose the little things, the frantic people in hiding, wrestling with everyday life, to shame the wise scholars of even today's Christendom prestige.

Likewise, God uses teens of the 2000's to speak to world leaders, using new technologies qualitatively characteristic of an age of computer communication, other times using music.

I write this foreword not because I am an intellectual and have studied the Psalms in great detail, nor because I have a degree in teenage psychology, or any such credentials. I speak in music with my seven cohorts of Five Iron Frenzy. But it would be a lie to say that we have created something out of nothing. God and Psalms and music He has inspired though the ages has inspired us, and always will.

If the Psalms mirror a person's life, then sadly many teens and musicians today are missing the hope and joy found in Psalms 47 and 150 while concentrating only on downbeat fragments of Psalm 88. We should seek to take in all that the Psalms have to show us about all of life. That takes much more than just one CD or one book. But Mark's one book digs deep into the Psalms' reflections on life, especially teen life.

God Knows What It's Like to be a Teenager sees all the Psalms, with all their highs and lows, as relevant today. This is the vital point. Weigh God's words against deceptions posing as "reality." And never forget the One who is really worthy to be deemed a role model.

Leanor "Jeff the Girl" Ortega
saxophone, Five Iron Frenzy
March, 2001

Read this first!! . . .

or you might not know what's going on when you read this book. God Knows is probably different than what you're used to, so listen up.

For each psalm (except for 119), you'll see the psalm itself written out, then you'll see my piece, say "FROM PSALM 77." In most of the "FROM" pieces, I respond to a psalm the way I think a teenager might. You'll see I try different things and different "voices."

But I want to be clear on something so no one feels misled: the teenagers talking in the pieces are hypothetical teenagers, not any particular ones I know. Although I got a lot of input from teens, I'm the one who wrote the pieces. If I mess up, that's my fault, not any teenager's fault. If you like what I wrote, remember God and a lot of teenagers helped me.

Speaking of which, some of the excellent poetry and lyrics I quote before the pieces is from teenagers.

In some of the book, I'm not taking on the role of a teenager, I'm simply talking to you. A few of the psalm pieces and all the general pieces, like "TRUSTING GOD", are that way. You'll probably be able to tell these just from reading them. But to be safe, I put my initials, M. M., at the end where it's just me talking.

One last thing, but it's important -- because God's word is much more important than whatever I write about it. For each psalm, be sure to read the actual psalm, not just my piece from it.

Thanks.

M. M.

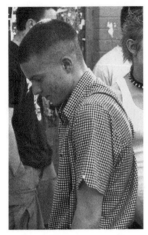

God Knows
What It's Like
To Be A Teenager

When you think about God, what do you think about?

A lot of people think about how powerful, infinite, and big He is. You might think about how He knows everything. Or how perfect and holy He is. Maybe you think about His love, how He cares.

But do you ever think of God as understanding? As someone who can relate to us? Do you think of God as someone who understands teenagers and can relate to them?

Most people don't see God that way, either because they just haven't thought of it or because they see God as so far above us that He just doesn't relate. Many wonder if He's there at all, much less there for us.

Then, of course, there are some funny ideas around about God. Like a few people think He gets up in the morning, stretches, then thinks, "Hmm. Who am I going to zap today?" They don't view God as very understanding.

Well, God isn't that way -- thank God.

God is high above us. Yet He knows us, far better than we know ourselves. Parents and other adults might not be able to figure you out, especially if you're a teenager, but God is able to. God understands us because He knows everything. He knows everything about you. After all, He created you. He knows your difficulties. He knows all your thoughts -- there's a scary thought. He knows and understands you like no one else can.

He's proven that to me in the Psalms. From my teen years on, no matter what I was feeling or thinking, no matter what I was going through, I've always been able to find a psalm that related to where I was at. I don't know how many times when I needed some encouragement from God or needed help to pray or just needed to know He cared, that I found what I needed in the Psalms.

That's why this book uses them. All the open emotions and

experiences of Psalms show God understands what it's like to be human. And with their being so intense, like being teen, they show He especially knows what it's like to be a teenager.

But what's even better is God more than knows.

For He doesn't just know us from far away. He's experienced being one of us.

For in Jesus, God came down and became one of us.

And He didn't take any shortcuts. He gave up all He had in heaven, came down here, and became a baby. And not some royal baby in a silk crib in a palace, although being King, He had every right to that. He was born in a barn, even in a feeding trough (That's what a "manger" is in the Christmas carol.) Although He was the Son of the King, He was born a carpenter's son.

He went through the humility of being a little child. He had to obey His parents like any other kid, and He did (Luke 2:51), even though He was the one who possessed all authority.

Jesus had to be different, and that made Him a target. So He perhaps got picked on and maybe beat up by other kids, though He had the power and the right to wipe them out.

But then, being an awesome friend, Jesus surely had close friends. Who wouldn't want to have the kid Jesus as a friend?

He experienced the joys of childhood and appreciated them more than the average kid. But those were nothing compared to the joys of heaven He gave up.

Then Jesus became -- a teenager.

Now the Bible doesn't say a whole lot about His teen years. One thing I definitely want to do in heaven is go back in time and see what the teenage Jesus was like.

But the Bible does give us a look at what Jesus was like right before He went teen. Luke 2: 41 - 52 tells us something that happened when He was 12.

41And His parents used to go to Jerusalem every year at the Feast of the Passover. 42And when He became twelve, they went up there according to the custom of the Feast; 43and as they were returning, after spending the full number of days, the boy Jesus stayed behind in Jerusalem. And His parents were unaware of it, 44but supposed Him to be in the caravan, and went a day's journey; and they began looking for Him among their relatives and acquaintances. 45And when they did not find Him, they returned to Jerusalem, looking for Him. 46And it came about that after three days they found Him in the temple, sitting in the midst of the teachers, both listening to them, and asking them questions. 47And all who heard Him were amazed at His understanding and His answers. 48And when they saw Him, they were astonished; and His mother said to Him, "Son, why have You treated us this way? Behold, Your father and I have been anxiously looking for You." 49And His said to them, "Why is it that you were looking for Me? Did you not know that I had to be in My Father's house?" (a more literal translation: "in the things of My Father?") 50And they did not understand the statement which He had made to them. 51And He went down with them, and came to Nazareth; and He continued in subjection to them; and His mother treasured all these things in her heart. 52And Jesus kept increasing in wisdom and stature, and in favor with God and men.

He and His family went to celebrate Passover in Jerusalem. Passover was the biggest Jewish holiday of the year. Now the custom was that a Jewish boy would first go up to Jerusalem for Passover at 12 or 13. His family lived a long journey away in Nazareth, so this was probably Jesus' first time to see the capital of Israel and the Temple. This was a big time for Him, like a kid's first visit to Disney World or Washington, D.C.

At the end of Passover, Jesus wasn't in a big hurry to go back home. He stayed behind while His parents began the journey home.

So Jesus had an independent streak that comes along near the beginning of the teen years. He doesn't want to be around mom and dad all the time. He honored His parents and obeyed them perfectly (yet more proof He was God). But He wants to do His thing, too. For Him, that meant being into "the things of My Father."

Do you want to do your thing? Do you have an urge to go beyond being just your mom's kid? Jesus can relate.

It took a day's journey for His parents to figure out He wasn't with them in the caravan. That's like your parents driving all day before they figured out you're not in the minivan and they left you behind.

Do your parents seem clueless sometimes? Jesus has been there.

When they finally found Him in the Temple and asked Him what He was doing there, He gave an honest answer -- which His parents didn't get at all.

Do your parents ever misunderstand you? Jesus really knows what that's like. Not only was He a twelve-year-old, He was God. So you can imagine how much His parents didn't understand Him.

And not just as a twelve-year-old, but His whole life, people didn't get Jesus. Even His brothers and disciples didn't get Him. Check it out in the gospels. He was probably the most misunderstood man who ever lived. Do you feel misunderstood?

Jesus knows where you're at -- because He has been there like nobody has.

Pretty soon after that Passover, Jesus became a teenager. Luke says in verse 52, "Jesus kept increasing in wisdom and stature, and in favor with God and men." Then we don't hear much else until he's around 30.

Still, Jesus was a real live teenager.

And He doesn't forget what it's like to be one like some adults do. He knows where you're at. He's been there, and He remembers.

Do you find your emotions are more up and down than they used to be back when you were just a kid? Are your emotions a real roller coaster sometimes? Well, that's something teens usually go through. Jesus experienced teenage emotions, too. He understands.

Do you want to be more independent? To have more freedom? And sometimes with those desires come conflict with parents and other authorities? Jesus had those desires, too. We saw even before 13 there was a little friction with his parents about what freedom is appropriate and what isn't. Jesus never sinned against his parents, but part of being teen is eagerly wanting more freedom when others are not eagerly giving it. Jesus has been there.

Have you ever had a zit? Well, Jesus probably did, too. He knows what that's like.

Jesus also experienced -- hormones. That's right. And He experienced all the craziness, emotion, energy, and yes, temptation that goes along with hormones.

What's amazing is He had a full set of teenage guy hormones -- and never sinned, not even in His thoughts. You might say, "Get out! Only God can do that." Well -- you're right!

Something important in the Bible to remember is in Hebrews 4:15. It says Jesus is not someone "who cannot sympathize with our weaknesses, but one who has been tempted in all things as we are, yet without sin." So Jesus didn't sin in any way, but He was tempted. And that includes sexual temptation, along with all the other temptations that come with being teen.

If anything, Jesus's temptations may have been more intense because He was a target of Satan. (Check out Luke 4:1-13 for starters.)

So if you've got teenage hormones and the craziness and temptations that come with them, Jesus can relate. He's been there.

And as you go through all the fun, intensity, hope, and difficulties of being teen, Jesus understands -- because He once was a teenager, too.

This is what is awesome about Christmas. God came down and became human. He became one of us. That's what Immanuel means: "God with us" -- He became one of us and lived with us. He didn't have to do that. He didn't have to love us like that. But He did. And He does.

There might be times when you feel nobody understands you. Times when your parents don't get you. Times when your friends look at you like you're a space alien. There may be times when even your dog doesn't understand you.

But you can know God understands what it's like to be you. Because He knows, not just in His head. He knows first hand what it's like to be one of us. Because in the person of Jesus, God became one of us.

In Jesus, God became one of you. He became a twelve-year-old. He became a teenager. That's how much He understands you. That's how much He loves you.

God knows what it's like to be you.

God knows what it's like to be a teenager.

Because He was one.

M. M.

Psalm 1

1   How blessed is the man who does not walk in the counsel of the
wicked, Nor stand in the path of sinners, Nor sit in the seat of scoffers!

2   But his delight is in the law of the LORD,
And in His law he meditates day and night.

3   He will be like a tree firmly planted by streams of water,
Which yields its fruit in its season
And its leaf does not wither;
And in whatever he does, he prospers.

4   The wicked are not so,
But they are like chaff which the wind drives away.

5   Therefore the wicked will not stand in the judgment,
Nor sinners in the assembly of the righteous.

6   For the LORD knows the way of the righteous,
But the way of the wicked will perish.

I will make a difference.

from PSALM 1

Sometimes, I wonder if it really makes a difference if I do the right thing.

I see people who are popular and have lots of friends. And they are popular because they do the wrong things. Then, I have friends or people I want to be my friends, and they make me choose between doing the right thing and them. 'Cause if I don't do what they do, I know they'll drop me. I have to admit, what they want to do usually looks fun, too. It's hard to not act like them, even if that's not who I am or who I want to be. They can make the wrong way look better.

But I know living straight and doing the right thing does make a difference, even if it doesn't seem so right now. My life will be where it belongs, not in some place where it will fall apart and be blown away.

God will lead me to where I belong. For I'll listen to Him; I'll get into His word every day. 'Cause I love what He says.

I will make a difference, not just always be chasing whatever I happen to crave. God meets my real needs better anyway. He will look after me, helping me grow and have the right kind of success. My life will be something awesome for the long run, not just for a few years of getting stupid.

If I live straight on the edge, listening to God's word and doing it, my life will make a difference, a difference that lasts.

Psalm 2

1   Why are the nations in an uproar
And the peoples devising a vain thing?
2   The kings of the earth take their stand
And the rulers take counsel together
Against the LORD and against His Anointed, saying,
3   "Let us tear their fetters apart
And cast away their cords from us!"

4   He who sits in the heavens laughs,
The Lord scoffs at them.
5   Then He will speak to them in His anger
And terrify them in His fury, saying,
6   "But as for Me, I have installed My King
Upon Zion, My holy mountain."

7   "I will surely tell of the decree of the LORD:
He said to Me, 'You are My Son,
Today I have begotten You.
8   'Ask of Me, and I will surely give the nations as Your inheritance,
And the very ends of the earth as Your possession.
9   'You shall break them with a rod of iron,
You shall shatter them like earthenware.'"

10   Now therefore, O kings, show discernment;
Take warning, O judges of the earth.
11   Worship the LORD with reverence
And rejoice with trembling.
12   Do homage to the Son, that He not become angry, and you perish
in the way,
For His wrath may soon be kindled.
How blessed are all who take refuge in Him!

The rulers of this world are not only evil; they're stupid.

from PSALM 2

When I was just a kid, I didn't pay any attention to the news, and I wondered why my parents got so worked up when it was on. Well, now that I'm not so clueless about what's going on in the world, I know. And I get even more worked up than they do.

It burns me how governments and rulers can be so evil. Some will stop at nothing. If they don't like an election, they'll cancel it or steal it. If they don't like someone's beliefs, they'll jail them or kill them. If they don't like an ethnic group, they'll enslave them, exile them, starve them, or massacre them.

It's not only foreign governments. Here, we've got jerks in power who won't lift a finger to protect children about to be born and then turn around and lie about it with a straight, oh-so-sincere face.

All they care about is their power and their evil desires. They don't care about justice, freedom, or rights; they don't care about right or wrong. They have no values and no God but themselves.

But one day, God will say to them: "I rule. And I've chosen Jesus as King, not you. Do you have a problem with that?"

But the rulers of this world are not only evil; they're stupid. They do have a problem with God and His rule. Because they think they should rule, not Jesus. They are so stupid, they will side with Satan against God and His Messiah.

God will laugh at those losers. He'll have a time making fun of those puny evil fools.

Then He'll destroy them.

Their time will be over. He will shatter them and their sick power trips. And He will raise up over them those they oppressed.

Then Jesus the Messiah, the King, will take His throne. He will make everything right. There will be no more oppression and no more wrong. There will be peace, justice, and love. Jesus will make everything perfect.

When He comes to take over, I'm going to be on His side. It doesn't take a genius to see that's the place to be.

I don't care if you're the President of the United States or the King of Swaziland -- you'd better get on His side, too.

Psalm 3
A Psalm of David, when he fled from Absalom his son.

1   O LORD, how my adversaries have increased!
Many are rising up against me.
2   Many are saying of my soul,
"There is no deliverance for him in God."   Selah.

3   But You, O LORD, are a shield about me,
My glory, and the One who lifts my head.
4   I was crying to the LORD with my voice,
And He answered me from His holy mountain.   Selah.
5   I lay down and slept;
I awoke, for the LORD sustains me.

6   I will not be afraid of ten thousands of people
Who have set themselves against me round about.

7   Arise, O LORD; save me, O my God!
For You have smitten all my enemies on the cheek;
You have shattered the teeth of the wicked.
8   Salvation belongs to the LORD;
Your blessing be upon Your people!   Selah.

from PSALM 3

O Lord, I'm in a tough spot. Everyone's on my case. I even have a gang threatening me. One of them thought I looked at him the wrong way at school, and now every time I walk down the hall, someone's telling me I'm dead meat.

But, Lord, You protect me. It's a good thing! You watch my back. You surround me with Your protection like body armor, better even.

If anything gets to me, it has to get through You first. Remembering that helps me sleep at night.

I've been in fixes before -- Lord, don't I know that -- I was down. But I prayed, and you answered me. You encouraged me and lifted my head up. You came through for me. It blows my mind, as big and lofty as You are, that You care about me that much.

Maybe I shouldn't be scared. I can get out of bed in the morning and face whatever comes down. Because all the gangs in the school, in the whole stinking town, are nothing compared to You. If You protect me, I'm protected. It could be thousands of them against You and me.

We have them outnumbered.

Still, I'm in a fix. I need Your help again. Please shield me and get me out of this mess. For You're the only one who can.

Psalm 4

For the choir director; on stringed instruments. A Psalm of David.

1   Answer me when I call, O God of my righteousness!
You have relieved me in my distress;
Be gracious to me and hear my prayer.

2   O sons of men, how long will my honor become a reproach?
How long will you love what is worthless and aim at deception?
Selah.
3   But know that the LORD has set apart the godly man for Himself;

The LORD hears when I call to Him.

4 Tremble, and do not sin;
Meditate in your heart upon your bed, and be still. Selah.
5 Offer the sacrifices of righteousness,
And trust in the LORD.

6 Many are saying, "Who will show us any good?"
Lift up the light of Your countenance upon us, O LORD!
7 You have put gladness in my heart,
More than when their grain and new wine abound.
8 In peace I will both lie down and sleep,
For You alone, O LORD, make me to dwell in safety.

from PSALM 4

I don't think I'll ever understand why some people do the things they do. These people at school are spreading lies about me. Even the good about me they twist into something bad.

Why do they get their kicks doing that? Why do they love doing what is sorry and worthless? Why do they always choose deception and lies over the truth?

Yet I know, even if they do their worst, the Lord looks after me and hears my prayers. I belong to Him; He'll take care of me.

Still, what they're doing seriously ticks me off. About all I can do is try to calm down and be cool -- and pray. Instead of doing something stupid out of anger, I need to keep on doing right, even if I might not feel like it and even if others don't like it. And I need to keep on trusting God.

Lord, no matter what they say, You know me as I really am. You understand me. And, even when it seems I can't trust anyone, I can trust you.

When things are bad, like now, I can feel like things will never be good again. But, sometimes sooner, sometimes later, they always are. The light of Your smile makes everything all right in the end.

They think its fun to trash people, to trash me. But the gladness You give me inside dogs any jollies they get.

No matter how crazy life gets, You give me peace, too. So I'm gonna lie down and sleep well. Because I know You protect me. You make me feel safe like no one else can.

Psalm 5

For the choir director; for flute accompaniment. A Psalm of David.

1   Give ear to my words, O LORD,
   Consider my groaning.
2   Heed the sound of my cry for help, my King and my God,
   For to You I pray.
3   In the morning, O LORD, You will hear my voice;
   In the morning I will order my prayer to You and eagerly watch.

4   For You are not a God who takes pleasure in wickedness;
   No evil dwells with You.
5   The boastful shall not stand before Your eyes;
   You hate all who do iniquity.
6   You destroy those who speak falsehood;
   The LORD abhors the man of bloodshed and deceit.
7   But as for me, by Your abundant lovingkindness I will enter Your
   house,
   At Your holy temple I will bow in reverence for You.

8   O LORD, lead me in Your righteousness because of my foes;
   Make Your way straight before me.
9   There is nothing reliable in what they say;
   Their inward part is destruction itself.
   Their throat is an open grave;
   They flatter with their tongue.
10   Hold them guilty, O God;
   By their own devices let them fall!
   In the multitude of their transgressions thrust them out,
   For they are rebellious against You.

11   But let all who take refuge in You be glad,
   Let them ever sing for joy;
   And may You shelter them,
   That those who love Your name may exult in You.
12   For it is You who blesses the righteous man, O LORD,
   You surround him with favor as with a shield.

Lord, I try to live right.

from PSALM 5

God, I need to talk to You. Please listen and help me. I'm gonna pray straight with You, then watch and wait for Your answer.

Lord, I try to live right. But every time I turn around, something's trying to trip me up. There are so many things pulling me where I know I shouldn't go.

I want to be honest, but when a test or a big paper comes up, I'm tempted to cheat. A lot of my friends do it and get away with it -- while I'm busting my brain studying or giving up all my free time writing a dumb paper. Then they want me to help them cheat. What am I supposed to do? They're my friends.

Then there's, uh, sex. I know it's smart to wait. But everything -- TV, magazines, ads, friends talking, girls who look just too fine -- everything says, "Do it!" And what am I supposed to do with all these desires I have? What I am supposed to say to friends who think there's something wrong with you if don't lose it?

I try to keep my mind clean -- I don't know why, it seems to be no use. Still I try. But sometimes when I'm with my friends, there's movies I shouldn't watch or drinking or worse.

Everything and everyone is pulling at me. Everyone acts like they like me and want the best for me. Half the time, you can't trust what they say. They make what's wrong seem so right. Lately, I think I don't even know the difference anymore.

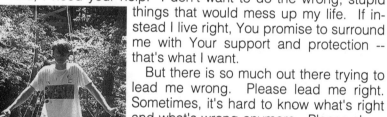

Lord, I need your help. I don't want to do the wrong, stupid things that would mess up my life. If instead I live right, You promise to surround me with Your support and protection -- that's what I want.

But there is so much out there trying to lead me wrong. Please lead me right. Sometimes, it's hard to know what's right and what's wrong anymore. Please show me. When I think about it, I know Your way is the best. Make it clear and straight for me.

Then give me the brains and the guts to live Your way. Because I don't want to mess up my life. I want it to be the best.

Psalm 6
For the choir director; with stringed instruments, upon an eight-string lyre.
A Psalm of David.

1   O LORD, do not rebuke me in Your anger,
  Nor chasten me in Your wrath.
2   Be gracious to me, O LORD, for I am pining away;
  Heal me, O LORD, for my bones are dismayed.
3   And my soul is greatly dismayed;
  But You, O LORD—how long?

4   Return, O LORD, rescue my soul;
       Save me because of Your lovingkindness.
5   For there is no mention of You in death;
       In Sheol who will give You thanks?

6   I am weary with my sighing;
       Every night I make my bed swim,
       I dissolve my couch with my tears.
7   My eye has wasted away with grief;
       It has become old because of all my adversaries.

8   Depart from me, all you who do iniquity,
       For the LORD has heard the voice of my weeping.
9   The LORD has heard my supplication,
       The LORD receives my prayer.
10   All my enemies will be ashamed and greatly dismayed;
       They shall turn back, they will suddenly be ashamed.

Why does my heart feel so bad?
Why does my soul feel so bad?

Moby "Why Does My Heart Feel So Bad?"
from *Play*

from PSALM 6

I am so depressed.

A week ago, I could tell you what I was down about. Now? -- I don't know. This heavy weight presses down upon me. It feels like it's about to crush the inside of me.

It's because of everything. It's because of nothing.

I don't want to do anything anymore. I hardly want to eat. I don't want anything, except to sleep, and someday wake up happy again. I've practically forgotten what happy is, except it's something I'm not.

I cry myself to sleep every night. When I wake, my pillow is still wet.

Oh Lord, do you really care for me? I know you do -- but then my life is like this, and I wonder. Why do you let me get so down? So down I feel like I'm dying? What good does it do? Why, Lord? How long do I have to be this way?

Lord, I know You hear me. You know my tears. And I know You answer prayer. Please do answer soon. Come and change my life because of Your love -- before I sink too far.

Psalm 7

A Shiggaion of David, which he sang to the LORD concerning Cush, a Benjamite.

1   O LORD my God, in You I have taken refuge;
Save me from all those who pursue me, and deliver me,
2   Or he will tear my soul like a lion,
Dragging me away, while there is none to deliver.

3   O LORD my God, if I have done this,
If there is injustice in my hands,
4   If I have rewarded evil to my friend,
Or have plundered him who without cause was my adversary,
5   Let the enemy pursue my soul and overtake it;
And let him trample my life down to the ground
And lay my glory in the dust.   Selah.

6   Arise, O LORD, in Your anger;
Lift up Yourself against the rage of my adversaries,
And arouse Yourself for me; You have appointed judgment.
7   Let the assembly of the peoples encompass You,
And over them return on high.
8   The LORD judges the peoples;
Vindicate me, O LORD, according to my righteousness and my integrity
that is in me.
9   O let the evil of the wicked come to an end, but establish the righteous;
For the righteous God tries the hearts and minds.
10   My shield is with God,
Who saves the upright in heart.
11   God is a righteous judge,
And a God who has indignation every day.

12   If a man does not repent, He will sharpen His sword;
He has bent His bow and made it ready.
13   He has also prepared for Himself deadly weapons;
He makes His arrows fiery shafts.
14   Behold, he travails with wickedness,
And he conceives mischief and brings forth falsehood.
15   He has dug a pit and hollowed it out,
And has fallen into the hole which he made.
16   His mischief will return upon his own head,
And his violence will descend upon his own pate.

17   I will give thanks to the LORD according to His righteousness
And will sing praise to the name of the LORD Most High.

from PSALM 7

O Lord, I'm coming to You for protection -- 'cause I need it. This thug and his friends want to kill me for something I didn't do. They were looking for an excuse to get me. So a couple of them made up this story against me, then spread it around. I told him it wasn't true, but he wouldn't listen. He doesn't care about the truth. He cares about beating me to a pulp.

God, if what they say is true, if I actually did what they say, then let them beat me up. Because if I did it, I would be so stupid, I would deserve to get beat up. But You know me, inside and out. You know I didn't do it -- even if no one else does.

So Lord, will You stick up for me and be my protection?

I'm glad You're just. I need some justice right about now. You care, too. You're not simply way up there being holy, not caring about what happens down here the way some people think You are. Instead every day, You're ticked about the evil man does. That includes the evil these goons want to do to me.

Lord, I hope they change their minds or find something better to do. But if they don't, stop them! Cause whatever plans they have against me to fail and backfire on them.

You are my shield, my firewall even. Thanks I can trust You. You are righteous. Your name is the highest.

Psalm 8
For the choir director; on the Gittith. A Psalm of David.

1   O LORD, our Lord,
How majestic is Your name in all the earth,
Who have displayed Your splendor above the heavens!
2   From the mouth of infants and nursing babes You have established strength
Because of Your adversaries,
To make the enemy and the revengeful cease.

3   When I consider Your heavens, the work of Your fingers,
The moon and the stars, which You have ordained;
4   What is man that You take thought of him,
And the son of man that You care for him?
5   Yet You have made him a little lower than God,
And You crown him with glory and majesty!
6   You make him to rule over the works of Your hands;
You have put all things under his feet,
7   All sheep and oxen,
And also the beasts of the field,

8   The birds of the heavens and the fish of the sea,
Whatever passes through the paths of the seas.

9   O LORD, our Lord,
How majestic is Your name in all the earth!

our imaginations run wild
two innocent children
idealistic dreams
and all that stuff
that becomes distorted
as time goes on
and truth begins to show
and we hide because it hurts
and its easier to run away
pretend that we're still worth something
and not go out on clear nights
because the infinite stars
show our smallness and frailness
and i'd rather make snow angels with you
on a cloudy, snowy night
with the street lights of this small town
shining down

joshua stevens, age 15, from "untitled"

from PSALM 8

One night I was camping out. It was warm so I slept outside my tent. I lay there in my sleeping bag on the grass. For a long time, I looked up at the stars.

The sky was incredible. It was real clear, like perfect crystal. There must have been thousands of stars out. The whole sky was sparkling.

As I lay there, looking up, I thought about how awesome God must be to create all those stars. And He created trillions of more stars I could not see. To make something as huge and as beautiful as the universe -- it almost gave me a headache thinking about it. God is so -- big.

Then I thought, we're like a speck of dust compared to God and all He's created. I wondered why we would be important to Him. He has the whole universe to care for and enjoy. Why would He care about us? We're so small. I'm so small.

But the same creativity He used in creating the universe, He uses in creating us. There are billions of people. Yet we're all different. We all have ways in which we're cool. All of us: from certain ones who look so good to friends who may not get as much attention but work with the poor and are just awesome friends; from athletes to artists; from Shara and her voice to Fred and his musical burps. He's made us all unique. He's created us all in His image. I don't think I'll ever completely understand what that means, but it's got to be special.

He's given us the whole world to take care of and enjoy. He's given us intelligence and creativity, including the ability to put up those satellites I saw moving across the sky. He's even given us fun camping overnights, like that night.

He does care about us. He made us. He provides for us.

He even died for us.

To me, that's what makes God great. He's big enough to create an entire universe -- a thousand universes if He wants. Yet He's so cool, even though we're so small compared to Him, He loves us and cares about us.

He cares about me.

SIGNIFICANCE

A deep need most of us have is the need to be significant. Most people strive to be significant their whole lives. Little kids often want to be the center of attention and will get obnoxious to get the attention they want. Older kids and teens try to gain status through looking good. They focus a lot on their styling, their clothes, their hair, and, of course, mirrors. Or they may try to become significant through sports or grades or a cool boyfriend or girlfriend. Older teenagers may try to be something by driving a cool car.

Adults, too, often try to build themselves up through what they own. They work hard to make money to buy more and more. Adults also try to gain significance through becoming important. They strive for success in their work, maybe hoping to get a fancy title, like chairman or chief executive officer. Or they might seek importance through politics, social climbing, or even good things, such as civic organizations, like the Mooses, the Kiwanis, or even church positions.

There's one slight problem with all these and a lot of other ways of trying to gain significance.

They don't work.

Let me save you a lot of trouble. If you get what I'm about to tell you, you'll be way ahead of a lot of adults, because a lot of them waste most or even all of their lives before they get this: When someone actually does achieve all the success they want in their self-centered striving to be something -- then they want more. And then when they get more success -- they want more. And they get more and more until, one day, they think,

"Is this all there is?"

And instead of feeling significant, they feel empty.

This world and all the things and ego trips in this world cannot give us the significance we need.

Real significance comes from God. It comes from Him creating you in His image, with God-like qualities like creativity and intelligence. It comes from Him loving you so much He even died for you. And if you trust in Jesus and His death for you, you discover He chose you to be His child long before you were born and has already prepared important work for you to do. (Ephesians 2: 8-10)

Imagine the President of the United States calls you into the Oval Office. Imagine he's a great president you have the highest respect for. (And, depending on when you're reading this, that may take a lot of imagination.) He tells you, "You may not realize it, but my men and I have been watching you since you were born. And yes, we know you're the one who set that fire. You know what fire I'm talking about. I know everything else about you, too.

"But in spite of all that, I want you to join my team. I'm not going to hold any of your past against you. And I have an important assignment I've chosen you for."

You would feel pretty stinking important. Well, God has done all that and more for you and for everyone who comes to Jesus.

I know for me personally, the times when I feel the most important and loved is when I know God is using me in others' lives, especially when those others let me know in their own way I'm important to them. Sometimes, maybe after just a phone call with a brother I'm working with, I could walk on air. It's hard to beat knowing God has chosen you to make a difference in people's lives. It surely thrashes trying to be something by being self-centered.

More even than that, God adopts us into His family, even making us co-heirs with Jesus! That means, for starters, when Jesus comes back to rule, we'll rule, too. (Romans 8: 16-17; Revelation 5: 9-10 and 22:5)

You can't get any more significant than that.

I've only begun talking about the significance God gives us through Jesus. So if you want to spend a lot of time in front of the mirror styling your hair, or if you want to risk your life and go out for football, or if you want to work to get that hot car, or if you enjoy being popular, that's O.K. Just don't try to gain your value or importance from these things. Your real value comes from God. Trust in Him and put Him first, and you will be more significant than you or even your mom can imagine.

M. M.

Psalm 9
For the choir director; on Muth-labben. A Psalm of David.

1   I will give thanks to the LORD with all my heart;
I will tell of all Your wonders.
2   I will be glad and exult in You;
I will sing praise to Your name, O Most High.

3   When my enemies turn back,
They stumble and perish before You.
4   For You have maintained my just cause;
You have sat on the throne judging righteously.
5   You have rebuked the nations, You have destroyed the wicked;
You have blotted out their name forever and ever.
6   The enemy has come to an end in perpetual ruins,
And You have uprooted the cities;
The very memory of them has perished.

7   But the LORD abides forever;
He has established His throne for judgment,
8   And He will judge the world in righteousness;
He will execute judgment for the peoples with equity.
9   The LORD also will be a stronghold for the oppressed,
A stronghold in times of trouble;
10   And those who know Your name will put their trust in You,
For You, O LORD, have not forsaken those who seek You.

11   Sing praises to the LORD, who dwells in Zion;
Declare among the peoples His deeds.
12   For He who requires blood remembers them;
He does not forget the cry of the afflicted.
13   Be gracious to me, O LORD;
See my affliction from those who hate me,
You who lift me up from the gates of death,

14   That I may tell of all Your praises,
      That in the gates of the daughter of Zion
      I may rejoice in Your salvation.
15   The nations have sunk down in the pit which they have made;
      In the net which they hid, their own foot has been caught.
16   The LORD has made Himself known;
      He has executed judgment.
      In the work of his own hands the wicked is snared.   Higgaion Selah.

17   The wicked will return to Sheol,
      Even all the nations who forget God.
18   For the needy will not always be forgotten,
      Nor the hope of the afflicted perish forever.
19   Arise, O LORD, do not let man prevail;
      Let the nations be judged before You.
20   Put them in fear, O LORD;
      Let the nations know that they are but men.   Selah.

Knowing You is the best.

from PSALM 9
Note: In Hebrew thought, a "name" refers to one's character. For example, to say, "His name is trustworthy" is to say His character is trustworthy.

O God, You are wonderful. You do awesome things all the time. You do them for me and for anyone who sincerely prays and seeks You. I can't keep it to myself.

So many times, You've answered my prayers and helped me when I was hurting. I used to wonder if You really cared. Now I know better. Because now I know You better. I know I can trust You to be there for me and never forget me. I know, just because of who You are.

I remember one time when I was way down. I was thinking about death a lot and even felt close to it. But I cried and prayed to You. And You lifted me up. Before long, I was happy even. Now when I have a down time, knowing You're really there for me makes it easier.

You give me so much to be happy about. Knowing You is the best. Who You are makes me jam. For Your name is the Most High over everything else. You rule forever!

And You have made Yourself known, through Your justice, through taking up for Your people, through helping out me -- through all Your awesome acts in history and in people's lives.

Thanks for letting me know You, not only in the Bible, but in my life.

Psalm 10

1   Why do You stand afar off, O LORD?
Why do You hide Yourself in times of trouble?
2   In pride the wicked hotly pursue the afflicted;
Let them be caught in the plots which they have devised.

3   For the wicked boasts of his heart's desire,
And the greedy man curses and spurns the LORD.
4   The wicked, in the haughtiness of his countenance, does not seek Him.
All his thoughts are, "There is no God."

5   His ways prosper at all times;
Your judgments are on high, out of his sight;
As for all his adversaries, he snorts at them.
6   He says to himself, "I will not be moved;
Throughout all generations I will not be in adversity."
7   His mouth is full of curses and deceit and oppression;
Under his tongue is mischief and wickedness.
8   He sits in the lurking places of the villages;
In the hiding places he kills the innocent;
His eyes stealthily watch for the unfortunate.
9   He lurks in a hiding place as a lion in his lair;
He lurks to catch the afflicted;
He catches the afflicted when he draws him into his net.
10   He crouches, he bows down,
And the unfortunate fall by his mighty ones.
11   He says to himself, "God has forgotten;
He has hidden His face; He will never see it."

12   Arise, O LORD; O God, lift up Your hand.
Do not forget the afflicted.
13   Why has the wicked spurned God?
He has said to himself, "You will not require it."
14   You have seen it, for You have beheld mischief and vexation to take it
into Your hand.
The unfortunate commits himself to You;
You have been the helper of the orphan.
15   Break the arm of the wicked and the evildoer,
Seek out his wickedness until You find none.

16   The LORD is King forever and ever;
Nations have perished from His land.
17   O LORD, You have heard the desire of the humble;
You will strengthen their heart, You will incline Your ear
18   To vindicate the orphan and the oppressed,
So that man who is of the earth will no longer cause terror.

from PSALM 10

Where are you, Lord? What gives? I just don't get it. I have friends, good friends who are way down under it, and it's not their fault at all. Just the opposite -- they're really cool. But they're going through their parents divorcing, or through their own break-ups. Or there's a bad illness. I know one girl whose mom has cancer. Some are just real lonely. They're hurting.

Then I see sleazy guys who are thugs. They're the reason some of my friends are down. These jerks brag about how bad they are and about the sorry things they do. They don't care about right and wrong, or about the people they hurt. They sure don't care about God.

And their life is good! They're popular. They have the coolest clothes and drive hot cars. They get everything they want. For some reason, there's always girls who like to hang with them. They get away with everything. And they think they always will. Because they think You're not there; or if You are, that You don't care.

Do You? I know You do. So where are You, then? It seems You stand far away and watch.

Half the reason they do what they do is they think they'll get away with it. And they do -- for now. I thank You that, sooner or later, You're going to teach them. You'll catch them even if no one else does. Sorry guys like these make me glad You're the God of justice. I just wish it would be sooner. Would You come and help my friends and take the thugs out of action? My friends have enough adversity without these guys.

Then take Satan out. He's the biggest thug. Brothers and sisters are hurting, Lord, because of the evil he brings into their lives. They need Your help. And so do I.

Thanks that You know what's up. You know what my friends are going through. You care, and You've got the power. I can trust You to help them out, and to help me out, and to make things right.

Psalm 11
For the choir director. A Psalm of David.

1   In the LORD I take refuge;
  How can you say to my soul, "Flee as a bird to your mountain;
2   For, behold, the wicked bend the bow,
  They make ready their arrow upon the string
  To shoot in darkness at the upright in heart.
3   If the foundations are destroyed,
  What can the righteous do?"

4   The LORD is in His holy temple; the LORD'S throne is in heaven;
  His eyes behold, His eyelids test the sons of men.
5   The LORD tests the righteous and the wicked,
  And the one who loves violence His soul hates.
6   Upon the wicked He will rain snares;
  Fire and brimstone and burning wind will be the portion of their cup.
7   For the LORD is righteous, He loves righteousness;
  The upright will behold His face.

And time stands still when no one understands you
When you don't quite understand yourself
But just know this that God is faithful
Even if you don't have faith yourself
MxPx "Tomorrow's Another Day"
from *Slowly Going the Way of the Buffalo*

from PSALM 11
especially verse 1

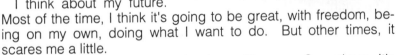

When I'm down or just want to be alone, I go off by myself to a favorite place. It might be the woods, or it might be my room. I play my guitar, draw, or listen to music. I lay back and think.

I think about my future. Most of the time, I think it's going to be great, with freedom, being on my own, doing what I want to do. But other times, it scares me a little.

I think about things happening in my life now. Sometimes, it's exciting, like when a really nice girl likes me, or a big game's tomorrow, or a cool trip is coming up. When stuff like that's happening, it's about all I can think about. Then, other not-so-good times, things happening can be hard to understand. And it can be hard to figure out what to do about them. So I think a lot. I think about God. I wonder about what He's like. I wonder what He feels about me.

I know He loves me and all, but -- I don't know -- I don't understand some of the things He does and lets happen in my life. I think about those things and try to figure them out, but a lot of times I can't.

Still, I know I can trust Him, though sometimes it's not exactly easy to.

But one night, I was laying back and thinking about God. After a while, I felt like I was laying back on Him. I went to sleep that way. It felt good resting on Him. It was about the best sleep I've ever had.

He is always there for me -- even when I don't understand Him from things being tough. I guess I really don't always have to understand Him -- because I can trust Him. I can rest on Him.

And one day, I'll see Him.

Psalm 12
For the choir director; upon an eight-stringed lyre. A Psalm of David.

1   Help, LORD, for the godly man ceases to be,
For the faithful disappear from among the sons of men.
2   They speak falsehood to one another;
With flattering lips and with a double heart they speak.
3   May the LORD cut off all flattering lips,
The tongue that speaks great things;
4   Who have said, "With our tongue we will prevail;
Our lips are our own; who is lord over us?"
5   "Because of the devastation of the afflicted, because of the groaning of the needy,
Now I will arise," says the LORD; "I will set him in the safety for which he longs."

6   The words of the LORD are pure words;
As silver tried in a furnace on the earth, refined seven times.
7   You, O LORD, will keep them;
You will preserve him from this generation forever.
8   The wicked strut about on every side
When vileness is exalted among the sons of men.

Even if I can't trust anyone else, I can trust You, Lord.

from PSALM 12

I can't trust anyone anymore!

I found out today someone I thought I could trust flat out lied to me. I guess I should have known better. He and his friends lie to each other all the time. Then there's this guy who's always talking to me like I'm the greatest -- I found out yesterday he's been going around bad-mouthing me behind my back.

There are so many like that. They sweet talk you, then lie behind your back. They'll lie to your face, too. They lie everywhere! After today, I feel like there's no one I can trust anymore. It seems everyone lies or cheats or is two-faced. It makes me wonder if I should bother being straight with anyone. I don't want to have to distrust everyone. That's no way to live. But I don't want to be lied to and back-stabbed anymore either. I need friends I can trust. Help!

Even if I can't trust anyone else, I can trust You, Lord. Your words are awesome and perfect and can always be trusted. You keep Your word. And Your word encourages me, telling me You'll take care of me and give me peace and a great future. After a rough day like today, it helps me and calms me to go to my room and read my Bible for a while. It's good to hear some truth and to hear good things that are for real, not cover up or buttering up.

It's good to hear from You, someone I know really cares about me instead of wanting to take advantage of me. Thank You for Your word. Thanks You're always straight with me.

Psalm 13
For the choir director. A Psalm of David.

1   How long, O LORD? Will You forget me forever?
How long will You hide Your face from me?
2   How long shall I take counsel in my soul,
Having sorrow in my heart all the day?
How long will my enemy be exalted over me?

3   Consider and answer me, O LORD my God;
Enlighten my eyes, or I will sleep the sleep of death,
4   And my enemy will say, "I have overcome him,"
And my adversaries will rejoice when I am shaken.

5   But I have trusted in Your lovingkindness;
     My heart shall rejoice in Your salvation.
6   I will sing to the LORD,
     Because He has dealt bountifully with me.

When I was young, the smallest trick of light, Could catch my eye.
Then life was new and every new day, I thought that I could fly.
I believed in what I hoped for, And I hoped for things unseen.
I had wings and dreams could soar.
I just don't feel like flying anymore.

Five Iron Frenzy "Every New Day"
from *Our Newest Album Ever*

from PSALM 13

Have you ever looked forward to getting older?

One of the cool things about being teenage and younger is having an optimism that whenever you finally get older and have more freedom, your life will be great.

At some point, though, there also come times when you not only think your life stinks, you're afraid it will always stink. And you get way down. For a lot of people, this first happens during their teenage years.

I don't want to be a downer. But unless you are so happy all the time it makes everyone hate you, you will have down times like this. It's part of being human.

So what do you do when you have those down times? Should you have a big pity party?

Well, Psalm 13, in only six verses, shows a much better way than a pity party to handle life's bummer times.

When David wrote this psalm, he was way down about the way his life was going. You may have noticed he was down when he wrote some other psalms, too. ("No kidding!" I hear someone say.) And he was up front in talking to God about it.

One of the things I love about the Bible, especially the Psalms, is how honest it is. The Bible is not sugar-coated. It's not about nice, holy people thinking nice, holy thoughts and acting nice and holy. It's about real life and real people with problems and the real God who loves them.

In all its honesty, this psalm doesn't seem all that uplifting when you first read it, does it? But did you notice God chose to have this placed in His word? Why do you think He did that?

I think God wants us to know when we're down about life, He

understands us. I think He wants us to know that even people He greatly used, like David, felt low. So it's O.K. to be that way at times.

And I think God wants us to be open and honest with Him, like David was, when we're down.

Notice God did not rebuke David for his hard, honest questions. God did not break in and say, "How dare you be impatient with Me, thou vile infidel!"

David realized he didn't know everything, but God does. So in verse 3, he prays for wisdom to understand his situation.

That's important, because when things are bad, we tend to get tunnel vision, where all our focus is on what's got us down. We tend to see our problem as bigger than it is. And we tend to see God as smaller than He is. At the same time, we think we know everything about our situation, and everything is wrong! That combination can get just a little depressing.

We need God's help with our vision, to see things as they really are, to see the big picture, not just our problems, and to see God as He really is. So when you're down, pray for wisdom to understand your situation. Instead of being so sure you're right when you think everything is wrong, instead of getting tunnel vision, pray for God to open your eyes.

In verses 5 and 6, David does something else we all need to do: take our main focus off our problems and put our focus on God. This doesn't mean ignore your problems. But remember -- God and His love is bigger than your problems.

In verse 5, David expresses his trust in God's love. Like him, we've got to trust God no matter what. Things were dark for David, but deep inside he still had confidence in God.

Now, you'd think it would be easy to trust God -- who's more trustworthy than God? But there's something stupid inside us that makes it difficult to really trust Him. Take me for example. When I was 14, I trusted God with my death, that when I die, I'd go to heaven because of what Jesus did for me. With God's help, it was pretty easy for me once I knew the facts.

But trusting God with my life has been a struggle for me. A lot of times, I've been so afraid He was going to drop the ball on me, afraid I'd end up with a lousy life. It wasn't until recent years I've had anywhere near a grip on trusting God with my life. I can tell you from experience, having confidence in God dogs being afraid God might do me wrong.

Please learn faster than I did. (And, yes, I still need to learn this better.) This is important. It will come up again and again in

Psalms. God wants you to get this. So do I. Especially when we're down, we need to **trust God**.

I'll beat you up some more on this later.

David also remembers past times when God had acted in his life. When we're low, get tunnel vision, and aren't thinking at our best, it's easy to forget these times. So we need to remind ourselves. That's one reason I recommend keeping a journal. When we remember past times when God has been good to us, it makes it easier to trust God to be good to us now and in the future.

David specifically remembers God's salvation. That's important when we're down. When we remember how God has loved us in saving us, it doesn't make sense to think He'll then turn around and forget us. Or as Paul put it, "He who did not spare His own Son, but delivered Him up for us all, how will He not also with Him freely give us all things?" (Romans 8:32)

There it is -- in just six verses, David shows us some good ways to deal with being down about life.

Again, this psalm just being here shows God understands when we're down. He cares, and He's there for us.

M. M.

Psalm 14
For the choir director. A Psalm of David.

1   The fool has said in his heart, "There is no God."
They are corrupt, they have committed abominable deeds;
There is no one who does good.
2   The LORD has looked down from heaven upon the sons of men
To see if there are any who understand,
Who seek after God.
3   They have all turned aside, together they have become corrupt;
There is no one who does good, not even one.
4   Do all the workers of wickedness not know,
Who eat up my people as they eat bread,
And do not call upon the Lord?
5   There they are in great dread,
For God is with the righteous generation.
6   You would put to shame the counsel of the afflicted,
But the LORD is his refuge.

7   Oh, that the salvation of Israel would come out of Zion!
When the LORD restores His captive people,
Jacob will rejoice, Israel will be glad.

Save me from myself

from PSALM 14
(See also PSALM 53)

People are pretty sad. I once thought most people were basically good. Not anymore. So many I thought were O. K. have shown me different. Oh yeah, there are people who are good by our standards or by their own standards. But how good are those? If people are lame, their standards are lame, too. Now God's standards, those are the one's that count. And the more I learn about them, the more I know nobody really measures up. There's not anyone really good. Even those that seem to live right and do good, their thoughts and motives aren't so hot on the inside. You probably don't want to know what goes on in their minds. I sure don't want anyone to know what goes on inside mine.

Those are the few we think are good. What about everyone else? People act like right and wrong don't exist. People act like God doesn't exist. They lie, cheat, steal, and worse. People suck. When God looks down and sees all the evil down here, it's amazing He doesn't just toast us. I would.

When He looks down and sees there's hardly anyone who really seeks Him; there's nobody who loves Him with a whole heart, even though He loves us so much He gave His only Son for us...I wonder if there's tears in His eyes.

Whenever I start looking down on people, I end up doing something or saying something stupid that shows me "There is no one who does good, not even one" includes me. I believe in God, and think He's great and loving. But how often do I act like He's not there at all? Every day. I hate lying and cheating. But if the truth and being honest is just a little too inconvenient, I bail. I know I'm supposed to love everyone, like God does. But too often I'm sorry even to my own family. Sometimes, I don't even love God.

Every once in a while, I get it in my mind I'm going to live right. But I always just end up falling on my face worse than ever. I'm not any good. I'm no better than anybody else.

Jesus, I need your help. I need you to forgive me. I can't live this life worth anything. I try, but it doesn't do any good. Because I suck. Please save me from myself. Please forgive me. Because if You don't, I'll go to hell and deserve it.

I can't do it myself. Please forgive me and help me. Please save me from myself.

Psalm 15
A Psalm of David.

1   O LORD, who may abide in Your tent?
Who may dwell on Your holy hill?
2   He who walks with integrity, and works righteousness,
And speaks truth in his heart.
3   He does not slander with his tongue,
Nor does evil to his neighbor,
Nor takes up a reproach against his friend;
4   In whose eyes a reprobate is despised,
But who honors those who fear the LORD;
He swears to his own hurt and does not change;
5   He does not put out his money at interest,
Nor does he take a bribe against the innocent.
He who does these things will never be shaken.

I want to be more like You.

from PSALM 15

Lord, thanks I get to be with You forever. Because You have forgiven me and saved me so I can be with You. You want me to be with You.

I want to say "thank You" with my life, not just my words. I want the way I live to be the best for You. You've changed my life; I want it to show. If I turned around after all You've done and went back to doing wrong, living my life like nothing happened -- that wouldn't be right.

Yet I find myself doing some of those old things, even though now I know they're wrong. I especially have trouble with my big mouth. Like I catch myself talking behind people's backs, even my friends' backs. I've been getting better about that, but it still stinks. I feel awful after I do stuff like that.

Lord, I don't want to be a hypocrite. I want to live the way a Christian should. I will walk and talk straight. I will do right for others, not take advantage of them. I will live, not as just a hearer of Your word and not as just a talker, but as a doer of Your word.

Jesus, I want to be more like You and less like the old me. Will You help me to? I want to live right. I want my life to be straight in line with Your word and my beliefs. I want my life to say "thank You" that I get to be with You.

Psalm 16
A Mikhtam of David.

1   Preserve me, O God, for I take refuge in You.
2   I said to the LORD, "You are my Lord;
I have no good besides You."
3   As for the saints who are in the earth,
They are the majestic ones in whom is all my delight.
4   The sorrows of those who have bartered for another god will be multi-plied;
I shall not pour out their drink offerings of blood,
Nor will I take their names upon my lips.

5   The LORD is the portion of my inheritance and my cup;
You support my lot.
6   The lines have fallen to me in pleasant places;
Indeed, my heritage is beautiful to me.

7   I will bless the LORD who has counseled me;
Indeed, my mind instructs me in the night.
8   I have set the LORD continually before me;
Because He is at my right hand, I will not be shaken.
9   Therefore my heart is glad and my glory rejoices;
My flesh also will dwell securely.
10   For You will not abandon my soul to Sheol;
Nor will You allow Your Holy One to undergo decay.
11   You will make known to me the path of life;
In Your presence is fullness of joy;
In Your right hand there are pleasures forever.

Oh Lord, You're beautiful.   Your face is all I seek.
For when Your eyes are on this child,
Your grace abounds to me.

Keith Green "Oh Lord You're Beautiful"
from *So You Wanna Go Back to Egypt*

from PSALM 16

Lord, I'm so glad You're my God. My life would be zero with-out You. Those who don't have You, who have other things as their gods, like money or themselves -- I can't see how they really enjoy life. I know I couldn't. I'm not going to make anything my god, except You.

I am glad I have You. You are so good to me. You help me out. You cause things to work out for me. You give me a life and a future I'm excited about.

You counsel me when I need to know what to do. A lot of times, it's from Your word. Sometimes, it's through good advice from a friend, a brother, or a sister, or even a parent. Then there's times when I'm lying in my bed at night, thinking, and the answer just comes to me like out of nowhere. But I know it's not out of nowhere.

Everywhere I go I see You. I see You in creation, in the cool brothers and friends You give me, in You looking out for me, in things happening that show Your word is right, in Your keeping all Your promises -- You are so beautiful. And You are always with Me. I can hardly describe the joy You give me, and how secure I am because of You.

And I know You will show me how to really live my life. I know You will show me an excellent life if I stick with You. I am hyped! You're my God and You're with me. With You, there is real happiness -- forever!

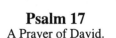

Psalm 17
A Prayer of David.

1   Hear a just cause, O LORD, give heed to my cry;
Give ear to my prayer, which is not from deceitful lips.
2   Let my judgment come forth from Your presence;
Let Your eyes look with equity.
3   You have tried my heart;
You have visited me by night;
You have tested me and You find nothing;
I have purposed that my mouth will not transgress.
4   As for the deeds of men, by the word of Your lips
I have kept from the paths of the violent.
5   My steps have held fast to Your paths.
My feet have not slipped.

6   I have called upon You, for You will answer me, O God;
Incline Your ear to me, hear my speech.
7   Wondrously show Your lovingkindness,
O Savior of those who take refuge at Your right hand
From those who rise up against them.
8   Keep me as the apple of the eye;
Hide me in the shadow of Your wings
9   From the wicked who despoil me,
My deadly enemies who surround me.
10   They have closed their unfeeling heart,
With their mouth they speak proudly.

11   They have now surrounded us in our steps;
   They set their eyes to cast us down to the ground.
12   He is like a lion that is eager to tear,
   And as a young lion lurking in hiding places.

13   Arise, O LORD, confront him, bring him low;
   Deliver my soul from the wicked with Your sword,
14   From men with Your hand, O LORD,
   From men of the world, whose portion is in this life,
   And whose belly You fill with Your treasure;
   They are satisfied with children,
   And leave their abundance to their babes.
15   As for me, I shall behold Your face in righteousness;
   I will be satisfied with Your likeness when I awake.

from PSALM 17

Lord, I'm calling to You, because I can pray to You with confidence. You do answer prayers, especially when they're straight and honest like mine is now. I can remember times when You've shown Your unstoppable love and answered prayers in awesome ways. Because You're awesome.

I can talk straight with You and be open with You. Sometimes, it's hard for me to open up to people, but I can with You. You know everything about me anyway. So You already know I mess up, but that I'm sincere, I'm not two-faced, and I try to follow You, to do things Your way.

Right now, I'm really thankful for the way You answer my prayers and help me out. Because I'm in a fix. Will You protect me from these guys who want to do me in? They are on me bad. And they don't care about right or wrong. Their fat hearts are as caring as their stunted brains are intelligent. All they care about is doing what they want to do and getting what they want to get. I guess I shouldn't talk, because I used to be that way. But now, I've got more important things than just what I can do or get in this life -- more important things like You.

Will You take up for me? For You are just. You're the Savior of all those who run to You. You're my Savior.

Oh God, thanks I get to see You through the way You answer prayer. And I thank You that, one day, I get to see You face to face. What a wake-up that will be!

Psalm 18

For the choir director. A Psalm of David the servant of the LORD, who spoke to the LORD the words of this song in the day that the LORD delivered him from the hand of all his enemies and from the hand of Saul. And he said,

1   "I love You, O LORD, my strength."
2   The LORD is my rock and my fortress and my deliverer,
    My God, my rock, in whom I take refuge;
    My shield and the horn of my salvation, my stronghold.
3   I call upon the LORD, who is worthy to be praised,
    And I am saved from my enemies.

4   The cords of death encompassed me,
    And the torrents of ungodliness terrified me.
5   The cords of Sheol surrounded me;
    The snares of death confronted me.
6   In my distress I called upon the LORD,
    And cried to my God for help;
    He heard my voice out of His temple,
    And my cry for help before Him came into His ears.

7   Then the earth shook and quaked;
    And the foundations of the mountains were trembling
    And were shaken, because He was angry.
8   Smoke went up out of His nostrils,
    And fire from His mouth devoured;
    Coals were kindled by it.
9   He bowed the heavens also, and came down
    With thick darkness under His feet.
10   He rode upon a cherub and flew;
    And He sped upon the wings of the wind.
11   He made darkness His hiding place, His canopy around Him,
    Darkness of waters, thick clouds of the skies.
12   From the brightness before Him passed His thick clouds,
    Hailstones and coals of fire.
13   The LORD also thundered in the heavens,
    And the Most High uttered His voice,
    Hailstones and coals of fire.
14   He sent out His arrows, and scattered them,
    And lightning flashes in abundance, and routed them.
15   Then the channels of water appeared,
    And the foundations of the world were laid bare
    At Your rebuke, O LORD,
    At the blast of the breath of Your nostrils.

16   He sent from on high, He took me;
    He drew me out of many waters.
17   He delivered me from my strong enemy,

And from those who hated me, for they were too mighty for me.
18   They confronted me in the day of my calamity,
But the LORD was my stay.
19   He brought me forth also into a broad place;
He rescued me, because He delighted in me.

20   The LORD has rewarded me according to my righteousness;
According to the cleanness of my hands He has recompensed me.
21   For I have kept the ways of the LORD,
And have not wickedly departed from my God.
22   For all His ordinances were before me,
And I did not put away His statutes from me.
23   I was also blameless with Him,
And I kept myself from my iniquity.
24   Therefore the LORD has recompensed me according to my righteousness,
According to the cleanness of my hands in His eyes.

25   With the kind You show Yourself kind;
With the blameless You show Yourself blameless;
26   With the pure You show Yourself pure,
And with the crooked You show Yourself astute.
27   For You save an afflicted people,
But haughty eyes You abase.
28   For You light my lamp;
The LORD my God illumines my darkness.
29   For by You I can run upon a troop;
And by my God I can leap over a wall.

30   As for God, His way is blameless;
The word of the LORD is tried;
He is a shield to all who take refuge in Him.
31   For who is God, but the LORD?
And who is a rock, except our God,
32   The God who girds me with strength
And makes my way blameless?
33   He makes my feet like hinds' feet,
And sets me upon my high places.
34   He trains my hands for battle,
So that my arms can bend a bow of bronze.
35   You have also given me the shield of Your salvation,
And Your right hand upholds me;
And Your gentleness makes me great.
36   You enlarge my steps under me,
And my feet have not slipped.

37   I pursued my enemies and overtook them,
And I did not turn back until they were consumed.

38   I shattered them, so that they were not able to rise;
   They fell under my feet.
39   For You have girded me with strength for battle;
   You have subdued under me those who rose up against me.
40   You have also made my enemies turn their backs to me,
   And I destroyed those who hated me.
41   They cried for help, but there was none to save,
   Even to the LORD, but He did not answer them.
42   Then I beat them fine as the dust before the wind;
   I emptied them out as the mire of the streets.

43   You have delivered me from the contentions of the people;
   You have placed me as head of the nations;
   A people whom I have not known serve me.
44   As soon as they hear, they obey me;
   Foreigners submit to me.
45   Foreigners fade away,
   And come trembling out of their fortresses.

46   The LORD lives, and blessed be my rock;
   And exalted be the God of my salvation,
47   The God who executes vengeance for me,
   And subdues peoples under me.
48   He delivers me from my enemies;
   Surely You lift me above those who rise up against me;
   You rescue me from the violent man.
49   Therefore I will give thanks to You among the nations, O LORD,
   And I will sing praises to Your name.
50   He gives great deliverance to His king,
   And shows lovingkindness to His anointed,
   To David and his descendants forever.

Isn't that what darkness wants for me to play   the role of a victim,
But I'm a child of Light   no longer bound by slavery.
I say oh death where is your sting,
And oh hades where is your victory?

John Reuben "Draw Near"
from *Are We There Yet?*

from PSALM 18

I love You, Lord. You rock. I can run to You. For Your love for me is strong. You've protected me and answered my prayer.

I was in a bad fix. I thought I was dead meat. But I prayed, and You came through for me in a big way. You took my dark situation and turned it into a bright, sunny day. You took care of me way beyond what I expected. Now things are O.K., better even. I feel free and peaceful now, like I feel when I'm walking way out in the country. Because you freed me from my trouble. You lifted me out of it and above it.

Because -- You really do love me.

You are so good to me, especially when I'm put down. And You are just. Those who treat people right, You treat them right. Those who are stuck up and always putting people down, You put them down.

God rules. He is God and nobody else! No one can be trusted like Him. No one is strong like Him. With Him, there is no wall or mountain high enough to keep me from where He wants me to go.

For You are strong for me. Yet You are gentle toward me. It's a good thing -- as powerful as You are, if You weren't easy with me, I'd be blown off the face of the earth! Instead of being too hard on me when I mess up or get myself in a fix, You help me out and make me stronger and teach me how to live smarter. Your gentleness and patience is making me cool. Most important of all, You forgive me and save me, instead of zapping me. And You know I've deserved to get zapped a few times.

I can't thank You enough -- You are so good to me. Thanks You are for real. You live and get things done, and not just in church or Sunday School or in ancient Bible times. You take up for me and lift me up. You live today and in my life. You are the best and always will be.

Psalm 19
For the choir director. A Psalm of David.

1   The heavens are telling of the glory of God;
     And their expanse is declaring the work of His hands.
2   Day to day pours forth speech,
     And night to night reveals knowledge.
3   There is no speech, nor are there words;
     Their voice is not heard.
4   Their line has gone out through all the earth,
     And their utterances to the end of the world.
     In them He has placed a tent for the sun,
5   Which is as a bridegroom coming out of his chamber;
     It rejoices as a strong man to run his course.
6   Its rising is from one end of the heavens,
     And its circuit to the other end of them;
     And there is nothing hidden from its heat.

7　The law of the LORD is perfect, restoring the soul;
　The testimony of the LORD is sure, making wise the simple.
8　The precepts of the LORD are right, rejoicing the heart;
　The commandment of the LORD is pure, enlightening the eyes.
9　The fear of the LORD is clean, enduring forever;
　The judgments of the LORD are true; they are righteous altogether.
10　They are more desirable than gold, yes, than much fine gold;
　Sweeter also than honey and the drippings of the honeycomb.
11　Moreover, by them Your servant is warned;
　In keeping them there is great reward.
12　Who can discern his errors? Acquit me of hidden faults.
13　Also keep back Your servant from presumptuous sins;
　Let them not rule over me;
　Then I will be blameless,
　And I shall be acquitted of great transgression.
14　Let the words of my mouth and the meditation of my heart
　Be acceptable in Your sight,
　O LORD, my rock and my Redeemer.

from PSALM 19

Creation is pretty amazing when you think about it. When you're out in the country, check out the sky. At night, there's all those stars, and they're different brightnesses and colors. Some have planets, and those are all different. Most of those planets have moons of all sorts like in our solar system.

I wonder what all those planets and moons are like. Just the ones in our solar system are strange enough. There's Saturn with it's rings and Venus with it's soupy thick atmosphere and a ground temperature hot enough to melt lead. There's Io with it's sulfur volcanoes and Europa with it's criss-crossed surface of massive ice blocks. No one can live in weird places like those, but God created them anyway because He wanted to. Hey, He's creative. No telling how weird the planets and moons are around those stars up there.

That's just the stars we can see. There are galaxies of billions and billions of stars we can't see, not to mention wild stuff like quasars, supernovas, and comets and . . . it will make your brain hurt if you think about it too much.

Or just think about our days. They're set up close to perfect for us. If the earth's rotation were slower, it would get hotter during the day and colder at night. If our going around the sun were slower, we'd freeze worse during the longer winters and burn up during the longer summer. (And, no, the schools still wouldn't give us longer summer vacations.) If the sun were much hotter or much colder, or if the sun were much closer or much farther away, we'd burn up like the closer planets or freeze our rears off like the farther planets.

What about our atmosphere? If it were real thin or didn't exist, like on the moon, it would get up to 200 degrees during the day, then minus 200 degrees at night. Think about that the next time you're whining about the temperature. Or if our atmosphere were soupy, like Venus, it might be so hot all the time, tires would melt. Heck, the roads would melt. How would you cruise then?

So the sun, the earth, the atmosphere, and the days and nights are set up close to perfect for us. That's not even mentioning how we are made and how the rest of nature is made.

Now, could all that have just -- happened? Could all this be the result of some random series of cosmic accidents that just happened to come out O. K.? I - don't - think - so. If all this doesn't tell you there's a God and He's awesome, then you're not listening.

God, You **are** awesome. And Your word and standards are so perfect and smart. I want to live by them.

But Lord, I am not perfect. Sometimes, I'm so clueless, I do wrong, sometimes big time, and don't even know it -- until it's too late and I feel super stupid. Forgive me and keep me from doing dumb too bad. That will keep me from a lot of wrong -- and a lot of guilt and embarrassment.

I pray that not only how I act on the outside, but what I say and how I am on the inside is how You created me to be -- and makes You happy You made me.

Psalm 20
For the choir director. A Psalm of David.

1   May the LORD answer you in the day of trouble!
    May the name of the God of Jacob set you securely on high!
2   May He send you help from the sanctuary
    And support you from Zion!
3   May He remember all your meal offerings
    And find your burnt offering acceptable!   Selah.

4   May He grant you your heart's desire
    And fulfill all your counsel!
5 We will sing for joy over your victory,
    And in the name of our God we will set up our banners.
    May the LORD fulfill all your petitions.

6   Now I know that the LORD saves His anointed;
     He will answer him from His holy heaven
     With the saving strength of His right hand.
7   Some boast in chariots and some in horses,
     But we will boast in the name of the LORD, our God.
8   They have bowed down and fallen,
     But we have risen and stood upright.
9   Save, O LORD;
     May the King answer us in the day we call.

You can't escape your thinkin
All you've ever been taught
Is that you walk this way
You talk this way
You front this way
You pose this way
You act this way
Na, na that's not me.
I got to be who God created me to be.

John Reuben "Do Not"
from *Are We There Yet?*

from PSALM 20

At school, there sure is a lot of bragging going on, a lot of trying to impress. It seems almost everyone tries to impress through looks and clothes. Then some try to build themselves up through athletics. Others brag about what they can get away with. And, of course, some guys brag about how they do with girls.

I used to think these were the ways to be somebody hot. I think different now. God is way more important than football or looks -- or even girls. What's cool with Him is what counts. What impresses others doesn't impress me much anymore. He can build someone up far better than sports or anything else can.

Knowing that has really freed me. Instead of being all into myself and worrying about what others think of me, I get into God and what He thinks. And with God, you don't have to worry about styles and fads that change every month.

I get into others, not to make them think I'm cool, but to really be interested in them and where they're coming from. I can relax around them and be real. That's much more fun than being all self-conscious and worried about what others think about me, the way I used to be.

I guess I needed to be freed from myself and from what others think. And God did it.

So let others try to be big shots and brag about things that impress some people, but aren't that important. I'll be real. I'll be who God made me to be. If other people, if the whole world doesn't like it, too bad.

If I'm going to brag, I'll brag about what's important– God.

Psalm 21
For the choir director. A Psalm of David.

1   O LORD, in Your strength the king will be glad,
    And in Your salvation how greatly he will rejoice!
2   You have given him his heart's desire,
    And You have not withheld the request of his lips.   Selah.
3   For You meet him with the blessings of good things;
    You set a crown of fine gold on his head.
4   He asked life of You,
    You gave it to him,
    Length of days forever and ever.
5   His glory is great through Your salvation,
    Splendor and majesty You place upon him.
6   For You make him most blessed forever;
    You make him joyful with gladness in Your presence.

7   For the king trusts in the LORD,
    And through the lovingkindness of the Most High he will not be shaken.
8   Your hand will find out all your enemies;
    Your right hand will find out those who hate you.
9   You will make them as a fiery oven in the time of your anger;
    The LORD will swallow them up in His wrath,
    And fire will devour them.
10   Their offspring You will destroy from the earth,
    And their descendants from among the sons of men.
11   Though they intended evil against You
    And devised a plot,
    They will not succeed.
12   For You will make them turn their back;
    You will aim with Your bowstrings at their faces.
13   Be exalted, O LORD, in Your strength;
    We will sing and praise Your power.

from PSALM 21

Oh Lord, You are strong. Am I glad. I'm especially hyped that Your love is strong. Nobody has both strength and love like You. Nobody even comes close.

You show me Your strong love by answering my prayers way beyond what I expect or even imagine, by being incredibly good to me. You're always so cool to me.

Best of all, when I asked for forgiveness and real life that lasts forever, You answered. You just gave me a new life. All I had to do was pray and trust in You. I sure didn't earn it. Jesus, thanks You earned it for me. Now I'm psyched about my future. To save me like You did -- now that takes strength.

Not only that, You're making me into something studly. You're making me more and more like You, Jesus. That takes a lot of strength and patience, too. Only You could do that. I sure couldn't on my own.

More even than that, You've given me You! I get to enjoy Your love and Your being cool to me in this life. I'll get to enjoy You even more in heaven. I get to enjoy being with You forever!

Your greatness, Your love, strength, and power make me want to yell it and sing it, even if my voice cracks all over the place.

Thank You so much for Your strong love for me. Show Your strength and power even more, Lord, so everybody will know You rule.

Psalm 22
For the choir director; upon Aijeleth Hashshahar.
A Psalm of David.

1　　My God, my God, why have You forsaken me?
Far from my deliverance are the words of my groaning.
2　　O my God, I cry by day, but You do not answer;
And by night, but I have no rest.
3　　Yet You are holy,
O You who are enthroned upon the praises of Israel.
4　　In You our fathers trusted;
They trusted and You delivered them.
5　　To You they cried out and were delivered;
In You they trusted and were not disappointed.

6　　But I am a worm and not a man,
A reproach of men and despised by the people.
7　　All who see me sneer at me;
They separate with the lip, they wag the head, saying,
8　　"Commit yourself to the LORD; let Him deliver him;
Let Him rescue him, because He delights in him."
9　　Yet You are He who brought me forth from the womb;
You made me trust when upon my mother's breasts.

10   Upon You I was cast from birth;
        You have been my God from my mother's womb.

11   Be not far from me, for trouble is near;
        For there is none to help.
12   Many bulls have surrounded me;
        Strong bulls of Bashan have encircled me.
13   They open wide their mouth at me,
        As a ravening and a roaring lion.
14   I am poured out like water,
        And all my bones are out of joint;
        My heart is like wax;
        It is melted within me.
15   My strength is dried up like a potsherd,
        And my tongue cleaves to my jaws;
        And You lay me in the dust of death.
16   For dogs have surrounded me;
        A band of evildoers has encompassed me;
        They pierced my hands and my feet.
17   I can count all my bones.
        They look, they stare at me;
18   They divide my garments among them,
        And for my clothing they cast lots.

19   But You, O LORD, be not far off;
        O You my help, hasten to my assistance.
20   Deliver my soul from the sword,
        My only life from the power of the dog.
21   Save me from the lion's mouth;
        From the horns of the wild oxen You answer me.

22   I will tell of Your name to my brethren;
        In the midst of the assembly I will praise You.
23   You who fear the LORD, praise Him;
        All you descendants of Jacob, glorify Him,
        And stand in awe of Him, all you descendants of Israel.
24   For He has not despised nor abhorred the affliction of the afflicted;
        Nor has He hidden His face from him;
        But when he cried to Him for help, He heard.

25   From You comes my praise in the great assembly;
        I shall pay my vows before those who fear Him.
26   The afflicted will eat and be satisfied;
        Those who seek Him will praise the LORD.
        Let your heart live forever!
27   All the ends of the earth will remember and turn to the LORD,
        And all the families of the nations will worship before You.
28   For the kingdom is the LORD'S

And He rules over the nations.
29   All the prosperous of the earth will eat and worship,
   All those who go down to the dust will bow before Him,
   Even he who cannot keep his soul alive.
30   Posterity will serve Him;
   It will be told of the Lord to the coming generation.
31   They will come and will declare His righteousness
   To a people who will be born, that He has performed it.

and now, i look in Your eyes
and wonder; if Your arms weren't
nailed down to a tree
would You still embrace me
knowing all the pain i've caused,
and all the things i've done that hurt You...t

joshua stevens "on falling in love"

from PSALM 22
Note:
   Much of Psalm 22 was fulfilled when Jesus was crucified. A number of specific events of the crucifixion are foretold by this psalm hundreds of years before it happened. Check some of the verses out for yourself: Verse 1 -- see Mark 15:34. Verses 7 and 8 -- see Matthew 27:39-43. Verse 16 -- "They pierced my hands and my feet." Verse 18 -- see Matthew 27:35.

   When I was a kid, one Bible verse stumped me more than any other -- Jesus saying on the cross, "My God, My God, why hast Thou forsaken Me?"

   What? God abandoning Jesus?

   Since then, I've found out the pain Jesus experienced on the cross was much more than only physical pain, though the physical pain was complete agony.
   When Jesus was on the cross, He took the punishment we all deserve for the wrong we've done. That punishment is being totally separated from God, which is what hell basically is.
   Jesus suffered so much in His life and in His death. Just to go from the awesomeness of heaven to this earth must have been hard. And, being God's Son, He was so misunderstood down here. Not even His best friends understood Him.
   He was alone a lot. He spent forty days alone in the wilderness

without any food. Though He was great, loved people, and did incredible things for them, He was rejected again and again.

But His worst suffering, His deepest pain, aloneness, and rejection, came the moment He began taking our punishment, the moment He became separated from His Father. When Jesus was carrying all our evil upon Himself on the cross, the Father, who loves His Son but hates evil, turned away from Jesus.

It's hard for us to understand how bad that was for Jesus because we're so out of it. We often don't have a clue whether God's around or not. And a lot of times, we really don't care.

But imagine having a perfect relationship with the Father from infinity back in time, from way before there was an earth or even a universe. Imagine being really tight with God, sharing everything, talking about anything, having perfect closeness -- perfect love -- with never a fight or even a disagreement between you. It would be like having the best time hanging with your best friend as long as you want, except a thousand times better. Or like having the perfect father.

But, in a moment, the closeness is gone. The friendship is lost. Instead, there is sudden and total separation.

And the awful loss and aloneness is agony never before experienced. And as you're dying, you want your friend, your Father back with you so bad. But he's gone -- gone. And you cry out to Him.

"My God! My God! Why hast Thou forsaken Me?"

It cannot be imagined.

We cannot even begin to comprehend it. It is too unspeakably terrible and holy.

That is what Jesus went through for us.

Sometimes I feel alone, and rejected. But the aloneness Jesus experienced on the cross -- being totally separated from His Father, who He had been close to forever, and dying there in darkness -- no one but He has ever been alone and rejected like that.

That is the ultimate aloneness, the ultimate separation Jesus endured so we, instead of being alone, can have friendship, even closeness with God.

When Jesus decided to come down to this earth, He knew what was going to happen. He knew He would have a difficult life, completely unlike heaven. He knew He would be misunderstood, instead of being perfectly understood and loved as in heaven; homeless, instead of in His perfect home; lonely and abandoned by even His closest friends; and He knew those He wanted to help would, in the end, reject Him and kill Him. And He knew the agony that lonely death would be.

What maybe is most amazing, He knew all the people He would die for, when they would be born, where they would live -- and every wrong thing they would ever do -- all the wrong they would do, all the wrong I would do. He knew they, I, deserved neither heaven nor His love. And He knew how awful it would be to take on the punishment they did deserve upon Himself and die on the cross -- though He never did anything wrong.

But He came down here, and He lived and He died for us anyway.

Jesus went though it all for us -- for me.

My mind can't comprehend it and never will.

Jesus -- thank you.

Psalm 23
A Psalm of David.

1   The LORD is my shepherd,
  I shall not want.
2   He makes me lie down in green pastures;
  He leads me beside quiet waters.
3   He restores my soul;
  He guides me in the paths of righteousness
  For His name's sake.

4   Even though I walk through the valley of the shadow of death,
  I fear no evil, for You are with me;
  Your rod and Your staff, they comfort me.
5   You prepare a table before me in the presence of my enemies;
  You have anointed my head with oil;
  My cup overflows.
6   Surely goodness and lovingkindness will follow me all the days of my life,
  And I will dwell in the house of the LORD forever.

from PSALM 23

The Lord looks after me. He's my protection and guide.

He meets all my needs. He is what I need. I have Him, and that's the best. Why should I want anything else?

He gives me cool places to hang out. He meets my physical needs, like food, soda, and sleep. It's a good thing, because I eat, drink, and sleep a lot.

When things get a little too crazy, He gives me peace. He calms me when I'm nervous about everything. He lifts me up when I'm down.

He helps me to live right. He counsels me so I'll know the right ways to go.

Jesus has the name above every other name, and He's going to live up to it. He'll take care of me and the rest of His people. So I want my life to honor Him, not disrespect His name or cause anyone to bad-mouth Him.

When things get dark, I don't fear; I'm confident and peaceful deep inside, because You are always with me. It calms me and helps me to know You're there.

Even when I'm surrounded by those who want to do me wrong, You do me right. When they try to trash me, You bring honor to me. When they try to intimidate me, You give me strength and peace. When they try to steal from me, You meet my needs and a lot more. For every difficulty I have, You do more good for me than I can take in. You are so generous. Even my pizza buffet plate overflows.

Lord, You are so awesome to me. I know I'll experience Your goodness and love my whole life.

And then I'll get to be with You forever.

Psalm 24
A Psalm of David.

1   The earth is the LORD'S, and all it contains,
The world, and those who dwell in it.
2   For He has founded it upon the seas
And established it upon the rivers.
3   Who may ascend into the hill of the LORD?
And who may stand in His holy place?
4   He who has clean hands and a pure heart,
Who has not lifted up his soul to falsehood
And has not sworn deceitfully.
5   He shall receive a blessing from the LORD
And righteousness from the God of his salvation.
6   This is the generation of those who seek Him,
Who seek Your face—even Jacob.   Selah.

7   Lift up your heads, O gates,
    And be lifted up, O ancient doors,
    That the King of glory may come in!
8   Who is the King of glory?
    The LORD strong and mighty,
    The LORD mighty in battle.
9   Lift up your heads, O gates,
    And lift them up, O ancient doors,
    That the King of glory may come in!
10   Who is this King of glory?
    The LORD of hosts,
    He is the King of glory.   Selah.

from PSALM 24

The whole earth and everything on it belongs to God. He created it all.

Sometimes, you wouldn't know it though. Man has messed things up so much with his pollution and everything. Man is messed up. He's not who God created him to be.

Yet as messed up as we are, God's still there for those who seek Him; for anyone who trusts Him and has an honest, pure heart toward Him.

One day, God is coming back to make things right. It's going to be something to see. This world has never seen anything that comes close to touching it. With His power, with His might -- and with His glory, He's going to come, take over, and rule.

For the power and the glory belong to the Lord Jesus. He is King!

Get ready, world. You can't keep the door closed on Him.

And He's going to make man right again. He's going to make Earth new again, make it perfect. He's going to make everything the way it should be.

    Jesus rules.

Psalm 25
A Psalm of David.

1   To You, O LORD, I lift up my soul.
2   O my God, in You I trust,
    Do not let me be ashamed;
    Do not let my enemies exult over me.
3   Indeed, none of those who wait for You will be ashamed;
    Those who deal treacherously without cause will be ashamed.

4   Make me know Your ways, O LORD;
Teach me Your paths.
5   Lead me in Your truth and teach me,
For You are the God of my salvation;
For You I wait all the day.
6   Remember, O LORD, Your compassion and Your lovingkindnesses,
For they have been from of old.
7   Do not remember the sins of my youth or my transgressions;
According to Your lovingkindness remember me,
For Your goodness' sake, O LORD.

8   Good and upright is the LORD;
Therefore He instructs sinners in the way.
9   He leads the humble in justice,
And He teaches the humble His way.
10   All the paths of the LORD are lovingkindness and truth
To those who keep His covenant and His testimonies.
11   For Your name's sake, O LORD,
Pardon my iniquity, for it is great.

12   Who is the man who fears the LORD?
He will instruct him in the way he should choose.
13   His soul will abide in prosperity,
And his descendants will inherit the land.
14   The secret of the LORD is for those who fear Him,
And He will make them know His covenant.
15   My eyes are continually toward the LORD,
For He will pluck my feet out of the net.

16   Turn to me and be gracious to me,
For I am lonely and afflicted.
17   The troubles of my heart are enlarged;
Bring me out of my distresses.
18   Look upon my affliction and my trouble,
And forgive all my sins.
19   Look upon my enemies, for they are many,
And they hate me with violent hatred.
20   Guard my soul and deliver me;
Do not let me be ashamed, for I take refuge in You.
21   Let integrity and uprightness preserve me,
For I wait for You.
22   Redeem Israel, O God,
Out of all his troubles.

**I'm still young and I'd like to stay that way
Cause growing up won't make everything o.k.**
MxPx "Responsibility"
from *The Ever Passing Moment*

from PSALM 25

Note: "Ashamed" in this psalm can also be translated to mean "dis-appointed."

Lord, I want to talk to You about my life. I can come and talk real honest with You because I can trust You. It seems I can't trust in much else anymore.

I used to think I'd be a kid forever, and if I ever did get older, it would be way cool. I thought life would get better and better. Sometimes I still think that way, but not now. I didn't have any worries. Not anymore.

I'm afraid life isn't going to be nearly as hot as I thought. I know it's going to be great in the end when I get to be with You. But that's a long time from now. Until then, I'm afraid life's going to be a big disappointment.

Right now, it already is. I thought being a teenager would be great, especially hanging out and doing things with my friends, and going out on dates. Instead, I'm so lonely and down.

And it's getting harder and harder to stay out of trouble and keep from doing stupid, wrong things. I thought I had a hard time with that when I was a little kid. Now that I'm a teenager, it's a lot worse. All the time I say or do stupid things that drag me down, and I wonder, "Why did I do that?"

I keep waiting for my life to get better. I still look forward to my being more together and having great times. I wonder if I'm waiting for something that will never come.

I think it's time I start waiting for You.

Lord, please turn to me and look with mercy and under-standing upon me and my messed-up life. I need your forgive-ness. I need your help. I'm so down about my life. Please bring me out of my depression and make my life better. I want to be confident about my future again. I need your help to live smart. I thought I knew everything. I've found out the hard way I don't. You know how to live. Please teach me Your way. It's got to be way better than my way.

Lord, please don't let me be disappointed with myself or with my life. Sometimes, life scares me. And I'm afraid to really trust You with it the way I should. But I know if I trust You, You won't let me down. I know if I follow You, You'll lead me right.

Psalm 26
A Psalm of David.

1   Vindicate me, O LORD, for I have walked in my integrity,
And I have trusted in the LORD without wavering.
2   Examine me, O LORD, and try me;
Test my mind and my heart.
3   For Your lovingkindness is before my eyes,
And I have walked in Your truth.
4   I do not sit with deceitful men,
Nor will I go with pretenders.
5   I hate the assembly of evildoers,
And I will not sit with the wicked.
6   I shall wash my hands in innocence,
And I will go about Your altar, O LORD,
7   That I may proclaim with the voice of thanksgiving
And declare all Your wonders.

8   O LORD, I love the habitation of Your house
And the place where Your glory dwells.
9   Do not take my soul away along with sinners,
Nor my life with men of bloodshed,
10   In whose hands is a wicked scheme,
And whose right hand is full of bribes.
11   But as for me, I shall walk in my integrity;
Redeem me, and be gracious to me.
12   My foot stands on a level place;
In the congregations I shall bless the LORD.

Your ways really are the best.

from PSALM 26

Lord, thank You for helping me live right. The way You've helped me shows me I can trust in You and Your ways.

You know I was afraid doing things Your way would not be as fun as doing them my way. I've found out different. Your ways really are the best. For one thing, I can be real. Before, it seemed I was always trying to cover up something. That gets pretty old, and almost impossible, after a while. Now I don't have to, because I've got nothing to hide. I like it a lot better being real that way.

And You've helped me get better friends to hang with. The guys I thought were cool friends turned out to be a bunch of posers. They were dishonest, including with me. They led me into some things I don't need to do. Then when I got hurt and got in trouble because of going along with them, they didn't care that much. I got some real friends now.

Most important, I'm closer to You now -- and I love it.

Don't get me wrong. I don't think I'm perfect or anything. I still need Your guidance and forgiveness every day. So check me out. If there's something I'm doing I need to change, show me and help me with it.

Thanks for already helping me so much to live right. Now my life is cool and steady, like it ought to be. Now I'm more excited about life -- and about You.

Psalm 27
A Psalm of David.

1   The LORD is my light and my salvation;
     Whom shall I fear?
     The LORD is the defense of my life;
     Whom shall I dread?
2   When evildoers came upon me to devour my flesh,
     My adversaries and my enemies, they stumbled and fell.
3   Though a host encamp against me,
     My heart will not fear;
     Though war arise against me,
     In spite of this I shall be confident.

4   One thing I have asked from the LORD, that I shall seek:
     That I may dwell in the house of the LORD all the days of my life,
     To behold the beauty of the LORD
     And to meditate in His temple.
5   For in the day of trouble He will conceal me in His tabernacle;
     In the secret place of His tent He will hide me;
     He will lift me up on a rock.
6   And now my head will be lifted up above my enemies around me,
     And I will offer in His tent sacrifices with shouts of joy;
     I will sing, yes, I will sing praises to the LORD.

7   Hear, O LORD, when I cry with my voice,
     And be gracious to me and answer me.
8   When You said, "Seek My face," my heart said to You,
     "Your face, O LORD, I shall seek."
9   Do not hide Your face from me,
     Do not turn Your servant away in anger;
     You have been my help;
     Do not abandon me nor forsake me,
     O God of my salvation!

10   For my father and my mother have forsaken me,
     But the LORD will take me up.

11   Teach me Your way, O LORD,
     And lead me in a level path
     Because of my foes.
12   Do not deliver me over to the desire of my adversaries,
     For false witnesses have risen against me,
     And such as breathe out violence.
13   I would have despaired unless I had believed that I would see the
     goodness of the LORD
     In the land of the living.
14   Wait for the LORD;
     Be strong and let your heart take courage;
     Yes, wait for the LORD.

from PSALM 27

"Seek Me. Talk to Me."

That's what You say to me, Lord. You, the King of the universe, want me to spend time with You, to talk to You. I'm that important to You, even though You're God.

Yes, I want to be with You and talk with You. How can I feel any other way? You are so awesome.

You'll listen to me and respond out of your infinite love and strength. I know You won't blow me off. Everyone else, even my parents, might blow me off. But You won't.

When I asked You to come into my life and forgive Me, You didn't tell me to go away, though I didn't deserve You to save me. You did forgive me and changed my life. And when I was in a tough situation and I prayed, You responded then, too, and became my protection. It was like You took me and hid me in Your secret place away from trouble. Then You lifted me up above it all. You are my salvation, for both this life and forever.

Things are rough again, Lord. I feel the whole world is against me. But I'm still confident, because I know You are for me. That's what counts. You defend me. So there'll be no fear here.

Lord, You care for me and are good to me -- and not just when I die. If I thought I'd have to wait until heaven to experience You and Your goodness, if I thought You wouldn't be with me and help me out in this life -- that would be a serious downer. I would really be depressed about life, because living without You would be one long downer.

But You are good to me in this life and forever. You are strong for me, and will help me be strong. So I can look up to You and be courageous. I can look forward with anticipation to what You're going to do.

Psalm 28
A Psalm of David.

1   To You, O LORD, I call;
My rock, do not be deaf to me,
For if You are silent to me,
I will become like those who go down to the pit.
2   Hear the voice of my supplications when I cry to You for help,
When I lift up my hands toward Your holy sanctuary.
3   Do not drag me away with the wicked
And with those who work iniquity,
Who speak peace with their neighbors,
While evil is in their hearts.
4   Requite them according to their work and according to the evil of their practices;
Requite them according to the deeds of their hands;
Repay them their recompense.
5   Because they do not regard the works of the LORD
Nor the deeds of His hands,
He will tear them down and not build them up.

6   Blessed be the LORD,
Because He has heard the voice of my supplication.
7   The LORD is my strength and my shield;
My heart trusts in Him, and I am helped;
Therefore my heart exults,
And with my song I shall thank Him.
8   The LORD is their strength,
And He is a saving defense to His anointed.
9   Save Your people and bless Your inheritance;
Be their shepherd also, and carry them forever.

God of creation it s you whom I seek.
Lord I feel strapped n tied down and my strength is weak.
Oh Lord when I cry out please hear what I speak.

John Reuben "Draw Near"
from *Are We There Yet?*

from PSALM 28

Am I glad God answers prayers. And not just righteous holy people's prayers, but my prayers.

I was low and going lower. It got to the point where about all I knew to do was call out to God and pray. So I did -- in a big way. I was a bit afraid God wouldn't answer. I would have really gone down then.

But God answered my prayer and brought me out of my pit. He did even more than I expected. My trust in Him wasn't real strong, but it was in the right guy. He is strong. And did He ever help me! God knew what I needed even better than I did, and He came through with it. Every time I think about what He did, I'm thanking Him.

What's the best is not everything being cool now, although that is excellent. What's the best is God cares about me so much, and He showed me! His caring and love for me isn't just some religious thoughts to me any more. It's for real.

Now I can trust Him, thank Him, and appreciate Him for real. God rocks! And He's my rock.

Psalm 29
A Psalm of David.

1   Ascribe to the LORD, O sons of the mighty,
Ascribe to the LORD glory and strength.
2   Ascribe to the LORD the glory due to His name;
Worship the LORD in holy array.

3   The voice of the LORD is upon the waters;
The God of glory thunders,
The LORD is over many waters.
4   The voice of the LORD is powerful,
The voice of the LORD is majestic.
5   The voice of the LORD breaks the cedars;
Yes, the LORD breaks in pieces the cedars of Lebanon.
6   He makes Lebanon skip like a calf,
And Sirion like a young wild ox.
7   The voice of the LORD hews out flames of fire.
8   The voice of the LORD shakes the wilderness;

The LORD shakes the wilderness of Kadesh.
9   The voice of the LORD makes the deer to calve
And strips the forests bare;
And in His temple everything says, "Glory!"

10   The LORD sat as King at the flood;
Yes, the LORD sits as King forever.
11   The LORD will give strength to His people;
The LORD will bless His people with peace.

from PSALM 29

We had a **bad** thunderstorm the other night. I was asleep when a loud lightning strike jolted me awake. When I got my head together enough, I noticed the lightning was going non-stop. I always sleep through storms, which amazes my parents. But even I wasn't going to sleep through this one. I got up and looked out my window.

The wind was blowing hard. Trees were swingin' and swayin' all over the place. It was just beginning to rain, but after a minute it was pouring down. It made lots of streaks in the lightning. We were in the middle of it then. The sky was one big strobe light. Everything looked weird. A lot of the lightning was close. One split a tree down the street. And the thunder from them was loud! It shook the house!

The coolest was when one hit this transformer on a telephone pole close to my house. It sounded different, I guess from being so close, not like a crash or a rumble, more like a big crack. And when it hit the box, it blew up, throwing sparks all over the place. We didn't have electricity for hours, but it was awesome!

I kept on watching the storm out my window. It was beautiful in a way. After a while, I thought how powerful and beautiful God must be. The storm I was watching was just a part of His creation. If just that part was so incredible, I thought how incredible God the creator must be. If one storm could do what that one did, then the sound, breath, and power of God's voice would blow anything away. If the lightning show I was watching was so cool that all I wanted to do was keep on watching it, I thought how cool God must be to watch and be with.

And though the world was going crazy outside, I felt peaceful there at the window watching it.

Even though I had to help with the clean-up the next day, it was cool seeing and hearing a part of God's power that night.

Psalm 30

A Psalm; a Song at the Dedication of the House.
A Psalm of David.

1   I will extol You, O LORD, for You have lifted me up,
And have not let my enemies rejoice over me.
2   O LORD my God,
I cried to You for help, and You healed me.
3   O LORD, You have brought up my soul from Sheol;
You have kept me alive, that I would not go down to the pit.
4   Sing praise to the LORD, you His godly ones,
And give thanks to His holy name.
5   For His anger is but for a moment,
His favor is for a lifetime;
Weeping may last for the night,
But a shout of joy comes in the morning.

6   Now as for me, I said in my prosperity,
"I will never be moved."
7   O LORD, by Your favor You have made my mountain to stand strong;
You hid Your face, I was dismayed.
8   To You, O LORD, I called,
And to the Lord I made supplication:
9   "What profit is there in my blood, if I go down to the pit?
Will the dust praise You? Will it declare Your faithfulness?

10   "Hear, O LORD, and be gracious to me;
O LORD, be my helper."
11   You have turned for me my mourning into dancing;
You have loosed my sackcloth and girded me with gladness,
12   That my soul may sing praise to You and not be silent.
O LORD my God, I will give thanks to You forever.

If my life is good, it's because of God.

from PSALM 30

Being a teenager is great. But one problem with being teen-age is I get some ideas I have to learn the hard way are off. Like one thing that's cool about being teen is I have a lot of energy, more than I know what to do with sometimes. I feel strong and am getting stronger. My parents tell me that's not normal for regular people. But I feel like I'll never get old like them, although I know I will -- a long time from now.

In all my teenage studliness, I thought, "I'm a stud. Nothing can touch me." I found out quick that attitude was off. Out of no-where, I got real sick and felt like I was dying. Heck, I wanted to

die. I had a fever of 1-Oh-4 and was barfing all over the place. Then, I remembered I needed God. Duh! So I prayed to Him, and moaned and groaned a bit, too. And He healed me up.

After going through that, I haven't forgotten if my life is good, it's because of God being good to me, not because I'm so studly. If He's not helping me and looking out for me, I'm in trouble. Now I'm glad I got sick to teach me a lesson, and to make me appreciate feeling good. Most importantly, I appreciate God more now and Him being good to me.

Psalm 31
For the choir director. A Psalm of David.

1   In You, O LORD, I have taken refuge;
Let me never be ashamed;
In Your righteousness deliver me.
2   Incline Your ear to me, rescue me quickly;
Be to me a rock of strength,
A stronghold to save me.
3   For You are my rock and my fortress;
For Your name's sake You will lead me and guide me.
4   You will pull me out of the net which they have secretly laid for me,
For You are my strength.
5   Into Your hand I commit my spirit;
You have ransomed me, O LORD, God of truth.

6   I hate those who regard vain idols,
But I trust in the LORD.
7   I will rejoice and be glad in Your lovingkindness,
Because You have seen my affliction;
You have known the troubles of my soul,
8   And You have not given me over into the hand of the enemy;
You have set my feet in a large place.

9   Be gracious to me, O LORD, for I am in distress;
My eye is wasted away from grief, my soul and my body also.
10   For my life is spent with sorrow
And my years with sighing;
My strength has failed because of my iniquity,
And my body has wasted away.

11 Because of all my adversaries, I have become a reproach,
Especially to my neighbors,
And an object of dread to my acquaintances;
Those who see me in the street flee from me.
12 I am forgotten as a dead man, out of mind;
I am like a broken vessel.
13 For I have heard the slander of many,
Terror is on every side;
While they took counsel together against me,
They schemed to take away my life.

14 But as for me, I trust in You, O LORD,
I say, "You are my God."
15 My times are in Your hand;
Deliver me from the hand of my enemies and from those who persecute
me.
16 Make Your face to shine upon Your servant;
Save me in Your lovingkindness.
17 Let me not be put to shame, O LORD, for I call upon You;
Let the wicked be put to shame, let them be silent in Sheol.
18 Let the lying lips be mute,
Which speak arrogantly against the righteous
With pride and contempt.

19 How great is Your goodness,
Which You have stored up for those who fear You,
Which You have wrought for those who take refuge in You,
Before the sons of men!
20 You hide them in the secret place of Your presence from the con-
spiracies of man;
You keep them secretly in a shelter from the strife of tongues.
21 Blessed be the LORD,
For He has made marvelous His lovingkindness to me in a besieged city.
22 As for me, I said in my alarm,
"I am cut off from before Your eyes";
Nevertheless You heard the voice of my supplications
When I cried to You.

23 O love the LORD, all you His godly ones!
The LORD preserves the faithful
And fully recompenses the proud doer.
24 Be strong and let your heart take courage,
All you who hope in the LORD.

My life is in your hands.

from PSALM 31

I'm coming to You, Lord, and praying. My trust is in You. I don't know anywhere else to go. Please don't let me walk away dejected.

My eyes are red and spent with crying. Depression has sapped my energy and desire to do anything. All I want to do is lie down on my bed and be by myself. The only thing keeping me going is You see my tears. You know what I'm going through.

You have even gone through it Yourself. Jesus, You know what it's like for people to reject You and tell all sorts of lies about You. They did it while You were down here. They are still doing it.

You were strong and handled it perfectly. And now You have a reputation, a name above anybody else's. But, Jesus, I am weak. I can't handle this and I don't know how. I need You to be strong for me.

I'm crying on the outside, but deep inside, I know You'll live up to Your name in my life, too. You'll help me and lead out of this dark time. I pray it's real soon, Lord, while I still have a life and a reputation left.

When I walk down the halls at school, I can hear the whispering. Why can't anyone talk to my face instead of behind my back? Even those who know me avoid me. Hardly anyone hangs with me anymore. No one takes up for me.

With the rumors and everything else, I'm afraid I'll never have a life at that school. Every day there, I'm treated like trash. I dread school. I wish I could go some place far away.

But there have been times before when I said to myself, "My life is ruined." Yet You heard my prayers and made things right again. When I thought evil was closing in on me, You took me and placed me in peaceful, wide open spaces. I know Your love for me is strong, even when my faith is weak.

Lord, I'm real down again. But I trust in You. You are my God. My life is in Your hands.

I know You can shelter me even from lying mouths and words. Do protect me from the lies going around about me. I pray the liars would be so exposed and so ashamed they would shut up, and people wouldn't believe what they say about me.

Lord, thanks for listening to me and knowing where I'm at. I love You. Thanks that even though some of my "friends" have forgotten me, You haven't and You won't. Help me to be strong, to keep hoping in You.

Psalm 32
A Psalm of David. A Maskil.

1   How blessed is he whose transgression is forgiven,
Whose sin is covered!
2   How blessed is the man to whom the LORD does not impute iniquity,
And in whose spirit there is no deceit!

3   When I kept silent about my sin, my body wasted away
Through my groaning all day long.
4   For day and night Your hand was heavy upon me;
My vitality was drained away as with the fever heat of summer.   Selah.

5   I acknowledged my sin to You,
And my iniquity I did not hide;
I said, "I will confess my transgressions to the LORD";
And You forgave the guilt of my sin.   Selah.
6   Therefore, let everyone who is godly pray to You in a time when You
may be found;
Surely in a flood of great waters they will not reach him.
7   You are my hiding place; You preserve me from trouble;
You surround me with songs of deliverance.   Selah.

8   I will instruct you and teach you in the way which you should go;
I will counsel you with My eye upon you.
9   Do not be as the horse or as the mule which have no understanding,
Whose trappings include bit and bridle to hold them in check,
Otherwise they will not come near to you.
10   Many are the sorrows of the wicked,
But he who trusts in the LORD, lovingkindness shall surround him.
11   Be glad in the LORD and rejoice, you righteous ones;
And shout for joy, all you who are upright in heart.

Today didn't have to be this way
Tomorrow is another day
Another chance to make things right
A chance to fully live your life
MxPx "Tomorrow's Another Day"
from *Slowly Going the Way of the Buffalo*

from PSALM 32

I'm through with covering up. I've found out the hard way faking doesn't fly.

Two weeks ago I did something stupid and wrong. What was stupider than stupid is I decided to cover it up. First thing that happened is I was nervous all the time that somebody -- like my parents -- was going to find out. So I told one little lie, then another and another to keep them off track.

Then guilt started eating away at me inside -- guilt from what I did, then guilt from lying about it to those I care about. That guilt kept getting heavier and heavier. So I tried to tell myself what I was doing wasn't that bad. I was deceiving myself now. Then I even tried to talk God into thinking what I was doing was O.K. That was brilliant. Like God's going to fall for that. Pretty soon, I wasn't praying at all. I couldn't face God, I was feeling so guilty.

Everything I did to cover up and escape my wrong made things worse. All this ate at me. I got way down.

I even lost my appetite. Then my parents knew something was wrong. They asked me real nice, but I said nothing was wrong -- and they trusted me and believed me. Then I just went up to my room. I'm really feeling like a low-life now. Here my Mom and Dad are, trusting me, and I lie to their faces.

So here I am, lying and laying on my bed, feeling awful. After actually thinking a while, I see that all my faking had done is make me even more guilty and miserable. So I think, "Maybe it would be better if I just 'fessed up." Duh!

If I mess up, I'm going to 'fess up.

So I prayed and 'fessed up first to God -- and I prayed my parents wouldn't go postal. Then I went downstairs and told them everything. It wasn't as bad as I was afraid it was going to be. They weren't near as upset as I thought they would be. They even appreciated me being straight with them, even if it took me a while. I got grounded, but not for the rest of my life or anything.

What was best was I felt like this big load of guilt was taken off me. It's like after you've had to wear a suit where the tie and shoes and everything was all sweaty and too tight, and then you finally get to take it off and put on your worn loose jeans. It felt great!

I knew God forgave me. Not because I'm good, but because Jesus is good and took care of my forgiveness on the cross. I could talk to Him and pray again. What's the best is God doesn't forgive the way some people forgive, where they say they forgive you, but then keep on holding it against you and aren't cool to you like before. Instead, God helped me make things right and helps me live smarter so I don't do something so stupid again. He's been good to me in a lot of ways. I'm so much happier now.

Being honest and forgiven dogs being fake and guilty any day.
I've learned my lesson. I hope I don't screw up again like I did.
But if I mess up, I'm going to 'fess up.

Psalm 33

1 Sing for joy in the LORD, O you righteous ones;
Praise is becoming to the upright.
2 Give thanks to the LORD with the lyre;
Sing praises to Him with a harp of ten strings.
3 Sing to Him a new song;
Play skillfully with a shout of joy.
4 For the word of the LORD is upright,
And all His work is done in faithfulness.
5 He loves righteousness and justice;
The earth is full of the lovingkindness of the LORD.

6 By the word of the LORD the heavens were made,
And by the breath of His mouth all their host.
7 He gathers the waters of the sea together as a heap;
He lays up the deeps in storehouses.
8 Let all the earth fear the LORD;
Let all the inhabitants of the world stand in awe of Him.
9 For He spoke, and it was done;
He commanded, and it stood fast.
10 The LORD nullifies the counsel of the nations;
He frustrates the plans of the peoples.
11 The counsel of the LORD stands forever,
The plans of His heart from generation to generation.
12 Blessed is the nation whose God is the LORD,
The people whom He has chosen for His own inheritance.

13 The LORD looks from heaven;
He sees all the sons of men;
14 From His dwelling place He looks out
On all the inhabitants of the earth,
15 He who fashions the hearts of them all,
He who understands all their works.
16 The king is not saved by a mighty army;
A warrior is not delivered by great strength.
17 A horse is a false hope for victory;
Nor does it deliver anyone by its great strength.

18 Behold, the eye of the LORD is on those who fear Him,
On those who hope for His lovingkindness,
19 To deliver their soul from death
And to keep them alive in famine.

20   Our soul waits for the LORD;
He is our help and our shield.
21   For our heart rejoices in Him,
Because we trust in His holy name.
22   Let Your lovingkindness, O LORD, be upon us,
According as we have hoped in You.

from PSALM 33

A lot of times, I get kind of ho-hum about God. And I need to remind myself how great He is.

Like how great His word is. Nobody is like God, who created the universe just by His word. He said "Let there be light," and there was light, simple as that. Then He said let there be the earth, the sun, the moon, the stars, galaxies, black holes, orangutans, salamanders and no telling what weird things we haven't even discovered yet -- and it was so, just because He said so. Now, who else can do that?

When God says something, it's done. And that's that.

Big-headed fools might think they run things. But it's God who rules. If He doesn't like their plans, He can stop them with the tip of His little finger. His word and His plans are the ones that count.

What's better is His word is not only powerful, it's always right. He's not like some dictator who uses the power of his orders for evil. You can trust that God's Word is good and comes out of His love.

The same goes for His plans. I know His plans for me are good, even when they mean I have to experience tough times. But when the tough times do come, I know He'll get me through them.

Because another thing great about God is He looks down and sees all the people of the world, all six billion of them. Yet He watches out for me. He watches out for each and every one who hopes in Him. He helps me; He shields me. And He understands me. He's always faithful to me in everything He does in my life.

He's my God, and I re-joice. For He is Lord, and I trust Him. I have an awesome life to look forward to because of Him -- because of His love -- because of Who He is.

Psalm 34

A Psalm of David when he feigned madness before
Abimelech, who drove him away and he departed.

1   I will bless the LORD at all times;
His praise shall continually be in my mouth.
2   My soul will make its boast in the LORD;
The humble will hear it and rejoice.
3   O magnify the LORD with me,
And let us exalt His name together.

4   I sought the LORD, and He answered me,
And delivered me from all my fears.
5   They looked to Him and were radiant,
And their faces will never be ashamed.
6   This poor man cried, and the LORD heard him
And saved him out of all his troubles.
7   The angel of the LORD encamps around those who fear Him,
And rescues them.

8   O taste and see that the LORD is good;
How blessed is the man who takes refuge in Him!
9   O fear the LORD, you His saints;
For to those who fear Him there is no want.
10   The young lions do lack and suffer hunger;
But they who seek the LORD shall not be in want of any good thing.
11   Come, you children, listen to me;
I will teach you the fear of the LORD.
12   Who is the man who desires life
And loves length of days that he may see good?
13   Keep your tongue from evil
And your lips from speaking deceit.
14   Depart from evil and do good;
Seek peace and pursue it.

15   The eyes of the LORD are toward the righteous
And His ears are open to their cry.
16   The face of the LORD is against evildoers,
To cut off the memory of them from the earth.
17   The righteous cry, and the LORD hears
And delivers them out of all their troubles.
18   The LORD is near to the brokenhearted
And saves those who are crushed in spirit.

19   Many are the afflictions of the righteous,
But the LORD delivers him out of them all.
20   He keeps all his bones,
Not one of them is broken.

21 Evil shall slay the wicked,
And those who hate the righteous will be condemned.
22 The LORD redeems the soul of His servants,
And none of those who take refuge in Him will be condemned.

I'm always having a tough time with something.

from PSALM 34
Sometimes, it seems like I'm always having a tough time with something. It's a good thing I can always talk to God and ask Him for help. I used to be afraid He wouldn't really care about my prayers or my situation, that He would just leave me stuck there, but not any more. He has come through for me so many times.

There have definitely been times when I've been down in it and fearful. But I prayed hard, and God listened and got me out of my troubles. He encouraged me and answered my prayers -- a lot of times way better than I imagined he would. It's so cool when God does that.

It is awesome God really listens when I pray. He's the King of everything -- He's God -- and He has a whole universe of things to be concerned about and has millions of prayers coming up to Him. A lot of them probably are more important than mine. Yet He listens to me. Not only that, He's always watching out for me and is always ready to listen to me. It's not like I have to get obnoxious to get his attention like I do with my dad sometimes.

I know God's not a genie or a slot machine, and He's too cool to become one. But I've found out He sure is good. There are some bad things that can't be undone. He still listens and helps me even then. Like when I was dumped by the first one I've ever really fell in love with. I was hurting. I found out what it means to have your heart broken. But when I prayed about it, I sensed Jesus was there with me. And He healed me inside. It didn't happen overnight. Still, before I knew it, I was happy and my old self again. Considering how broken-hearted and in love I was, that's a miracle!

So like I said, it seems like I'm always having a tough time with something. But the Lord listens and brings me out of it every time.

Psalm 35
A Psalm of David.

1   Contend, O LORD, with those who contend with me;
Fight against those who fight against me.
2   Take hold of buckler and shield
And rise up for my help.
3   Draw also the spear and the battle-axe to meet those who pursue me;
Say to my soul, "I am your salvation."
4   Let those be ashamed and dishonored who seek my life;
Let those be turned back and humiliated who devise evil against me.
5   Let them be like chaff before the wind,
With the angel of the LORD driving them on.
6   Let their way be dark and slippery,
With the angel of the LORD pursuing them.
7   For without cause they hid their net for me;
Without cause they dug a pit for my soul.
8   Let destruction come upon him unawares,
And let the net which he hid catch himself;
Into that very destruction let him fall.

9   And my soul shall rejoice in the LORD;
It shall exult in His salvation.
10   All my bones will say, "LORD, who is like You,
Who delivers the afflicted from him who is too strong for him,
And the afflicted and the needy from him who robs him?"
11   Malicious witnesses rise up;
They ask me of things that I do not know.
12   They repay me evil for good,
To the bereavement of my soul.
13   But as for me, when they were sick, my clothing was sackcloth;
I humbled my soul with fasting,
And my prayer kept returning to my bosom.
14   I went about as though it were my friend or brother;
I bowed down mourning, as one who sorrows for a mother.
15   But at my stumbling they rejoiced and gathered themselves together;
The smiters whom I did not know gathered together against me,
They slandered me without ceasing.
16   Like godless jesters at a feast,
They gnashed at me with their teeth.

17   Lord, how long will You look on?
Rescue my soul from their ravages,
My only life from the lions.
18   I will give You thanks in the great congregation;
I will praise You among a mighty throng.
19   Do not let those who are wrongfully my enemies rejoice over me;
Nor let those who hate me without cause wink maliciously.

20   For they do not speak peace,
But they devise deceitful words against those who are quiet in the land.
21   They opened their mouth wide against me;
They said, "Aha, aha, our eyes have seen it!"

22   You have seen it, O LORD, do not keep silent;
O Lord, do not be far from me.
23   Stir up Yourself, and awake to my right
And to my cause, my God and my Lord.
24   Judge me, O LORD my God, according to Your righteousness,
And do not let them rejoice over me.
25   Do not let them say in their heart, "Aha, our desire!"
Do not let them say, "We have swallowed him up!"
26   Let those be ashamed and humiliated altogether who rejoice at my distress;
Let those be clothed with shame and dishonor who magnify themselves over me.

27   Let them shout for joy and rejoice, who favor my vindication;
And let them say continually, "The LORD be magnified,
Who delights in the prosperity of His servant."
28   And my tongue shall declare Your righteousness
And Your praise all day long.

I don't care if we're punk, or ska, or hardcore,
enough for you,
it's sad but true,
you can call us names till your face turns blue.
Our assurance comes from God,
it's nothing new,
we'll never care 'cause we're never cool enough for you.
Five Iron Frenzy "Cool Enough for You"
from *Upbeats and Beatdowns*

from PSALM 35

Lord, You're on the side of average guys and girls who trust You and try to live right. A lot of people care about those who are popular, athletic, or rich. But those things aren't important to You. You care about average people like me.

And right now, I am glad about that. Because I need You to take up for me, Lord.

Part of that "cool" crowd is making my life miserable. Every day, they're threatening me and telling lies about me. I don't even know why, except they're jerks. Other than that, I don't think there is a reason why.

I try to mind my business and live my life without causing too much trouble. Yet they say all sorts of things about me. Most of it, I don't even know what they're talking about. Yet they're treating me like I did something awful.

Instead, I've been good to them. I was friends with a couple of them when we were younger. We were tight, too. We had great times. And I stuck with them when they were going through some tough times.

But then they got all concerned about their image and popularity, and became too cool to hang with me. That hurt. What they're doing now makes the hurt worse.

They have so many lies going around about me. Sometimes I feel even who I am is being torn away from me.

Lord, I need your help. They are too strong for me. But You are too strong for them. I know You can stop them.

Not only stop them; make them fully see their wrong so they'll be ashamed and maybe turn in the right direction.

I especially want that for my old friends.

Thanks for taking up for me.

Psalm 36
For the choir director. A Psalm of David the servant of the LORD.

1   Transgression speaks to the ungodly within his heart;
There is no fear of God before his eyes.
2   For it flatters him in his own eyes
Concerning the discovery of his iniquity and the hatred of it.
3   The words of his mouth are wickedness and deceit;
He has ceased to be wise and to do good.
4   He plans wickedness upon his bed;
He sets himself on a path that is not good;
He does not despise evil.

5   Your lovingkindness, O LORD, extends to the heavens,
Your faithfulness reaches to the skies.
6   Your righteousness is like the mountains of God;
Your judgments are like a great deep.
O LORD, You preserve man and beast.
7   How precious is Your lovingkindness, O God!
And the children of men take refuge in the shadow of Your wings.
8   They drink their fill of the abundance of Your house;
And You give them to drink of the river of Your delights.
9   For with You is the fountain of life;
In Your light we see light.

10   O continue Your lovingkindness to those who know You,
   And Your righteousness to the upright in heart.
11   Let not the foot of pride come upon me,
   And let not the hand of the wicked drive me away.
12   There the doers of iniquity have fallen;
   They have been thrust down and cannot rise.

from PSALM 36

I can't understand some people, who love evil. They don't feel good unless they're doing bad. All they can think about is doing wrong and hurting others. Probably even when they're lying in their beds at night, they're planning what evil they want to do. They fool themselves to think their wrong will never be discovered. They think God will just look the other way and do nothing. They don't fear Him at all. They're evil; I didn't say they're smart.

And their mouths are like trash cans. Sorry, I shouldn't say that. That's an insult to trash cans. You ought to hear them talk. Actually, maybe you shouldn't.

I don't understand them. Don't they see the way they're going is going to hurt them in the end?

You Lord, on the other hand, are righteous. And not just a follow-the-rules righteousness, but a deep, soaring righteousness and holiness that loves far beyond what I can imagine. You are so good and faithful to Your children. You save all who come to You. You protect them.

Your righteousness is generous. You meet our needs. You give us so much to enjoy. You give us real life, not just existence. Not like just a trickle of water to keep us barely alive, but like a jamming water park and a bright summer day, You give us life big time -- abundant life. Your light makes my life so bright, I need Songlasses.

When I think about guys who are against God and into wrong, when I think about the darkness they're heading for and the harm they could do me if You weren't looking out for me -- and to be honest, when I think about my own wrong -- I'm overwhelmed You're so good to me. I could easily be messed up by them. I could easily be them. I could be surrounded by darkness.

Instead, You give me Your light. My life is good only because of Your righteous love toward me.

TRUSTING GOD

Us Christians can be pretty funny. We trust God to get us to heaven. Considering we've never seen heaven and don't know where it is, and considering all God has to forgive us for before we get there, that's a lot of trust. But we trust Jesus and His word, so most of us are confident about heaven. Because our confidence is in Jesus.

Yet most of us have a hard time trusting God with this life. We trust God with our afterlife, but we're afraid He might mess up this one. We're afraid that, after dying for us and rising again for us and everything else He's done for us, that now He's going to drop the ball on us. We get all anxious as if He might make a big mistake or just doesn't care or something. Go figure.

If we don't trust Jesus with this life, that's what can mess it up, as surely as not trusting Jesus for the next life will mess that one up. I know. I was what I'm talking about, confident in God for heaven, but not for this life.

When I was a teenager, I was seriously down at times, contemplating suicide even, because I was afraid God was giving me a sorry life. I was especially unhappy with not having a girlfriend. Later when I was pushing 30, I went through some dark periods of depression. During one stretch, I cried driving to church three straight Sundays. My life was in a rut, I feared the future, and I was **not** content with being single.

It wasn't until I was 33 (I can be a little slow sometimes.) that I saw I had a big blind spot -- I didn't trust God with my life, with my future. But God did some unusual things in my life to show me I can trust Him. He didn't have to do that, but He did. After I confessed I didn't trust Him the way I should, He increased my faith and trust.

Now, I'm not perfect in this. From time to time, that old distrust tries to slip back into my mind. But I'm a lot happier now. I'm even content being a single guy, if you can believe that. I used to think if God didn't come through for me the way I think He should, especially in the area of marriage, my life would be sorry. Now I know it's God who can and will meet my needs, not some future wife, and not my little blueprint on how I'd like my life to go. He knows what's best for me far better than I do.

And maybe it's just my perception, but it seems God's doing more in my life now. If so, that's in line with passages like Hebrews 11:6, James 1: 5-8, and Matthew 17:20. Don't get me wrong -- I totally reject "Have faith and you'll be healed of zits and get a brand new car!" theology. God is not a Coke machine. Still, there is a link between faith and God's provision. One very big example is You have to trust in Jesus to receive eternal life with Him. I think a lot of things in this life are that way, too.

So how do you trust God with your life, especially when it can get scary? Something that's helped me a lot is remembering times when God has acted in my life in the past. Many psalms do that, too. When things got tough, the psalmists recalled past acts of God and were encouraged. When you remember what God has done for you in the past, it doesn't make much sense to think He won't take care of you now.

You'd think if God has done something cool in your life, you'd remember it. But you'd be surprised how easy it is to forget. Have you ever prayed for something, and God answered? But by the time He answered, you hardly noticed because you forgot you had prayed about it? I plead "Guilty" to that one. Or when you're deep in the dumps, do you find it hard to think about anything good -- anything? That's one reason I recommend keeping a journal. When God does something awesome, write it down so you won't forget. And then it will be there to encourage you and help you trust Him when you need it.

What's even more important is to focus on God and who He is, instead of just on whatever's got you bummed. That's sounds simple. But when worried or down, most people tend to get tunnel vision, where all they can see is what's got them down. I know I've had several bad cases of tunnel vision. But instead of focusing on just your bad circumstances, focus on God. That's what David did back in Psalm 27: 1-3. His attitude was God takes care of me, so I'm not going to fear but be confident, no matter what. Also check out Psalm 46 and Colossians 3: 1-2. God is bigger and better than whatever stuff you're going through, so focus on Him. Then it will be easier to trust Him to bring you through.

Before we move on, let's be honest about something. A lot of teenagers focus on what they don't have -- a boyfriend or girl-friend, a nice car, magazine cover looks, whatever -- and they think if they only had whatever, then they'd be happy for life. Wrong! Only God can meet our deepest needs. We need to trust Him, not things or circumstances or getting whatever, to make our lives good.

In fact, Psalm 37 talks about that, so check it out.

M. M.

Psalm 37
A Psalm of David.

1   Do not fret because of evildoers,
Be not envious toward wrongdoers.
2   For they will wither quickly like the grass
And fade like the green herb.
3   Trust in the LORD and do good;
Dwell in the land and cultivate faithfulness.
4   Delight yourself in the LORD;
And He will give you the desires of your heart.
5   Commit your way to the LORD,
Trust also in Him, and He will do it.
6   He will bring forth your righteousness as the light
And your judgment as the noonday.

7   Rest in the LORD and wait patiently for Him;
Do not fret because of him who prospers in his way,
Because of the man who carries out wicked schemes.
8   Cease from anger and forsake wrath;
Do not fret; it leads only to evildoing.
9   For evildoers will be cut off,
But those who wait for the LORD, they will inherit the land.
10   Yet a little while and the wicked man will be no more;
And you will look carefully for his place and he will not be there.
11   But the humble will inherit the land
And will delight themselves in abundant prosperity.

12   The wicked plots against the righteous
And gnashes at him with his teeth.
13   The Lord laughs at him,
For He sees his day is coming.
14   The wicked have drawn the sword and bent their bow
To cast down the afflicted and the needy,
To slay those who are upright in conduct.
15   Their sword will enter their own heart,
And their bows will be broken.

16   Better is the little of the righteous
Than the abundance of many wicked.
17   For the arms of the wicked will be broken,
But the LORD sustains the righteous.
18   The LORD knows the days of the blameless,
And their inheritance will be forever.
19   They will not be ashamed in the time of evil,
And in the days of famine they will have abundance.
20   But the wicked will perish;
And the enemies of the LORD will be like the glory of the pastures,

They vanish—like smoke they vanish away.
21 The wicked borrows and does not pay back,
But the righteous is gracious and gives.
22 For those blessed by Him will inherit the land,
But those cursed by Him will be cut off.
23 The steps of a man are established by the LORD,
And He delights in his way.
24 When he falls, he will not be hurled headlong,
Because the LORD is the One who holds his hand.
25 I have been young and now I am old,
Yet I have not seen the righteous forsaken
Or his descendants begging bread.
26 All day long he is gracious and lends,
And his descendants are a blessing.

27 Depart from evil and do good,
So you will abide forever.
28 For the LORD loves justice
And does not forsake His godly ones;
They are preserved forever,
But the descendants of the wicked will be cut off.
29 The righteous will inherit the land
And dwell in it forever.
30 The mouth of the righteous utters wisdom,
And his tongue speaks justice.
31 The law of his God is in his heart;
His steps do not slip.
32 The wicked spies upon the righteous
And seeks to kill him.
33 The LORD will not leave him in his hand
Or let him be condemned when he is judged.
34 Wait for the LORD and keep His way,
And He will exalt you to inherit the land;
When the wicked are cut off, you will see it.

35 I have seen a wicked, violent man
Spreading himself like a luxuriant tree in its native soil.
36 Then he passed away, and lo, he was no more;
I sought for him, but he could not be found.
37 Mark the blameless man, and behold the upright;
For the man of peace will have a posterity.
38 But transgressors will be altogether destroyed;
The posterity of the wicked will be cut off.
39 But the salvation of the righteous is from the LORD;
He is their strength in time of trouble.
40 The LORD helps them and delivers them;
He delivers them from the wicked and saves them,
Because they take refuge in Him.

would you understand

if i let you into me

and held your hand maybe

just for a day!

joshua stevens "Tell me something"

from PSALM 37

I get worried about my life and my future. I know I shouldn't, but I do. I used to think getting older would be cool, and in a lot of ways it is. But there are a lot more things to worry about, more heavy stuff going on, more things that can go wrong.

Then the truth sinks in -- I'm not going to be a kid or teenager forever. Who knows what my life is going to be like then?

When I think about these things, it's good to know I can hold on to God and hold on to His promises to me.

It's good to know He holds on to me.

There are times I see my life as a string of random events, accidents even, that could go in any direction. But it isn't that way. God has excellent plans for me. What's more, He actually enjoys guiding my life and watching me and looking out for me. He likes me and cares about my life that much. If -- I mean when -- I do trip up, He's there to keep me from falling too hard and to give me a hand to pull me up.

I don't have to rely on chance or worry about it. I don't even have to rely on myself. God is there for me. If I commit my life and my decisions to Him, He'll help me and make things right in the end.

Lately, I've been worrying about whether God will meet my needs and fulfill my desires. And I have to admit I get a little jealous when I see others whose lives seem perfect even though they don't care about God.

But I don't need to worry about God providing and being faithful to me, because He will and more. If I'm going to worry, I need to worry about being faithful to Him. He's awesome and deserves my best. And He is generous. If I am faithful and trust Him and put Him first, He'll meet my needs and more, even my deepest desires. And at just the right time, His timing. Sometimes His timing isn't exactly the time I would prefer. But whose timing is better, mine or God's? And some desires He'll change first, because sometimes what I want is not the best thing. I could never pay the insurance on a Ferrari, for example. Still,

God is so good and generous. Why do I get so stupid I'm afraid He'll drop the ball on me? It's dumb to be afraid He'll let me down.

Above all, He'll give me Himself. That's my deepest need and desire.

Jesus already has given Himself for me. He died for me on the cross. He gave His own life for me so I can live. It's hard for me to even imagine that kind of love.

If He loves me like that, it doesn't make any sense to worry He won't meet my other needs. So I don't need to worry. Jesus is there for me. I can relax. He won't forget me. I just need to give my worries a rest, live right, and love and trust Him.

PROMISES

Something else that can encourage you and help you trust God: remember His promises. When you know God has given His word about something, it helps you trust Him and hang in there in that area of your life. Instead of just being discouraged by bad circumstances you're going through, you can be encouraged by looking forward to good that God says is coming. It's like how a coming vacation makes school work easier to endure, except better.

I know His word has helped me that way many times. Probably my favorite promise in the Bible is Romans 8:28 -- "God causes all things to work together for good to those who love God." More than once, that verse has been about all I knew to hang on to. There have been times so dark when the only thing keeping me from giving up was knowing God would somehow turn my darkness into light. And every time, God kept His promise. Sooner or later, I've seen good come out of all my bad times.

One big good is my trust in Him has grown. I know His promise of Romans 8:28, and I've seen Him keep it again and again. God has proven Himself to me to be the greatest Promise Keeper of all time! I trust Him more now than before. Bad times are easier to handle now, because I'm confident He'll turn them into good.

And Romans 8:28 is only one promise. The Psalms, not to mention the rest of the Bible, are full of God's promises. You probably noticed a few just in Psalm 37. (If you didn't, read it again.) As you go through Psalms, if any promises get a hold on you, write them down so you can get a hold on them when you need it.

There are two things to be careful about, though. First, don't take a verse out of context and twist it into a promise you want it to be. For example, "Ask and you shall receive" is a great promise Jesus made. But I don't think He was talking about a Porshe. Sorry. Second, a lot of times, God does not fulfill a promise right away. Sometimes, the complete fulfillment of a promise doesn't even come in this life. Check out Hebrews 11: 13-16. Still, you can trust that His timing is the best and that He will keep His word.

God's word is stronger than any difficulties. Nothing will ever stop God from keeping His word. So hold on to it, no matter what.

M. M.

Psalm 38
A Psalm of David, for a memorial.

1   O LORD, rebuke me not in Your wrath,
And chasten me not in Your burning anger.
2   For Your arrows have sunk deep into me,
And Your hand has pressed down on me.
3   There is no soundness in my flesh because of Your indignation;
There is no health in my bones because of my sin.
4   For my iniquities are gone over my head;
As a heavy burden they weigh too much for me.
5   My wounds grow foul and fester
Because of my folly.
6   I am bent over and greatly bowed down;
I go mourning all day long.
7   For my loins are filled with burning,
And there is no soundness in my flesh.
8   I am benumbed and badly crushed;
I groan because of the agitation of my heart.

9   Lord, all my desire is before You;
And my sighing is not hidden from You.
10   My heart throbs, my strength fails me;
And the light of my eyes, even that has gone from me.
11   My loved ones and my friends stand aloof from my plague;
And my kinsmen stand afar off.
12   Those who seek my life lay snares for me;
And those who seek to injure me have threatened destruction,
And they devise treachery all day long.
13   But I, like a deaf man, do not hear;
And I am like a mute man who does not open his mouth.

14 Yes, I am like a man who does not hear,
And in whose mouth are no arguments.
15 For I hope in You, O LORD;
You will answer, O Lord my God.
16 For I said, "May they not rejoice over me,
Who, when my foot slips, would magnify themselves against me."
17 For I am ready to fall,
And my sorrow is continually before me.
18 For I confess my iniquity;
I am full of anxiety because of my sin.
19 But my enemies are vigorous and strong,
And many are those who hate me wrongfully.
20 And those who repay evil for good,
They oppose me, because I follow what is good.
21 Do not forsake me, O LORD;
O my God, do not be far from me!
22 Make haste to help me,
O Lord, my salvation!

*I told the world to bring it on
but
deep down I know I wasn't ready.
I said I couldn't be deceived
meanwhile
I'm walking into the same old traps.
I said I couldn't be broke
as
I watched my world collapse.*

John Reuben "X-ray"
from *Are We There Yet?*

from PSALM 38

Lord, I am low. And it's my fault. I'm in over my head because of my stupidity.

The wrong things I was into, I thought it didn't really matter. I thought I wouldn't get caught or hurt. Was I wrong!

I thought if things got rough, my friends would be there for me. But they act like they don't know me. I guess I shouldn't be mad at them. My life is so bad now, if I were them, I wouldn't want to be around me either. I don't like being around me anymore. But I picked the wrong kind of friends. And who's fault is that?

Lord, You know where I am. You know my pain. There's not much I can say, except I've blown it and I'm sorry. I can't blame You for letting things get so bad. The blame belongs to the guy in the mirror. I don't have any smooth arguments about why You should help me out. I deserve nothing from You.

But I'm praying anyway, because I hope in You. You're my only hope. I know, Jesus, when You died for me, You knew every bad thing I would ever do. Yet You died for me anyway. You went through hell on the cross, which You never deserved, to save me from hell, which I do deserve.

If You were that incredible of a friend to me then, I know You're still a friend to me now, even if I've lost all my other friends -- even if I've been a sorry friend to You.

Jesus, I'm scared. But I know You won't forget me. I know You'll come close and help me.

Psalm 39
For the choir director, for Jeduthun. A Psalm of David.

1   I said, "I will guard my ways
That I may not sin with my tongue;
I will guard my mouth as with a muzzle
While the wicked are in my presence."
2   I was mute and silent,
I refrained even from good,
And my sorrow grew worse.
3   My heart was hot within me,
While I was musing the fire burned;
Then I spoke with my tongue:
4   "LORD, make me to know my end
And what is the extent of my days;
Let me know how transient I am.
5   "Behold, You have made my days as handbreadths,
And my lifetime as nothing in Your sight;
Surely every man at his best is a mere breath.   Selah.
6   "Surely every man walks about as a phantom;
Surely they make an uproar for nothing;
He amasses riches and does not know who will gather them.

7   "And now, Lord, for what do I wait?
My hope is in You.
8   "Deliver me from all my transgressions;
Make me not the reproach of the foolish.
9   "I have become mute, I do not open my mouth,
Because it is You who have done it.
10   "Remove Your plague from me;
Because of the opposition of Your hand I am perishing.

11   "With reproofs You chasten a man for iniquity;
    You consume as a moth what is precious to him;
    Surely every man is a mere breath.   Selah.

12   "Hear my prayer, O LORD, and give ear to my cry;
    Do not be silent at my tears;
    For I am a stranger with You,
    A sojourner like all my fathers.
13   "Turn Your gaze away from me, that I may smile again
    Before I depart and am no more."

I'm a nobody.
I'm so lost in the crowd, I can't even find myself.

from PSALM 39

I used to think I could do anything I wanted to. I thought I could be somebody and make a difference in this world.

But I can't even keep from screwing up. I said to myself, "I'm going to watch myself and keep my mouth shut so I'll stop making a fool of myself." But it just made things worse. Not only did I keep screwing up anyway, I got so into myself and was so afraid to be me, I made myself distant from friends and from good things I was involved in. I got frustrated with -- life. I felt a searing emptiness inside. I felt a burning desire shut inside, but I didn't even know for what.

Now I feel useless. I feel I'm just taking up space and wasting oxygen. I'm a useless breathing machine . . . that will break down soon. Compared to You, I'm only a few breaths in time. I used to feel like I'd live forever -- used to.

And if I finally do something right, what good will that do? If I make straight A's, get successful, get popular, and make a million dollars, what good will that really do anybody? Especially after I'm dead.

I'm a nobody. I'm so lost in the crowd, I can't even find myself.

Lord, I don't have a lot of hope. But what hope I have is in You. I sure don't hope in myself anymore.

Maybe You're letting me go through all this to show me how much I need You. If You are, I don't blame You. I know now I need You to forgive me and rescue me from myself. And I know now only You can give my life real significance.

Would you?

I want to smile again.

Psalm 40
For the choir director. A Psalm of David.

1   I waited patiently for the LORD;
And He inclined to me and heard my cry.
2   He brought me up out of the pit of destruction, out of the miry clay,
And He set my feet upon a rock making my footsteps firm.
3   He put a new song in my mouth, a song of praise to our God;
Many will see and fear
And will trust in the LORD.

4   How blessed is the man who has made the LORD his trust,
And has not turned to the proud, nor to those who lapse into falsehood.
5   Many, O LORD my God, are the wonders which You have done,
And Your thoughts toward us;
There is none to compare with You.
If I would declare and speak of them,
They would be too numerous to count.

6   Sacrifice and meal offering You have not desired;
My ears You have opened;
Burnt offering and sin offering You have not required.
7   Then I said, "Behold, I come;
In the scroll of the book it is written of me.
8   I delight to do Your will, O my God;
Your Law is within my heart."

9   I have proclaimed glad tidings of righteousness in the great congregation;
Behold, I will not restrain my lips,
O LORD, You know.
10   I have not hidden Your righteousness within my heart;
I have spoken of Your faithfulness and Your salvation;
I have not concealed Your lovingkindness and Your truth from the great
congregation.

11   You, O LORD, will not withhold Your compassion from me;
Your lovingkindness and Your truth will continually preserve me.
12   For evils beyond number have surrounded me;
My iniquities have overtaken me, so that I am not able to see;
They are more numerous than the hairs of my head,
And my heart has failed me.

13   Be pleased, O LORD, to deliver me;
Make haste, O LORD, to help me.
14   Let those be ashamed and humiliated together
Who seek my life to destroy it;

Let those be turned back and dishonored
Who delight in my hurt.
15 Let those be appalled because of their shame
Who say to me, "Aha, aha!"
16 Let all who seek You rejoice and be glad in You;
Let those who love Your salvation say continually,
"The LORD be magnified!"
17 Since I am afflicted and needy,
Let the Lord be mindful of me.
You are my help and my deliverer;
Do not delay, O my God.

Forget religion. I'm into reality.

from PSALM 40

Note: Verse 6 -- "My ears Thou hast opened" or "pierced" may refer to the Jewish legal custom of Exodus 21: 5 - 6. If a freed slave loved his master and desired to continue to serve him, his master would pierce the slave's ear, and the slave stayed with him for life.

Forget religion. I'm into reality.
Forget acting all holy Sunday morning, but then not backing it up the rest of the week. I'm through with saying Jesus is my Lord during church, but then blowing Him off as soon as I'm out the door. I'm through with trusting in religion. I will trust in God.
So much of religion is trusting in one's own goodness and holiness to win brownie points with God. So much of it is trusting in one's own religious rituals and thoughts instead of trusting in God and what He thinks. Forget religion.
God's thoughts and acts are so many and so awesome. What we can think or do is nothing in comparison. Our religion is weak. It can't touch the reality of who God is. It can't even come close. God's thoughts -- our puny minds can not begin to comprehend them. Don't even try to get them all down or count them. His thoughts toward just me are mind-blowing.
God, You are so great, infinite in power, wisdom, righteousness, and love. You are so great to me. You deserve everything from me, all I have and all I am. But You don't want my religious ritual.
You want me.
You've got me, Lord.
I want to live my life the way You want me to. Not because I have to -- You've already forgiven me and given me Yourself and

heaven -- but because I want to.

I'm not going keep You to myself anymore. I'm going to tell others about You, Your truth, and Your love. Jesus, I'm going to tell people about how You loved us by dying for us, then rising again so we can live. I'm not going to just tell it. I'm going to live it.

You have given so much, even Your life for me. You didn't give me just a little religion, and religion is not what I'm going to give You. I want to give You myself. I want to live my life for You.

I belong to You now.

Thanks for giving me real life. Thanks for being the One worth living for.

Psalm 41
For the choir director. A Psalm of David.

1   How blessed is he who considers the helpless;
The LORD will deliver him in a day of trouble.
2   The LORD will protect him and keep him alive,
And he shall be called blessed upon the earth;
And do not give him over to the desire of his enemies.
3   The LORD will sustain him upon his sickbed;
In his illness, You restore him to health.

4   As for me, I said, "O LORD, be gracious to me;
Heal my soul, for I have sinned against You."
5   My enemies speak evil against me,
"When will he die, and his name perish?"
6   And when he comes to see me, he speaks falsehood;
His heart gathers wickedness to itself;
When he goes outside, he tells it.
7   All who hate me whisper together against me;
Against me they devise my hurt, saying,
8   "A wicked thing is poured out upon him,
That when he lies down, he will not rise up again."
9   Even my close friend in whom I trusted,
Who ate my bread,
Has lifted up his heel against me.

10   But You, O LORD, be gracious to me and raise me up,
That I may repay them.
11   By this I know that You are pleased with me,
Because my enemy does not shout in triumph over me.
12   As for me, You uphold me in my integrity,
And You set me in Your presence forever.

13   Blessed be the LORD, the God of Israel,
From everlasting to everlasting.
Amen and Amen.

Thanks for sticking with me, Lord.

from PSALM 41

When times are tough, you find out who your friends are. I sure have.

I did stupid and got into a bad spot. It was rough. What made things worse was all these guys who acted like my friends before, they started whispering behind my back and saying all sorts of things about me. They were getting their jollies out of my hurting.

What happened after I talked with a close friend hurt the worst. We were hanging out at my place, like we always did, and I opened up with him about where I was and how I was feeling. He acted like he so understood and sympathized with me.

But as soon as we said, "Later," he went out and blabbed everything all over the place. I was beyond humiliated. I couldn't believe he turned his back on me and kicked me like that.

Now I really appreciate those who stuck with me and were real friends to me. Because there sure are people who will kick you when you're down.

God stuck with me. He stuck with me even though I messed up and sinned. It was my bad, but He was good to me anyway and brought me through it. He even did so in a way that strengthened my reputation. So now I know God is with me. And now those who were running my rep down are feeling like the fools they are.

Thanks for sticking with me, Lord. Help me to be a faithful friend who sticks with You forever.

Psalm 42
For the choir director. A Maskil of the sons of Korah.

1   As the deer pants for the water brooks,
So my soul pants for You, O God.
2   My soul thirsts for God, for the living God;
When shall I come and appear before God?
3   My tears have been my food day and night,
While they say to me all day long, "Where is your God?"
4   These things I remember and I pour out my soul within me.
For I used to go along with the throng and lead them in procession to the
house of God,
With the voice of joy and thanksgiving, a multitude keeping festival.

5   Why are you in despair, O my soul?
And why have you become disturbed within me?
Hope in God, for I shall again praise Him
For the help of His presence.
6   O my God, my soul is in despair within me;
Therefore I remember You from the land of the Jordan
And the peaks of Hermon, from Mount Mizar.
7   Deep calls to deep at the sound of Your waterfalls;
All Your breakers and Your waves have rolled over me.
8   The LORD will command His lovingkindness in the daytime;
And His song will be with me in the night,
A prayer to the God of my life.

9   I will say to God my rock, "Why have You forgotten me?
Why do I go mourning because of the oppression of the enemy?"
10   As a shattering of my bones, my adversaries revile me,
While they say to me all day long, "Where is your God?"
11   Why are you in despair, O my soul?
And why have you become disturbed within me?
Hope in God, for I shall yet praise Him,
The help of my countenance and my God.

from PSALM 42

Note: If you're wondering who the sons of Korah were, go to "from PSALM 84."

Do you ever have times when you wonder where God is? When you feel like your prayers are bouncing off the walls of your room and not going anywhere? Have you even felt like God has forgotten you? Do you want to be close to God, but He seems so far away, and your life is so dry?

Or maybe you feel you're the one who's gotten far away from God. Even the most faithful, God-centered people feel that way at times. God having Psalm 42 in His word backs that up.

These times definitely happen for teenagers. Life probably is not as simple and easy as it used to be, before you were teen. Your faith and thoughts about God aren't as simple. Your emotions probably are more complex, too. So it's to be expected you'll have times when you feel God is distant, when you wonder where He is and whether He cares about you.

Being a new Christian can be tough, too. Yeah, it's great at first -- the emotions of becoming a Christian can make you high as a kite. But you don't stay high forever. You have to come down from the mountain top. You find out life still has problems. You still have to struggle with your actions and attitudes and with sin. And maybe you don't feel as close to God as you did at the beginning.

Well, if you ever feel this way -- who doesn't? -- you have good company. Not only the psalmists, but other giants of faith like Paul and Elijah struggled with spiritual down times. (I Kings 19: 1-14; Romans 7: 7-25 for starters) Still, these dry times might make you think you're not good enough for God, that He doesn't care about you or want to be around you. So you feel bad about yourself, making things worse.

Two things about that -- first, nobody is worthy of God's presence. Jesus comes into our lives not because we're so good, but because He is good and loves us. Second, if you are thirsty for God, that is a good sign about your relationship with Him. "Huh?", you say. That's right. If you are desiring and seeking God's presence, you are probably His child or are on the way to becoming His child. It's kinda like a little kid away at camp. When he gets homesick, does he miss his Aunt Gertrude, or his Uncle Hubert? No, he misses his mom and dad and his home. If you're missing God, probably one reason is He's your Father and your home is with Him; you belong to Him.

If you think about it, the ones who never miss God aren't godly people, but the ungodly. They don't care if God's around. In fact, they'd rather He'd not be around. That would make it easier for them to do wrong.

Yet even if you know you're His child, these dry times are rough. Your life and your faith feel like they're in a rut, or worse. And you don't know how long you're going to be stuck there. You may not even know why you're stuck there.

Life is difficult enough without God seeming distant. The waves of life can break over you like a stormy ocean, wave after wave overwhelming you (verse 7). In despair, you cry inside -- and out (verse 3). Even remembering past times when you've felt close to God can be tough (verse 4). You wonder why you and God aren't close that way now. And there are no easy answers.

So what do you do when you're down and God seems far away?

Keep on praying. And I don't mean pretty prayers of put-on piety. I mean honest prayers. In case you haven't noticed by now, the Psalms are full of prayers by people who were down and even frustrated with God and who were open and honest with Him about it. Being down and talking straight with Him about it is not on God's bad list. Instead, He honors that kind of openness in the Psalms. You, too, honestly talk to God about where you are at and how you're feeling. Maybe as you're drifting to sleep at night with wet eyes, talk to Him (verse 8). He can handle it.

Remind yourself that no matter how down you get, you can still hope in God (verses 5, 8, 11). Hope in God does not disappoint in the end. Like the guys who wrote this psalm, you'll probably have to remind yourself of this more than once.

Maybe the most important thing about God to remember is "He is a rewarder of those who seek Him." (Hebrews 11: 6) Verse 8 in this psalm says it in a different way -- God "commands His lovingkindness" to help His people. Jesus said if you'll keep on seeking God, you'll find Him (Matthew 7: 7-8). Because if you seek to get close to Him, He'll get close to you (James 4: 8). Best of all, Jesus said He will never reject the one who sincerely comes to Him (John 6:37).

Keep seeking Jesus, and the dry times will come to an end. For He will satisfy your inner thirst (John 4:14).

Yeah, there will be times when God seems distant. But, remember, He is there for you.

M. M.

Psalm 43

1   Vindicate me, O God, and plead my case against an ungodly nation;
O deliver me from the deceitful and unjust man!

2   For You are the God of my strength; why have You rejected me?
Why do I go mourning because of the oppression of the enemy?

3   O send out Your light and Your truth, let them lead me;
Let them bring me to Your holy hill
And to Your dwelling places.

4   Then I will go to the altar of God,
To God my exceeding joy;
And upon the lyre I shall praise You, O God, my God.

5   Why are you in despair, O my soul?
And why are you disturbed within me?
Hope in God, for I shall again praise Him,
The help of my countenance and my God.

clocks tick

    and tock

        over and

           over

time left without me long ago

    i cry caffeine and emotion at night,

        the tears

        fall splashing into puddles on the floor.

joshua stevens "untitled"

from PSALM 43

Life can get dark. I know mine has.

What gets me down bad is being rejected. What's worse is when I feel rejected by You. And I don't even know why.

I used to be strong because of You in my life.   Now I'm weak. I used to be confident about where my life was going. Now it's dark. I don't see anything to do or anywhere to go -- except to cry to You. I need Your light and joy again. I need You.

I know Your light can lead me out of my darkness. And Your truth can guide me like nothing else can. So send out Your light. I'll come running to it. Lead me to where I can see things as they really are.

I want to see You in my life again. You bring me real joy like nothing else. I want the light of Your presence. Then I get to be with You and worship You up close.

So yeah, I'm down. God understands. But maybe I shouldn't be so down in it. My hope is in Him. He helps me smile. He'll give me plenty to be happy about. He'll give me more than plenty to praise Him for. He gives me Himself.

Psalm 44

For the choir director. A Maskil of the sons of Korah.

1   O God, we have heard with our ears,
Our fathers have told us
The work that You did in their days,
In the days of old.

2   You with Your own hand drove out the nations;
Then You planted them;
You afflicted the peoples,
Then You spread them abroad.

3   For by their own sword they did not possess the land,
    And their own arm did not save them,
    But Your right hand and Your arm and the light of Your presence,
    For You favored them.

4   You are my King, O God;
    Command victories for Jacob.
5   Through You we will push back our adversaries;
    Through Your name we will trample down those who rise up against us.
6   For I will not trust in my bow,
    Nor will my sword save me.
7   But You have saved us from our adversaries,
    And You have put to shame those who hate us.
8   In God we have boasted all day long,
    And we will give thanks to Your name forever.   Selah.

9   Yet You have rejected us and brought us to dishonor,
    And do not go out with our armies.
10   You cause us to turn back from the adversary;
    And those who hate us have taken spoil for themselves.
11   You give us as sheep to be eaten
    And have scattered us among the nations.
12   You sell Your people cheaply,
    And have not profited by their sale.
13   You make us a reproach to our neighbors,
    A scoffing and a derision to those around us.
14   You make us a byword among the nations,
    A laughingstock among the peoples.
15   All day long my dishonor is before me
    And my humiliation has overwhelmed me,
16   Because of the voice of him who reproaches and reviles,
    Because of the presence of the enemy and the avenger.

17   All this has come upon us, but we have not forgotten You,
    And we have not dealt falsely with Your covenant.
18   Our heart has not turned back,
    And our steps have not deviated from Your way,
19   Yet You have crushed us in a place of jackals
    And covered us with the shadow of death.

20   If we had forgotten the name of our God
    Or extended our hands to a strange god,
21   Would not God find this out?
    For He knows the secrets of the heart.
22   But for Your sake we are killed all day long;
    We are considered as sheep to be slaughtered.
23   Arouse Yourself, why do You sleep, O Lord?
    Awake, do not reject us forever.

24 Why do You hide Your face
 And forget our affliction and our oppression?
25 For our soul has sunk down into the dust;
 Our body cleaves to the earth.
26 Rise up, be our help,
 And redeem us for the sake of Your lovingkindness.

from PSALM 44

God, You have been great to me in the past. Two thousand years ago, You died for me, Jesus. I never did anything to deserve that. You did it because You're that way; You love people like me that much. Then You worked in my life to bring me to You. You have been great to me and my family so many times and in so many ways. All the good I have is because of You. No matter what happens, I will always thank You.

But now I am low. Those who don't care about You and who hate me are on me all day. Any chance they have to bring me down, they do it. They steal from me. They badmouth me and laugh at me. They're always threatening me. I never know when they might carry out their threats. Every day, they find some way to humiliate me and make me feel like dirt.

I don't know why this is happening to me. Why have You allowed this? I've been faithful to You. I get into Your word and do my best to live by it. I haven't forgotten You. Why does it seem You've forgotten me?

Instead of suffering for something wrong I did, I suffer for You. Every day, I'm put down and kicked around because I'm a Christian. I've read in the Bible where You said I should rejoice if I suffer for Your name. I guess that's better than suffering for something wrong, but I sure don't feel like doing any rejoicing. Because of my belief in You, I'm a target.

So why don't You take up for me?

I'm confident You will take up for me. I don't know why You are delaying, but I do know You love me. You've already shown me love on the cross and in my life. It's hard for me to see it now, but I know You'll help me and bring me through this.

But please don't delay any longer. My life is low. I need You now.

Psalm 45

For the choir director; according to the Shoshannim. A Maskil of the sons
of Korah. A Song of Love.

1   My heart overflows with a good theme;
       I address my verses to the King;
       My tongue is the pen of a ready writer.
2   You are fairer than the sons of men;
       Grace is poured upon Your lips;
       Therefore God has blessed You forever.

3   Gird Your sword on Your thigh, O Mighty One,
       In Your splendor and Your majesty!
4   And in Your majesty ride on victoriously,
       For the cause of truth and meekness and righteousness;
       Let Your right hand teach You awesome things.
5   Your arrows are sharp;
       The peoples fall under You;
       Your arrows are in the heart of the King's enemies.

6   Your throne, O God, is forever and ever;
       A scepter of uprightness is the scepter of Your kingdom.
7   You have loved righteousness and hated wickedness;
       Therefore God, Your God, has anointed You
       With the oil of joy above Your fellows.
8   All Your garments are fragrant with myrrh and aloes and cassia;
       Out of ivory palaces stringed instruments have made You glad.
9   Kings' daughters are among Your noble ladies;
       At Your right hand stands the queen in gold from Ophir.

10   Listen, O daughter, give attention and incline your ear:
       Forget your people and your father's house;
11   Then the King will desire your beauty.
       Because He is your Lord, bow down to Him.
12   The daughter of Tyre will come with a gift;
       The rich among the people will seek your favor.

13   The King's daughter is all glorious within;
       Her clothing is interwoven with gold.
14   She will be led to the King in embroidered work;
       The virgins, her companions who follow her,
       Will be brought to You.
15   They will be led forth with gladness and rejoicing;
       They will enter into the King's palace.
16   In place of your fathers will be your sons;
       You shall make them princes in all the earth.
17   I will cause Your name to be remembered in all generations;
       Therefore the peoples will give You thanks forever and ever.

from PSALM 45

I am hyped Jesus is King. He's gonna rule! And His rule is going to be perfect, because He is perfect.

I can hardly wait until Jesus comes back (especially right before finals). I can't even imagine how awesome it will be. He will come riding in all His majesty to make things right. He will put evil where it belongs.

He won't take over because of a thirst for power or to oppress people like men do. He will ride and conquer for the cause of truth, righteousness, and peace -- real peace. It's like a superhero winning, except it's way better -- and it's for real -- and it's forever. He won't be coming for power or money. He'll come to take up for the weak and the poor. Those who have been put down unjustly by evil men in power will be put down no longer. Jesus will defeat evil governments for them. Then He'll crush Satan. The world will finally be safe for all who belong to Him.

His rule will be righteous! Things will finally be the way they ought to be. And we'll get to see Him -- to see Jesus! We'll get to enjoy how awesome He is as much as we want.

Then we won't have to worry anymore about presidents trashing what is right. We won't have to worry about bozos winning the next election. Because Jesus will rule not for just a few years, but forever and ever and ever. Yeah! I'm gonna thank Him forever, starting now!

Psalm 46
For the choir director.
A Psalm of the sons of Korah, set to Alamoth. A Song.

1   God is our refuge and strength,
A very present help in trouble.
2   Therefore we will not fear, though the earth should change
And though the mountains slip into the heart of the sea;
3   Though its waters roar and foam,
Though the mountains quake at its swelling pride.   Selah.

4   There is a river whose streams make glad the city of God,
The holy dwelling places of the Most High.
5   God is in the midst of her, she will not be moved;
God will help her when morning dawns.
6   The nations made an uproar, the kingdoms tottered;
He raised His voice, the earth melted.
7   The LORD of hosts is with us;
The God of Jacob is our stronghold.   Selah.

8   Come, behold the works of the LORD,
    Who has wrought desolations in the earth.
9   He makes wars to cease to the end of the earth;
    He breaks the bow and cuts the spear in two;
    He burns the chariots with fire.
10   "Cease striving and know that I am God;
    I will be exalted among the nations, I will be exalted in the earth."
11   The LORD of hosts is with us;
    The God of Jacob is our stronghold.   Selah.

"I am with you."

from PSALM 46

God is my protection and strength. When I'm in a tight spot, He is there to help me. In troubled times, He is very present, closer than any troubles.

My world could be shaken. My life may change faster than I can handle it. The world around me could come apart. Yet if it does, I will not fear. Because He is there for me.

God is with me. He gives me life to drink like a pure flowing river. He helps me from the beginning of the day to when I go to bed at night -- and then even in my sleep. I can go to Him anytime. If anything evil tries to do me in, all He has to do is say a word, and it melts away.

God is so powerful. What He has done and what He will do is so awesome. One day, He will end all war and violence. Yet there are times when I'm scared of what might happen in my life.

Then He says to me, "Relax and know for real I am God. I rule. I'm in control.

"And I am with you."

When He reminds me of that, I'm peaceful inside again.

God is with me. He is my security. He is my strength.

Psalm 47
For the choir director. A Psalm of the sons of Korah.

1   O clap your hands, all peoples;
    Shout to God with the voice of joy.
2   For the LORD Most High is to be feared,
    A great King over all the earth.
3   He subdues peoples under us
    And nations under our feet.

4   He chooses our inheritance for us,
     The glory of Jacob whom He loves.   Selah.

5   God has ascended with a shout,
     The LORD, with the sound of a trumpet.
6   Sing praises to God, sing praises;
     Sing praises to our King, sing praises.
7   For God is the King of all the earth;
     Sing praises with a skillful psalm.
8   God reigns over the nations,
     God sits on His holy throne.
9   The princes of the people have assembled themselves as the people of
     the God of Abraham,
     For the shields of the earth belong to God;
     He is highly exalted.

Psalm 48
A Song; a Psalm of the sons of Korah.

1   Great is the LORD, and greatly to be praised,
     In the city of our God, His holy mountain.
2   Beautiful in elevation, the joy of the whole earth,
     Is Mount Zion in the far north,
     The city of the great King.
3   God, in her palaces,
     Has made Himself known as a stronghold.

4   For, lo, the kings assembled themselves,
     They passed by together.
5   They saw it, then they were amazed;
     They were terrified, they fled in alarm.
6   Panic seized them there,
     Anguish, as of a woman in childbirth.
7   With the east wind
     You break the ships of Tarshish.
8   As we have heard, so have we seen
     In the city of the LORD of hosts, in the city of our God;
     God will establish her forever.   Selah.

9   We have thought on Your lovingkindness, O God,
     In the midst of Your temple.
10   As is Your name, O God,
     So is Your praise to the ends of the earth;
     Your right hand is full of righteousness.
11   Let Mount Zion be glad,
     Let the daughters of Judah rejoice
     Because of Your judgments.
12   Walk about Zion and go around her;

Count her towers;
13   Consider her ramparts;
Go through her palaces,
That you may tell it to the next generation.
14   For such is God,
Our God forever and ever;
He will guide us until death.

from PSALMS 47 and 48

In these two psalms, those sons of Korah get happy God is King. They definitely have a better grip than most people on how excellent it is that God rules, that He is in control (or, to use a big theological word, that He is sovereign).

One reason we don't have a grip is we've never seen a great King like Jesus. The sorry kings of history built strongholds and castles and forts to protect themselves and their power while regular people would get slaughtered in wars. Most kings don't risk their lives for the people. The people risk their lives for the kings. But Jesus laid his life down for us and He Himself is a stronghold for us (48:3).

And regular kings aren't very concerned about being loyal to the people. They are extremely concerned about the people being loyal to them. But God is faithful to us even when we aren't faithful to Him (2 Timothy 2:13).

Talking about faithfulness, a word that comes up in Psalm 48 and in a lot of psalms is "lovingkindness" (verse 9. The word might be different in some translations.). I know, I know. That's one of those words belonging with "Thee" and "Thou" in old hymns that are impossible to sing, especially when your voice is doing puberty leaps. Unfortunately, there isn't a good English word for what the original Hebrew means. The Hebrew word roughly means faithful, loyal love.

What? When the Bible talks about God having lovingkindness toward us, does that mean the King of the universe is faithful and loyal toward **us**? That's backwards. Yet that is exactly what it means. King Jesus proved it when He died for us, though He knew all the wrong we would ever do against Him. No one has ever been more faithful to us than that. As He said, "Greater love has no one than this, that one lay down his life for his friends." (John 15:13) God being that faithful and loving to us is just a little different than the rulers we read about in the newspapers and history books.

Are you getting glad God rules? Wait, there's more.

God is a King who is with us and "will guide us until death." (48:14) Now, regular kings and presidents don't care much about you as an individual. They might care about your money, especially at tax time or when they need a campaign contribution. They might care about your life -- when they want you to risk it for a stupid war. They might care about your choices -- when it's time to vote. But if you're too young to vote, to pay taxes or go to war, then they probably don't care about you at all.

But God cares about our lives enough to be there to guide us all the way through.

Now since they care about themselves a lot more than they care about you, regular kings and rulers aren't going to share with you the perks of ruling. You're not going to get your own room in the royal palace. You're not going to get a crown. You're not going to get a personal 747, not from anyone who rules a country today. And when the guy after him inherits being ruler and takes over, you're not going to get squat from him either.

But God is already preparing an inheritance for His people when Jesus takes over (Psalms 47:4, John 14:2-3). Romans 8:17 says His people are co-heirs with Jesus -- in other words, when Jesus inherits being ruler of everything, we inherit, too. There's a mind-blower! King Jesus will share with us all the benefits of His rule. He won't keep people far away from Him like regular rulers, but we'll get to be right there with Him. If we're faithful until we die, we'll even get to sit with Him on His throne (Revelation 4:21)!

Yet, even if we know all this and more, we've only begun to get a grip on how awesome it is and will be that God rules. He is the great King for all His people.

So let's get happy, too.

M. M.

Psalm 49
For the choir director. A Psalm of the sons of Korah.

1   Hear this, all peoples;
Give ear, all inhabitants of the world,
2   Both low and high,
Rich and poor together.
3   My mouth will speak wisdom,
And the meditation of my heart will be understanding.
4   I will incline my ear to a proverb;
I will express my riddle on the harp.

5   Why should I fear in days of adversity,
     When the iniquity of my foes surrounds me,
6   Even those who trust in their wealth
     And boast in the abundance of their riches?
7   No man can by any means redeem his brother
     Or give to God a ransom for him—
8   For the redemption of his soul is costly,
     And he should cease trying forever—
9   That he should live on eternally,
     That he should not undergo decay.

10   For he sees that even wise men die;
      The stupid and the senseless alike perish
      And leave their wealth to others.
11   Their inner thought is that their houses are forever
      And their dwelling places to all generations;
      They have called their lands after their own names.
12   But man in his pomp will not endure;
      He is like the beasts that perish.

13   This is the way of those who are foolish,
      And of those after them who approve their words.   Selah.
14   As sheep they are appointed for Sheol;
      Death shall be their shepherd;
      And the upright shall rule over them in the morning,
      And their form shall be for Sheol to consume
      So that they have no habitation.
15   But God will redeem my soul from the power of Sheol,
      For He will receive me.   Selah.

16   Do not be afraid when a man becomes rich,
      When the glory of his house is increased;
17   For when he dies he will carry nothing away;
      His glory will not descend after him.
18   Though while he lives he congratulates himself—
      And though men praise you when you do well for yourself—
19   He shall go to the generation of his fathers;
      They will never see the light.
20   Man in his pomp, yet without understanding,
      Is like the beasts that perish.

Won't let them teach me how to be a money tree.
MxPx "Money Tree"
from *Teenage Politics*

from **PSALM 49**

I used to think being rich meant being happy. And if I ever got rich, I would be real happy.

But a lot of the rich kids I know are messed up. The adults aren't any better. My folks have this rich couple as friends. He owns a company, and they are loaded. Yet most of the time, they seem more tired and bored with life than happy.

Even me -- if I make some money, I might be happy for a little while. But then I just want to get more.

So now I know different -- if money's all you got, you don't got much.

Dead rich people are still dead. But they're not rich anymore. So what good does it do to place your trust in money instead of Jesus? What good does it do to spend all your life making money and then go to hell?

All the money in the world can't buy a ticket to heaven. God isn't selling them anyway. Even the scalpers don't have them, although some might sell you fakes. Only Jesus can get you in. He's already paid the price.

Because He has, I know He'll receive me when I die. That's peace no amount of money can buy.

Some people just don't get it. At school, there are those who have enough money, or whose parents have enough money, that they have nice clothes and a nice car and all. That's O.K., but they get obsessed and stuck up about it. But their clothes are going to fall apart, if they don't get too fat for them first. And their cars will become scrap metal sooner or later. Maybe later than what I drive, but what's the difference?

The a-dolts are even more stupid. They bust their butts and spend all their time making money, but then ignore their families and ignore God. They don't do any good with their money, either. What they give to good causes is like a bad tip, if even that.

Yet they congratulate themselves. They put their shoulders out of joint patting themselves on the back. They fool themselves and each other into thinking they have really accomplished something. Oh boy! But in the end, they just leave bigger piles of money when they die. Their coffins are nicer and their funerals fancier than the average guy. But who cares?

I pray I never get like that. I hope I never let money blind me and keep me from what's important.

Jesus, may I never let money become anywhere near as important to me as You. Help me to focus on what is important. Help me to trust in what is forever. Help me to treasure You far above any material thing of this earth.

Psalm 50
A Psalm of Asaph.

1   The Mighty One, God, the LORD, has spoken,
And summoned the earth from the rising of the sun to its setting.
2   Out of Zion, the perfection of beauty,
God has shone forth.
3   May our God come and not keep silence;
Fire devours before Him,
And it is very tempestuous around Him.
4   He summons the heavens above,
And the earth, to judge His people:
5   "Gather My godly ones to Me,
Those who have made a covenant with Me by sacrifice."
6   And the heavens declare His righteousness,
For God Himself is judge.   Selah.

7   "Hear, O My people, and I will speak;
O Israel, I will testify against you;
I am God, your God.
8   "I do not reprove you for your sacrifices,
And your burnt offerings are continually before Me.
9   "I shall take no young bull out of your house
Nor male goats out of your folds.
10   "For every beast of the forest is Mine,
The cattle on a thousand hills.
11   "I know every bird of the mountains,
And everything that moves in the field is Mine.
12   "If I were hungry I would not tell you,
For the world is Mine, and all it contains.
13   "Shall I eat the flesh of bulls
Or drink the blood of male goats?
14   "Offer to God a sacrifice of thanksgiving
And pay your vows to the Most High;
15   Call upon Me in the day of trouble;
I shall rescue you, and you will honor Me."

16   But to the wicked God says,
"What right have you to tell of My statutes
And to take My covenant in your mouth?
17   "For you hate discipline,
And you cast My words behind you.
18   "When you see a thief, you are pleased with him,
And you associate with adulterers.

19   "You let your mouth loose in evil
   And your tongue frames deceit.
20   "You sit and speak against your brother;
   You slander your own mother's son.
21   "These things you have done and I kept silence;
   You thought that I was just like you;
   I will reprove you and state the case in order before your eyes.

22   "Now consider this, you who forget God,
   Or I will tear you in pieces, and there will be none to deliver.
23   "He who offers a sacrifice of thanksgiving honors Me;
   And to him who orders his way aright
   I shall show the salvation of God."

Real Christianity is 24/7.

from PSALM 50

God must get tired of all the religion down here.

I think He looks down and sees all the ritual, standing up and sitting down, long processions, boring music, unresponsive readings, offerings, holy-moly words, presumptuous proclamations, boring sermons, love offerings, pious looks, eternal altar calls, special offerings and says, "I am not impressed. If I ever got bored, I would really be bored right now. Now thankfulness, honesty, keeping your word, people taking the time to pray and just talk to me -- and I don't mean a lot of fancy words -- people honoring Me by the way they live every day -- now that's what I like. I sure would like to see more of that."

But what He sees instead are hypocrites forgetting Him and tossing His word behind them as soon as they step out of church. They might act all holy inside a church building, but they really hate God's standards -- and they live like it. Their businesses cheat people. They are always running their mouths and deceiving people. If their lips are moving -- and they usually are -- they're lying. They lie about others, bad-mouthing them. They even slander Christian brothers who are trying to live right.

Yet they think they're cool with God just because He lets them get away with it for a while, and because they go to church on Sunday.

Judgment Day is going to be interesting for them. I imagine God will say to them something like "So you thought, because I didn't zap you right away, everything was cool. You thought I was an overgrown version of you -- that, just like you, I only cared how holy you were for one hour, once a week, in a religious building, and I didn't care how sleazy you acted the rest of the week. Well -- **you're wrong**."

I imagine that will wipe the smug look off their faces real fast.

I'm not saying there isn't any religion that is for real and pleases God. But He cares more about how someone lives the whole week. So do I. Real Christianity is 24/7.

Psalm 51

For the choir director. A Psalm of David,
when Nathan the prophet came to him,
after he had gone in to Bathsheba.

1   Be gracious to me, O God, according to Your lovingkindness;
     According to the greatness of Your compassion blot out my transgressions.
2   Wash me thoroughly from my iniquity
     And cleanse me from my sin.
3   For I know my transgressions,
     And my sin is ever before me.
4   Against You, You only, I have sinned
     And done what is evil in Your sight,
     So that You are justified when You speak
     And blameless when You judge.

5   Behold, I was brought forth in iniquity,
     And in sin my mother conceived me.
6   Behold, You desire truth in the innermost being,
     And in the hidden part You will make me know wisdom.
7   Purify me with hyssop, and I shall be clean;
     Wash me, and I shall be whiter than snow.
8   Make me to hear joy and gladness,
     Let the bones which You have broken rejoice.
9   Hide Your face from my sins
     And blot out all my iniquities.

10   Create in me a clean heart, O God,
      And renew a steadfast spirit within me.
11   Do not cast me away from Your presence
      And do not take Your Holy Spirit from me.
12   Restore to me the joy of Your salvation
      And sustain me with a willing spirit.
13   Then I will teach transgressors Your ways,
      And sinners will be converted to You.
14   Deliver me from bloodguiltiness, O God, the God of my salvation;
      Then my tongue will joyfully sing of Your righteousness.
15   O Lord, open my lips,

That my mouth may declare Your praise.
16   For You do not delight in sacrifice, otherwise I would give it;
You are not pleased with burnt offering.
17   The sacrifices of God are a broken spirit;
A broken and a contrite heart, O God, You will not despise.

18   By Your favor do good to Zion;
Build the walls of Jerusalem.
19   Then You will delight in righteous sacrifices,
In burnt offering and whole burnt offering;
Then young bulls will be offered on Your altar.

If I could take what I've learned
From all the mistakes I've made
From the pages that I've turned
From the lost games that I've played

I'd be a better person for it
Better than deciding to ignore it
It meant so much to me
I want to make things right with you and me

MxPx "Misplaced Memories"
from *The Ever Passing Moment*

from PSALM 51

God, I've always believed You forgive people who sincerely come to You and 'fess up. I really hope that's true now.

Because what I did was worse than bad. Can you forgive me for even that? To forgive me, You'd have to really be loving and merciful -- but then, You really are loving and merciful.

I know I don't deserve You to forgive me, but I need You to. I feel so dirty. I wish I could forget what I did. I can't. It's like it's stuck to me. I can't keep from seeing it and smelling it. I can't stop thinking about the people I hurt. I wish I could take it all back. I can't. Worst of all, I can't keep from knowing it's ultimately against You I've sinned. It's hard for me to face You and pray, although I know I need to. So please don't turn away from me.

I feel so dirty.
But You can make me clean.
You and only You can make me pure. You can wash my sin

and guilt away. Wash me, and I'm clean. You can even make me happy again.

Will you?

I don't want to be forgiven to just go and do the same thing again. So teach me so I'll know how to live smart. Make me clean deep inside so I won't want to do stupid, wrong things. I know how someone is on the inside is what's most important anyway.

Be with me, to guide me and to give me the strength and the will to live right. I need Your presence to be happy for real, too. With You being there to help me, I can then help others, instead of hurting them.

I know what I did was way wrong. I also know if someone comes to You and is sad and broken over what they've done and wants to change, You won't reject them. But You'll forgive and accept them.

Thanks for forgiving and accepting me.

Psalm 52

For the choir director. A Maskil of David, when Doeg the Edomite came and told Saul and said to him, "David has come to the house of Ahimelech."

1   Why do you boast in evil, O mighty man?
The lovingkindness of God endures all day long.
2   Your tongue devises destruction,
Like a sharp razor, O worker of deceit.
3   You love evil more than good,
Falsehood more than speaking what is right.   Selah.
4   You love all words that devour,
O deceitful tongue.

5   But God will break you down forever;
He will snatch you up and tear you away from your tent,
And uproot you from the land of the living.   Selah.
6   The righteous will see and fear,
And will laugh at him, saying,
7   "Behold, the man who would not make God his refuge,
But trusted in the abundance of his riches
And was strong in his evil desire."
8   But as for me, I am like a green olive tree in the house of God;
I trust in the lovingkindness of God forever and ever.
9   I will give You thanks forever, because You have done it,
And I will wait on Your name, for it is good, in the presence of Your
godly ones.

from PSALM 52

There's these guys at school, they act like they rule the place. And, I'm sorry to say, they practically do. They're strong, do well in sports, and are popular.

And they brag. The only thing at school bigger than them is their egos. What gets me more is what they brag the most about. I mean, if I had to admit it, they have a lot to boast in with sports, cars and all. But what they brag the most about is the wrong they do.

You ought to hear them in the locker room gloating about the girls they use. They even brag about dropping them after they use them, as if that's something to be proud of. And they talk big about who they beat up or the stupid stuff they do on their drunken Saturday nights. If I did stuff like that, I'd be ashamed of it, not broadcasting it.

Their bucket mouths aren't much better when they're not bragging. They are constantly trashing other people and lying. They love to deceive and use. They sweet-talk people into giving them what they want, then turn around and bad-mouth them behind their backs.

Maybe I shouldn't be talking because too many times I say things I end up feeling bad about. But at least I feel bad about it. They love and brag about the evil they say and do.

They have a lot of four letter words in their vocabulary, but I don't think they've even heard of the word "humility." God's gonna teach it to them. They enjoy trashing and putting down people, and laughing at them -- one day, they're the ones who are going to be laughed at.

My dad told me about his high school reunion. He said it was funny how so many of the Big Guys who ruled his school and put everybody down are nobodies now. What goes around comes around.

As for me, if I'm going to brag, I'm going to brag about God and that I can trust in Him and in His love. His love is forever.

And I can trust Him to take care of these guys.

Thanks that I really can trust You, Lord. And I thank You for Your righteousness and justice, even if I don't see it all now. Because I know You're faithful and powerful, I also know Your justice is as good as done. So I'm waiting and watching for it. I'm waiting for You.

Psalm 53

For the choir director; according to Mahalath. A Maskil of David.

1   The fool has said in his heart, "There is no God,"
They are corrupt, and have committed abominable injustice;
There is no one who does good.
2   God has looked down from heaven upon the sons of men
To see if there is anyone who understands,
Who seeks after God.
3   Every one of them has turned aside; together they have become corrupt;
There is no one who does good, not even one.

4   Have the workers of wickedness no knowledge,
Who eat up My people as though they ate bread
And have not called upon God?
5   There they were in great fear where no fear had been;
For God scattered the bones of him who encamped against you;
You put them to shame, because God had rejected them.
6   Oh, that the salvation of Israel would come out of Zion!
When God restores His captive people,
Let Jacob rejoice, let Israel be glad.

From PSALM 53

(See also PSALM 14)

You may have noticed Psalms 14 and 53 are very similar. So why did God say the same thing twice? Probably because it's important we get what these say. If God says something twice, we better listen. And what these psalms say is we do not measure up to God's standards. In fact, Paul quoted these psalms to make that point (Romans 3: 10-12).

Why is it so important to realize we don't measure up? Because if we think we can somehow live up to God's standards and can earn our way to heaven by being "good" instead of trusting in Jesus -- well, we'll find out the hard way we are terribly wrong and end up in the place without air conditioning, if we don't get things straight in time.

Unfortunately, so many people don't get it straight, including a lot of church people. They actually think they can live up to God's high standards and earn heaven. Yeah, right.

In these two psalms, God says it as straight as it can be said -- without Jesus, we don't measure up. We need Jesus and His forgiveness.

M. M.

Psalm 54

For the choir director; on stringed instruments. A Maskil of David, when
the Ziphites came and said to Saul,
"Is not David hiding himself among us?"

1   Save me, O God, by Your name,
     And vindicate me by Your power.
2   Hear my prayer, O God;
     Give ear to the words of my mouth.
3   For strangers have risen against me
     And violent men have sought my life;
     They have not set God before them.   Selah.

4   Behold, God is my helper;
     The Lord is the sustainer of my soul.
5   He will recompense the evil to my foes;
     Destroy them in Your faithfulness.

6   Willingly I will sacrifice to You;
     I will give thanks to Your name, O LORD, for it is good.
7   For He has delivered me from all trouble,
     And my eye has looked with satisfaction upon my enemies.

I'm so confident You'll answer my prayer, I want to thank You ahead of time.

from PSALM 54

Lord, things are tough for me again, so I'm prayin'. Please listen up!

I thank you I can come to You and pray with confidence, with anticipation even. I can be confident in You because You are so cool and powerful. It's part of who You are to answer the prayers of those who come to You.

You help me. You keep me going.

Lord, because of who You are, I'm so confident You'll answer my prayer, I want to thank You ahead of time. So thank You for who You are, for being good, and for being good to me.

Psalm 55

For the choir director; on stringed instruments. A Maskil of David.

1   Give ear to my prayer, O God;
And do not hide Yourself from my supplication.
2   Give heed to me and answer me;
I am restless in my complaint and am surely distracted,
3   Because of the voice of the enemy,
Because of the pressure of the wicked;
For they bring down trouble upon me
And in anger they bear a grudge against me.

4   My heart is in anguish within me,
And the terrors of death have fallen upon me.
5   Fear and trembling come upon me,
And horror has overwhelmed me.
6   I said, "Oh, that I had wings like a dove!
I would fly away and be at rest.
7   "Behold, I would wander far away,
I would lodge in the wilderness.   Selah.
8   "I would hasten to my place of refuge
From the stormy wind and tempest."

9   Confuse, O Lord, divide their tongues,
For I have seen violence and strife in the city.
10   Day and night they go around her upon her walls,
And iniquity and mischief are in her midst.
11   Destruction is in her midst;
Oppression and deceit do not depart from her streets.

12   For it is not an enemy who reproaches me,
Then I could bear it;
Nor is it one who hates me who has exalted himself against me,
Then I could hide myself from him.
13   But it is you, a man my equal,
My companion and my familiar friend;
14   We who had sweet fellowship together
Walked in the house of God in the throng.
15   Let death come deceitfully upon them;
Let them go down alive to Sheol,
For evil is in their dwelling, in their midst.

16   As for me, I shall call upon God,
And the LORD will save me.
17   Evening and morning and at noon, I will complain and murmur,
And He will hear my voice.
18   He will redeem my soul in peace from the battle which is against me,
For they are many who strive with me.

19   God will hear and answer them—
 Even the one who sits enthroned from of old— Selah.
 With whom there is no change,
 And who do not fear God.
20   He has put forth his hands against those who were at peace with him;
 He has violated his covenant.
21   His speech was smoother than butter,
 But his heart was war;
 His words were softer than oil, Yet they were drawn swords.
22   Cast your burden upon the LORD and He will sustain you;
 He will never allow the righteous to be shaken.
23   But You, O God, will bring them down to the pit of destruction;
 Men of bloodshed and deceit will not live out half their days.
 But I will trust in You.

I thought he was my best friend ever.

from PSALM 55

I'm hurting, Lord. It's more than I can handle.

There's people bringing down trouble on me. If it were just the usual jerks, I could handle it. But it isn't, and I can't.

I'm restless and distracted. I try to think about something else, but all I can think about is this. When I lie awake at night, wishing I could just go to sleep, all I can think about is this. I can't take my mind off it; I can't get away from it. I wish I could. If I could, I'd get into my car and drive far away where nothing and no one could hurt me any more.

You see, it isn't just the usual jerks -- but my close friend.

We walked down the halls together. We hung out and had sleepovers. I trusted him, and we talked about anything and everything. And hanging and talking with him always made me feel all right.

Now he's turned around and stabbed me in the back. He's spreading around all my secrets we shared. He once told me straight up I was his best friend. Now I wonder if everything he told me is just a lie. I don't even know why he did it. Maybe it was to get in with the "cool" crowd, I don't know. What I do know is it hurts.

I feel like I can't trust anyone anymore. I trusted who I thought was my best friend ever, and look what he does. He talked to me like he was a faithful friend, but behind my back, his words were knives. He's made my life miserable. Who can I trust?

Lord, I dread going to school now. It's become a place of violence and strife for me. It's all I can do to make myself get up in the mornings and go there.

Having my secrets all over the place and not being able to trust anyone -- that's what scares me the most.

But I thank You that You're still in control, even though things seem totally off. I can come to You and pray straight about my troubles. I can lay it all on You. And You'll listen and protect me. You'll give me the peace and strength I need.

Even if I can't trust in a close friend, I can trust in You.

Psalm 56

For the choir director; according to Jonath elem rehokim.
A Mikhtam of David, when the Philistines seized him in Gath.

1   Be gracious to me, O God, for man has trampled upon me;
     Fighting all day long he oppresses me.
2   My foes have trampled upon me all day long,
     For they are many who fight proudly against me.
3   When I am afraid,
     I will put my trust in You.
4   In God, whose word I praise,
     In God I have put my trust;
     I shall not be afraid.
     What can mere man do to me?
5   All day long they distort my words;
     All their thoughts are against me for evil.
6   They attack, they lurk,
     They watch my steps,
     As they have waited to take my life.
7   Because of wickedness, cast them forth,
     In anger put down the peoples, O God!

8   You have taken account of my wanderings;
     Put my tears in Your bottle.
     Are they not in Your book?
9   Then my enemies will turn back in the day when I call;
     This I know, that God is for me.
10   In God, whose word I praise,
     In the LORD, whose word I praise,
11   In God I have put my trust, I shall not be afraid.
     What can man do to me?
12   Your vows are binding upon me, O God;
     I will render thank offerings to You.
13   For You have delivered my soul from death,
     Indeed my feet from stumbling,
     So that I may walk before God
     In the light of the living.

i've tried and pretended to be
too tough to cry
but i wasn't very good at it

joshua stevens, untitled

from PSALM 56

Life sure has me down lately. It seems everything and every-one is against me all day long. People are always on my case. Everything I say gets twisted and thrown back at me. It's always something.

At the end of some days, I'm so down under it, all I can do is go to my room and pray and cry.

But that's the best thing I can do. Because You care about me and my life like no one else does. You watch me and know everything I go through. And You remember and think about how my days go. Even if I forget about them, You don't. You even keep a book about my life.

And when I cry, You take my tears and put them in Your bottle. That's how much You care about me. You have a special bottle up there in heaven for me. Knowing me, it's probably pretty big, too.

You care so much about me. You've shown me that again and again, especially through what Jesus did. So I know, no matter how bad things get, You are for me. And if You are for me, what can bad things or bad people do to me? For You will always bring me through in the end.

When I am scared, I remember You and put my trust in You. For You always fulfill Your promises and Your word. Then my fears are overwhelmed by peace and confidence. Because of You, I won't be afraid of life or man. I trust in You. And You are for me. Who cares who's against?

Thanks for loving me and looking out for me. Because of what You do, my life is bright, not dark, under Your watchful eye.

Psalm 57

For the choir director; set to Al-tashheth. A Mikhtam of David, when he
fled from Saul in the cave.

1   Be gracious to me, O God, be gracious to me,
      For my soul takes refuge in You;
      And in the shadow of Your wings I will take refuge
      Until destruction passes by.
2   I will cry to God Most High,
      To God who accomplishes all things for me.
3   He will send from heaven and save me;
      He reproaches him who tramples upon me.   Selah.
      God will send forth His lovingkindness and His truth.

4   My soul is among lions;
      I must lie among those who breathe forth fire,
      Even the sons of men, whose teeth are spears and arrows
      And their tongue a sharp sword.
5   Be exalted above the heavens, O God;
      Let Your glory be above all the earth.
6   They have prepared a net for my steps;
      My soul is bowed down;
      They dug a pit before me;
      They themselves have fallen into the midst of it.   Selah.

7   My heart is steadfast, O God, my heart is steadfast;
      I will sing, yes, I will sing praises!
8   Awake, my glory!
      Awake, harp and lyre!
      I will awaken the dawn.
9   I will give thanks to You, O Lord, among the peoples;
      I will sing praises to You among the nations.
10   For Your lovingkindness is great to the heavens
      And Your truth to the clouds.
11   Be exalted above the heavens, O God;
      Let Your glory be above all the earth.

They make school a jungle for me.

from PSALM 57

There's these people at school who are always trying to get
me down. I'm surrounded by them. They've got razor tongues
and they're always cutting me with them. Every day, they snap
at me and run me down. They make school a jungle for me.
Sometimes, it's more like a Jurassic Park movie.

It's rough, and I get bummed about it. But I'm not going to let them keep me down. I can go to God, and He'll shelter me and take care of me at school and everywhere. He might run down those who try to run me down. He might just let them mess themselves up with their wrong, stupid ways. Maybe what they try to do to me will do themselves in. Whichever way He does it, I know His truth will defeat the lies they say about me. His powerful love will defeat their muscle and put them where they belong. I know He'll take care of me.

So forget them. Let them do their worst. I won't let them get to me. Instead of sleeping the day away like I do when I'm depressed, I'm going to get up with the sun and spend time with God, and praise Him and thank Him for the new day. I'm going to get happy because of Him at school, too, even in front of those people. That'll show 'em. They'll see for themselves they can't keep me down. They can give it up. They're no match for God and me.

Thanks, Lord, for being so much bigger than them. Thanks for giving me a joy nothing and nobody can take away from me. You are great. So be exalted in my life, at school and everywhere. Show people You rule.

Psalm 58
For the choir director; set to Al-tashheth. A Mikhtam of David.

1   Do you indeed speak righteousness, O gods?
Do you judge uprightly, O sons of men?
2   No, in heart you work unrighteousness;
On earth you weigh out the violence of your hands.
3   The wicked are estranged from the womb;
These who speak lies go astray from birth.
4   They have venom like the venom of a serpent;
Like a deaf cobra that stops up its ear,
5   So that it does not hear the voice of charmers,
Or a skillful caster of spells.

6   O God, shatter their teeth in their mouth;
Break out the fangs of the young lions, O LORD.
7   Let them flow away like water that runs off;
When he aims his arrows, let them be as headless shafts.
8   Let them be as a snail which melts away as it goes along,
Like the miscarriages of a woman which never see the sun.

9   Before your pots can feel the fire of thorns
He will sweep them away with a whirlwind, the green and the burning alike.
10   The righteous will rejoice when he sees the vengeance;
He will wash his feet in the blood of the wicked.
11   And men will say, "Surely there is a reward for the righteous;
Surely there is a God who judges on earth!"

from PSALM 58
Note: Check out Romans 12:19.

These evil sleazes think they are such studs.

They get their jollies from hurting people and doing wrong. They act like they were born evil. As a matter of fact, they were. And they've been getting worse ever since.

I want so bad to get back at those jerks for what they've done to me and my friends. It's hard not to. But that's God's job to do that, not mine. He's in charge of vengeance.

Besides, God's a lot better at payback than me. If He wants to, He can knock the teeth out of their garbage mouths and put pus-filled sores on their lying tongues. When they cuss every other word, He can cause all their cursing to fall back on them, giving them, among other things, a fatal outbreak of acne. Then He can break their jaws, so we don't have to listen to them at all or ever see their ugly smiles.

He can make them so sick, their day is a vomitarama, and they have to sleep in the bathroom. He can make slime like them melt away like slugs when you put salt on them. He can spill so much of their blood on the floor you can have sliding contests on it. He can send a tornado to suck them up and blow them away, never to be seen again.

He can make their lives so bad even I would feel sorry for them.

Or if He wants to, He can make them sorry, make them turn to Jesus, changing them. That's even better. Because that would ruin Satan's day, and he's the worst enemy of all.

Either way, though I'm real angry now, the day will come when I'll be so happy I'll feel like moshing. Because God will take care of them and all who love to do wrong. He is just. He will make things right.

Psalm 59

For the choir director; set to Al-tashheth. A Mikhtam of David, when Saul
sent men and they watched the house in order to kill him.

1   Deliver me from my enemies, O my God;
     Set me securely on high away from those who rise up against me.
2   Deliver me from those who do iniquity
     And save me from men of bloodshed.
3   For behold, they have set an ambush for my life;
     Fierce men launch an attack against me,
     Not for my transgression nor for my sin, O LORD,
4   For no guilt of mine, they run and set themselves against me.
     Arouse Yourself to help me, and see!
5   You, O LORD God of hosts, the God of Israel,
     Awake to punish all the nations;
     Do not be gracious to any who are treacherous in iniquity.   Selah.
6   They return at evening, they howl like a dog,
     And go around the city.
7   Behold, they belch forth with their mouth;
     Swords are in their lips,
     For, they say, "Who hears?"
8   But You, O LORD, laugh at them;
     You scoff at all the nations.

9   Because of his strength I will watch for You,
     For God is my stronghold.
10   My God in His lovingkindness will meet me;
     God will let me look triumphantly upon my foes.
11   Do not slay them, or my people will forget;
     Scatter them by Your power, and bring them down,
     O Lord, our shield.
12   On account of the sin of their mouth and the words of their lips,
     Let them even be caught in their pride,
     And on account of curses and lies which they utter.
13   Destroy them in wrath, destroy them that they may be no more;
     That men may know that God rules in Jacob
     To the ends of the earth.   Selah.
14   They return at evening, they howl like a dog,
     And go around the city.
15   They wander about for food
     And growl if they are not satisfied.

16   But as for me, I shall sing of Your strength;
     Yes, I shall joyfully sing of Your lovingkindness in the morning,
     For You have been my stronghold
     And a refuge in the day of my distress.
17   O my strength, I will sing praises to You;
     For God is my stronghold, the God who shows me lovingkindness.

from PSALM 59

Lord, I need Your help again. These guys at school -- they want to do me in.

They don't have any reason to want to get me, other than they love pointless violence. I've never done anything to them. I've never done anything to anybody that deserves what they're trying to do to me. Take a look, Lord, at their evil and take up for me!

They are such lowlifes. My friend, Josh, can burp at will, non-stop, as long as he likes. Well, these guys talk like that, except non-stop they belch out cussing and lies. Practically every word they say either disses You or hurts someone.

They think they'll always get away with it. They think, "Who cares? Who hears? Who will catch us?"

You care. You hear. You will catch them.

And You laugh at their stupidity, that they think You'll just look the other way and do nothing. One fine day, You'll show them different.

I am waiting and watching for that day! You will meet me in Your strong love. You will unleash Your strength and Your power upon their evil. Then we'll see who really rules the school. I don't know exactly how You're going to do it, but it's going to be cool. Maybe You'll split them up and put them in their place where they can't hurt anybody any more. Maybe their own words will get them in trouble they can't get out of. Or maybe You'll give them a taste of their own medicine and give them the beating they've given others. Whichever way You do it, I hope You do it in a way that makes everyone know it came from You.

I will know it came from You.

Thanks I can run to You when things get rough. Thanks for showing Your love and strength in my life.

Psalm 60

For the choir director; according to Shushan Eduth.
A Mikhtam of David, to teach; when he struggled with
Aram-naharaim and with Aram-zobah, and Joab returned,
and smote twelve thousand of Edom in the Valley of Salt.

1   O God, You have rejected us. You have broken us;
   You have been angry; O, restore us.
2   You have made the land quake, You have split it open;
   Heal its breaches, for it totters.

3   You have made Your people experience hardship;
    You have given us wine to drink that makes us stagger.
4   You have given a banner to those who fear You,
    That it may be displayed because of the truth.   Selah.
5   That Your beloved may be delivered,
    Save with Your right hand, and answer us!

6   God has spoken in His holiness:
    "I will exult, I will portion out Shechem and measure out the valley of
    Succoth.
7   "Gilead is Mine, and Manasseh is Mine;
    Ephraim also is the helmet of My head;
    Judah is My scepter.
8   "Moab is My washbowl;
    Over Edom I shall throw My shoe;
    Shout loud, O Philistia, because of Me!"

9   Who will bring me into the besieged city?
    Who will lead me to Edom?
10   Have not You Yourself, O God, rejected us?
    And will You not go forth with our armies, O God?
11   O give us help against the adversary,
    For deliverance by man is in vain.
12   Through God we shall do valiantly,
    And it is He who will tread down our adversaries.

*Man strugglin can start to take it s toll
16 years old tryin to change what you can t control*

John Reuben "No Regrets"
from *Are We There Yet?*

from PSALM 60

I can't get anything right! Everything I try blows up in my face. Like every chance I get to do something in sports, I either screw up and drop the ball or ride the bench.

What's worse is I'm a total loser with girls. I've heard every lame excuse there is for not going out with me. And don't ask me about grades. I get

enough about them from my parents. Speaking of parents, I can't seem to do anything right at home either.

It's all getting me down. I'm feeling more like a loser every day. Sometimes, I wonder what's the use of even trying.

Are You angry with me, God? I know things going so sorry wouldn't be happening if You haven't caused it or at least allowed it. I'm not blaming You. I'm sure You have good reasons. Maybe it's to remind me how much I need You. And I do know I need You, more than ever. But I feel like You've rejected me.

If there's anything wrong between us, show me the ways I need to change and to make it right. Make things the way they used to be between us, when I felt You smiled at me instead of frowned at me. Make me right so I'll stop screwing things up so bad and so things will be right between us.

God, I need Your help. Help me to live this life and do things right for a change. I know now if it's just me doing things, it isn't worth squat. Haven't I found that out the hard way!

But if You're with me and helping me, there's nothing I can't do. So please run with me, Lord.

ALL RIGHT. WHY ARE THERE SO MANY PSALMS ABOUT BAD DAYS?

You might have noticed in a lot of psalms, the psalmist just is not having a good day. Some of these make a goth look happy. So you might be asking, "Why are there so many 'Bad Day' psalms?"

Well, there are some good reasons:

1. David wrote a lot of them. He had some difficult experiences: being chased around the desert by Saul and other people who wanted to kill him; Saul using him for spear target practice; sons dying; one son, Absalom, trying to take the throne from him. That's for starters.

Some of David's psalms were written in the middle of these tough times.

Which leads to...

2. David was stuck hiding in caves a lot. He had to find something to do. He wrote on Psalm 57 in a cave. Who knows how many others. Caves didn't have TVs or computers back then.

3. Serious times inspire serious prayer.

Let's be honest. When things are good, it's easy to get slack about prayer. But when times are tough, we get more serious, more open, and probably more creative about prayer. Our prayers then become more than "Bless the food. Bless the meat. Good grief. Let's eat." That's human nature.

Likewise, some of the greatest prayers of the Bible, including some psalms, come out of difficulties and even tragedy.

4. God values the honesty of His people. God wants His people to be honest with Him when they are bummed about life. He's not into plastered-on happy faces.

So when David was writing one of his Bad Day psalms, God didn't say, "Hey David, I know you're stuck in caves a lot. And, yes, an army is trying to kill you. But lighten up, guy."

No, God instead put them in His word. The prayers of His people in down times mean a lot to Him.

5. We have down times, too. I think God put these psalms in to help us pray during those times. I know they have helped me a lot.

6. God wants us to know He understands and knows where we're at when we're having those down times.

7. This might be the biggest reason: God doesn't wimp out on what's called "The Problem of Evil." You may not have heard of that. It is a problem or tough question religious and intellectual people have wrestled with for centuries. It goes like this: If God is good, then why is there so much evil and suffering in the world?

Now, it would take another book -- a big book -- to go into how God's Word answers that. Even then, there are some things He doesn't let us know yet. But God does tackle that question. That's part of the honesty of His word. God doesn't take cop-outs some religions take. He doesn't pretend evil is an illusion or a result of your so-called past life or whatever. His word goes into how evil came into the world, how mankind suffers from it, how God has defeated it, and how He'll remove it in the end.

The Psalms deal with evil and suffering as well. They don't ignore it. A few even take on hard questions like why do good people have a hard time while evil people have a blast. Check out Psalm 73 for starters.

Part of the honesty and openness of God's word is His being real about evil and suffering and the tough questions their pain makes us ask.

There are surely a lot more reasons for all those tough-time psalms. God's thoughts toward us are more than we can count.

Among those thoughts are His understanding and readiness to help when we are suffering. He shows us that in many ways. He definitely shows us that in the Psalms.

M. M.

Psalm 61

For the choir director; on a stringed instrument. A Psalm of David.

1   Hear my cry, O God;
Give heed to my prayer.
2   From the end of the earth I call to You when my heart is faint;
Lead me to the rock that is higher than I.
3   For You have been a refuge for me,
A tower of strength against the enemy.
4   Let me dwell in Your tent forever;
Let me take refuge in the shelter of Your wings.   Selah.

5   For You have heard my vows, O God;
You have given me the inheritance of those who fear Your name.
6   You will prolong the king's life;
His years will be as many generations.
7   He will abide before God forever;
Appoint lovingkindness and truth that they may preserve him.
8   So I will sing praise to Your name forever,
That I may pay my vows day by day.

it's time to leave
i'd give up now
before time moves
and it's too late
the path's too narrow
you'll never make it
                    the
                        road's
            i   too
                see   steep
                    you
                        falling

        i feel like leaving
        giving up now
        i hope it's not too late
    to turn around
and head the other way
            the easy way
the path's too narrow
i'll never make it
the road's too steep

i'm
  falling
      down
the path's too narrow
i'll never make it
i'm falling down
        i'd like to enter
          it seems so nice
          inside the walls
          through the gate
          into the home
    i see in the distance
far away, far away
the path's too narrow
i can't keep up
the road's too steep
        stop me from falling
the road's too steep
      keep me from falling down
      `joshua stevens, "a word of encouragement"

from PSALM 61

Lord, I'm calling out to You. I'm crying in a distant place. Please hear me.

I'm so far down. I'm so far away -- far away from where I want to be. Where I want my life to be is far beyond the horizon, where I can not see it, where I can not reach it, where I can hardly even imagine it. I feel like I'm at the other horizon, standing at the edge of the world.

And I'm about to fall off.

I feel You're so far away. I want to get close to You, but I've wandered so far to a place unsheltered from the ocean storm. The tides and quick sands of my life pull me down. And the waves pulling me and beating on me drain me of hope and strength.

I need Your shelter. I need Your strong arms around me.

I thought I was so strong. Now I know I'm so weak. I'm worn down and overwhelmed by life. I'm so down under it. All I have the strength to do is call out to You.

From where You are, will You hear me? Will You come help

me? My life is a high, steep cliff at land's end. And I'm at the bottom of it. The waves are crashing in upon me. The cliff is steep and slippery -- and it looms high over me. I don't have the strength or the grip to climb it alone.

Lord, I need You. Will You come and lead me up? Lead me to a place higher than I, so high I can't even attain to it. Carry me up to a place where I can live, not just exist and die. Lift me up close to You.

I'm down now, but wherever I am, You know what I'm going through. I can call out to You, and You'll hear. And if You hear, You'll answer with love and truth to lead me. You'll lead me to a life that's awesome, that's with You, forever.

I'm calling out to You in fear now. But I know You'll bring me to a place of peace. Instead of being overwhelmed by difficulty, I'll be overwhelmed by You.

And my life will fulfill Your purposes for it day by day. My life will glorify You forever.

Psalm 62

For the choir director; according to Jeduthun. A Psalm of David.

1   My soul waits in silence for God only;
     From Him is my salvation.
2   He only is my rock and my salvation,
     My stronghold; I shall not be greatly shaken.

3   How long will you assail a man,
     That you may murder him, all of you,
     Like a leaning wall, like a tottering fence?
4   They have counseled only to thrust him down from his high position;
     They delight in falsehood;
     They bless with their mouth,
     But inwardly they curse.   Selah.

5   My soul, wait in silence for God only,
     For my hope is from Him.
6   He only is my rock and my salvation,
     My stronghold; I shall not be shaken.
7   On God my salvation and my glory rest;
     The rock of my strength, my refuge is in God.
8   Trust in Him at all times, O people;
     Pour out your heart before Him;
     God is a refuge for us.   Selah.

9   Men of low degree are only vanity and men of rank are a lie;
 In the balances they go up;
 They are together lighter than breath.
10   Do not trust in oppression
 And do not vainly hope in robbery;
 If riches increase, do not set your heart upon them.

11   Once God has spoken;
 Twice I have heard this:
 That power belongs to God;
12   And lovingkindness is Yours, O Lord,
 For You recompense a man according to his work.

from PSALM 62

Note: A lot of this is based on an experience a brother had with this psalm.

Everything is wrong. And there's nothing I can do to get things right. How long will I be pushed down? My life is so bad. I have trouble sleeping at night. It's all I can do to just get up in the morning. I feel like I have no reason to get up.

But I remember I still have God, even if I have nothing else. He still is there for me, even if no one else is. He alone will always be there for me. He alone saves me so I can be there with Him.

And I will wait for Him alone to save me now. Only He can make life right for me again.

God knows I've tried. So I will wait for Him in silence. Every time I've opened my mouth to defend myself or to make things better, it just makes things worse. So I'll pray to Him, and He'll defend me. Those who won't stop attacking me and telling lies about me, He will take care of them.

Still, when things are like they are now, it's too easy for me to get all anxious and for my faith to get weak. I have to remind myself my hope is in Him, not in the circumstances of my life. Even if everything is going wrong, He stays right and faithful. He is always there for me and will save me. He'll take care of me. He's like a rock for me that can not be moved and that nothing can get through. He surrounds me and protects me. So I won't get too shook up. I will trust in Him.

I can go to Him any time and talk to Him about anything going on in my life. No matter how down I am, I can talk it out with Him. He can handle it.

When I think about it, the things and people bothering me are all lighter than a burp compared to God. God's the one with the power, not them. All power belongs to Him. His love for me and faithfulness to me can not be stopped by anything or anyone.

Even if everything is wrong, He can make everything right. He will make everything right.

I will quietly wait for only Him. For all my hope comes from Him. He only is my rock and my salvation.

Psalm 63
A Psalm of David, when he was in the wilderness of Judah.

1   O God, You are my God; I shall seek You earnestly;
My soul thirsts for You, my flesh yearns for You,
In a dry and weary land where there is no water.
2   Thus I have seen You in the sanctuary,
To see Your power and Your glory.
3   Because Your lovingkindness is better than life,
My lips will praise You.
4   So I will bless You as long as I live;
I will lift up my hands in Your name.
5   My soul is satisfied as with marrow and fatness,
And my mouth offers praises with joyful lips.

6   When I remember You on my bed,
I meditate on You in the night watches,
7   For You have been my help,
And in the shadow of Your wings I sing for joy.
8   My soul clings to You;
Your right hand upholds me.

9   But those who seek my life to destroy it,
Will go into the depths of the earth.
10   They will be delivered over to the power of the sword;
They will be a prey for foxes.
11   But the king will rejoice in God;
Everyone who swears by Him will glory,
For the mouths of those who speak lies will be stopped.

*sometimes i wanted someone to hold
but sometimes i needed someone to hold me*

joshua stevens
from "on monsters and butterflies"

from PSALM 63

O God, You are my God. I love You. I want to be closer to You. I'm going to seek You and spend time with You everyday.

Yet sometimes I feel so far from You. And this is one of those times. I feel I barely know You. And my life is so dry when it's like this. My world is a desert without the water of Your life and presence.

I'm so thirsty for You. Where can I find You in this desert? I read my Bible, but lately it seems like just words, even though I know it's not. I pray, but my prayers just bounce off the walls and disappear into dry air. The dryness and heat of my life make me weak. It's all I can do to just make it through the day without You close by me.

But when my life got dry and barren before, You rained Your presence on me. Like lightning, You broke through, and I saw for myself how awesome and powerful You are. I saw Your power and love toward me.

That made me so excited about You and the life You give me. Your presence and Your love toward me is better than any lifetime without You. I used to think I could live large on my own without You. I know different now. I am glad You're in my life -- even during this dry time. I know this drought won't last forever, although it seems that way. You will satisfy me with Your goodness -- with Yourself.

Oh God, I appreciate Your presence in the past. And I look forward to an awesome future with You. But I need You in my life, not just in the past or in the future.

I need You now.

Lying in my bed at night drifting toward sleep, my thoughts drift toward You. I think about how awesome You are -- how infinite -- and how great it would be to be near You, to even see You. I wonder what You must be like up close. I could see You and know You for a hundred thousand years -- and there'd be so much more to know.

I think about how awesome You are toward me and how You've helped me. I think about Your watching over me. I remember times I've felt close to You. I remember feeling safe and loved underneath Your arms.

Even as I'm falling asleep, deep inside, I won't let go of You. You won't let go of me.

There in the dark, You feel close again. It feels like You're right there with me. I go to sleep feeling all peaceful because I'm holding on to You. And You're holding on to me.

Psalm 64
For the choir director. A Psalm of David.

1   Hear my voice, O God, in my complaint;
Preserve my life from dread of the enemy.
2   Hide me from the secret counsel of evildoers,
From the tumult of those who do iniquity,
3   Who have sharpened their tongue like a sword.
They aimed bitter speech as their arrow,
4   To shoot from concealment at the blameless;
Suddenly they shoot at him, and do not fear.
5   They hold fast to themselves an evil purpose;
They talk of laying snares secretly;
They say, "Who can see them?"
6   They devise injustices, saying,
"We are ready with a well-conceived plot";
For the inward thought and the heart of a man are deep.

7   But God will shoot at them with an arrow;
Suddenly they will be wounded.
8   So they will make him stumble;
Their own tongue is against them;
All who see them will shake the head.
9   Then all men will fear,
And they will declare the work of God,
And will consider what He has done.
10   The righteous man will be glad in the LORD and will take refuge in Him;
And all the upright in heart will glory.

from PSALM 64
and the last line of PSALM 63
Lies can be so deadly.

I have a friend. She's just a little different, but she's cool. And she's one of the best friends you could have.

There's this "in" group at school. They look down on everyone else. They don't like "different." And they decided they especially didn't like my friend. So they started false vicious rumors about her.

They hurt her bad. She hasn't been the same since. It's like they stole who she was from her. She's been "sick" a lot, missing school a lot. She really dreads school. When she comes, you can tell it's all she can do just to make it through the day. She's depressed a lot. It hurts to see her that way. She used to always be real happy.

Words can hurt so much.

God, protect my friend and protect me from the lies of this group of conceited lowlifes. How can we defend ourselves against rumors and lies like theirs? We might as well be fighting air. Only You can defend us. They are cowardly sneaks, but their cowardice makes them impossible to combat. They aim their lying tongues from where you can't see them. And their names are never attached to their lies. They gang together and gang up on the defenseless. The way they spread gossip and rumors together, their lies seem like truth "everybody knows" before you know it.

They think they will never be caught, that they will always get away with it. And unless You do something about it, Lord, they're probably right. How can we defend ourselves against the weapons of words, especially when we can't even see where they're coming from?

But one day, You will aim at them. And You never miss. Their own tongues -- which caused others so much hurt -- You will cause them to trip over their own lying tongues. Suddenly, they won't be "in" anymore. They will be so "out", the rest of the school will shake their heads when they talk about them. Nobody will listen to them anymore. Their lying mouths will be stopped.

My friend and I will be glad. We will know it's from You. I hope You make others know it's from You, too, so they'll think about You. And I hope people will think twice before they ever spread rumors again.

That includes me. The rumors I've helped spread in the past don't seem so harmless now.

Psalm 65

For the choir director. A Psalm of David. A Song.

1   There will be silence before You, and praise in Zion, O God,
And to You the vow will be performed.
2   O You who hear prayer,
To You all men come.
3   Iniquities prevail against me;

As for our transgressions, You forgive them.
4   How blessed is the one whom You choose and bring near to You
To dwell in Your courts.
We will be satisfied with the goodness of Your house,
Your holy temple.

5   By awesome deeds You answer us in righteousness, O God of our sal-
vation,
You who are the trust of all the ends of the earth and of the farthest sea;
6   Who establishes the mountains by His strength,
Being girded with might;
7   Who stills the roaring of the seas,
The roaring of their waves,
And the tumult of the peoples.
8   They who dwell in the ends of the earth stand in awe of Your signs;
You make the dawn and the sunset shout for joy.

9   You visit the earth and cause it to overflow;
You greatly enrich it;
The stream of God is full of water;
You prepare their grain, for thus You prepare the earth.
10   You water its furrows abundantly,
You settle its ridges,
You soften it with showers,
You bless its growth.
11   You have crowned the year with Your bounty,
And Your paths drip with fatness.
12   The pastures of the wilderness drip,
And the hills gird themselves with rejoicing.
13   The meadows are clothed with flocks
And the valleys are covered with grain;
They shout for joy, yes, they sing.

I'm in awe of you

from PSALM 65

When I think about You, God, sometimes I have to be silent.
Because nothing I can say can touch how great and infinite You
are. I am in awe of You.

Then other times, I have to let loose and praise You and thank
You again and again. Because I appreciate You and Your goodness so much, I can't keep it inside.

Now is one of those times.

You are so good to me and to all people. You hear my prayers,
even though You have a zillion prayers coming up at You. You
answer prayers in awesome ways I couldn't even imagine.

You especially answer my prayers for forgiveness. I try to live right. But sin and temptation are too big for me, and sooner or later, usually sooner, I fail big time. But because Jesus didn't fail, You forgive me. You've even chosen me to be one of Your children, and You bring me closer and closer to You.

You are beyond perfect. Everything You do is righteous. You can be trusted like nobody else.

You are strong and beautiful. You show that in the way You created the earth. To make a mountain -- every time I see mountains, I'm in awe of them -- how great and mighty You must be! I'm in awe of You. And You didn't just create things like mountains, You made them beautiful. And sunsets and sunrises (on those rare days I'm awake enough to see one), no human art can match them. They practically shout, "There's a Creator, and He's awesome!"

You could have created the earth only to get things done, to give man and animals only what they need. You could have created food without taste, birds and butterflies without color, beaches without sand, rivers without swimming holes. You didn't have to make the sky blue, cardinals red, or sunflowers yellow. You didn't have to create birds or flowers at all.

But You did and so much more. The earth overflows with Your creativity and goodness. The earth shows You are great, creative, generous, and fun even, and beautiful. And that's not even talking about the rest of the universe.

You are so generous to man to give us a planet like this. We sure don't deserve it.

We don't deserve You.

Creation sings of Your grace. I will come to You and sing, too.

Psalm 66
For the choir director. A Song. A Psalm.

1   Shout joyfully to God, all the earth;
2   Sing the glory of His name;
     Make His praise glorious.
3   Say to God, "How awesome are Your works!
     Because of the greatness of Your power Your enemies will give feigned
     obedience to You.
4   "All the earth will worship You,
     And will sing praises to You;
     They will sing praises to Your name."   Selah.

5   Come and see the works of God,
    Who is awesome in His deeds toward the sons of men.
6   He turned the sea into dry land;
    They passed through the river on foot;
    There let us rejoice in Him!
7   He rules by His might forever;
    His eyes keep watch on the nations;
    Let not the rebellious exalt themselves.   Selah.

8   Bless our God, O peoples,
    And sound His praise abroad,
9   Who keeps us in life
    And does not allow our feet to slip.
10   For You have tried us, O God;
    You have refined us as silver is refined.
11   You brought us into the net;
    You laid an oppressive burden upon our loins.
12   You made men ride over our heads;
    We went through fire and through water,
    Yet You brought us out into a place of abundance.
13   I shall come into Your house with burnt offerings;
    I shall pay You my vows,
14   Which my lips uttered
    And my mouth spoke when I was in distress.
15   I shall offer to You burnt offerings of fat beasts,
    With the smoke of rams;
    I shall make an offering of bulls with male goats.   Selah.

16   Come and hear, all who fear God,
    And I will tell of what He has done for my soul.
17   I cried to Him with my mouth,
    And He was extolled with my tongue.
18   If I regard wickedness in my heart,
    The Lord will not hear;
19   But certainly God has heard;
    He has given heed to the voice of my prayer.
20   Blessed be God,
    Who has not turned away my prayer
    Nor His lovingkindness from me.

You painted me a picture and showed me how to see
Though I just won't behold it
Unless it pertains to me

Jars of Clay "Unforgetful You"
from *If I Left the Zoo*

from PSALM 66

God is great. He's great, not just because He's up there being God. He is awesome in the many things He does for people.

I used not to think that. I thought God was up there being holy and doing whatever God does, but that He really didn't do much for me down here. I'd hear about the things He did in the Bible, like split the Red Sea to save Moses and the Hebrews. And I'd think that would have been something to see, but He doesn't do cool things like that today, especially not for me.

One time, my life was rough. I was really down in it. And I had an attitude toward God. I told Him, "God, all that stuff in the Bible is great. But what have You done for me lately?"

Yet God brought me through it and made things even better than before. He even took the bad things I was going through and turned them into good. Seeing Him come through for me like that, even if my attitude wasn't the best, made me appreciate Him more.

Now I notice things He does for me that I didn't pay much attention to before. There's all the prayers He answers. I don't know how many times I've prayed for something and when it happens, I forget God answered my prayer or even that I prayed for it at all. Now I'm better about appreciating and thanking Him for the way He answers my prayers. A lot of times He answers even better than I was hoping for.

Then there's the many things He does for me I don't think much about, but I should -- like His protection. Being a teenager, sometimes I feel I'm going to live forever, that nothing can touch me, and I think I don't need that much protection. But when I look back, there have been so many times when God was looking out for me. And it's a good thing. Sure, I had that broken arm, but things could have easily been so much worse the past few years with all the stupid things I've tried. Then there's all the times I wasn't thinking or paying attention to what I was doing. I've lost count of how many times I've nearly been run over. If my parents knew all the close calls I've had, they'd probably lock me up for my own protection until I'm 30.

But God has kept me alive and in one piece. He's kept my feet from slipping too far.

So when I think about it, He still does great works for people -- and for me. Just to keep me and my friends out of too much trouble probably takes enough power to split the Red Sea!

Psalm 67

For the choir director; with stringed instruments. A Psalm. A Song.

1   God be gracious to us and bless us,
And cause His face to shine upon us—   Selah.
2   That Your way may be known on the earth,
Your salvation among all nations.
3   Let the peoples praise You, O God;
Let all the peoples praise You.
4   Let the nations be glad and sing for joy;
For You will judge the peoples with uprightness
And guide the nations on the earth.   Selah.
5   Let the peoples praise You, O God;
Let all the peoples praise You.
6   The earth has yielded its produce;
God, our God, blesses us.
7   God blesses us,
That all the ends of the earth may fear Him.

From PSALM 67

Lord, I hope when You look down at me, You smile. I want my
life to make You glad. It's only
through Your smile and Your
blessing that my life can be good.

I want Your smile to shine on
me. And not just so my life will be
good, but so others can see You
in my life. I want to help others
know You, Your ways, and Your
salvation. If people see only me,
that won't help them come to know You.

I want You to bless me so I can be a blessing to others. I need
You to help me do well in school so I can become a doctor and
help people in poor countries who don't have good medical care
available. Or so I can do something even better if you have better in mind for me. I need You to help me earn some money so I
can go on that missions project I have a heart for. I need You to
help me always have time, patience, and a smile for those kids I
work with.

I want You to shine on me and use me to shine on others.

Thank You for being my God and for blessing my life. When I
think about You, and that I'm Yours and You're mine, and when I
think about how good You are to me -- I can hardly take it in.

I want to say thank You with my life. Take my life in Your
hands and use it to shine on many. Use me to show the way.

Psalm 68

For the choir director. A Psalm of David. A Song.

1   Let God arise, let His enemies be scattered,
And let those who hate Him flee before Him.
2   As smoke is driven away, so drive them away;
As wax melts before the fire,
So let the wicked perish before God.
3   But let the righteous be glad; let them exult before God;
Yes, let them rejoice with gladness.
4   Sing to God, sing praises to His name;
Lift up a song for Him who rides through the deserts,
Whose name is the LORD, and exult before Him.

5   A father of the fatherless and a judge for the widows,
Is God in His holy habitation.
6   God makes a home for the lonely;
He leads out the prisoners into prosperity,
Only the rebellious dwell in a parched land.

7   O God, when You went forth before Your people,
When You marched through the wilderness,   Selah.
8   The earth quaked;
The heavens also dropped rain at the presence of God;
Sinai itself quaked at the presence of God, the God of Israel.
9   You shed abroad a plentiful rain, O God;
You confirmed Your inheritance when it was parched.
10   Your creatures settled in it;
You provided in Your goodness for the poor, O God.

11   The Lord gives the command;
The women who proclaim the good tidings are a great host:
12   "Kings of armies flee, they flee,
And she who remains at home will divide the spoil!"
13   When you lie down among the sheepfolds,
You are like the wings of a dove covered with silver,
And its pinions with glistening gold.
14   When the Almighty scattered the kings there,
It was snowing in Zalmon.

15   A mountain of God is the mountain of Bashan;
A mountain of many peaks is the mountain of Bashan.
16   Why do you look with envy, O mountains with many peaks,
At the mountain which God has desired for His abode?
Surely the LORD will dwell there forever.
17   The chariots of God are myriads, thousands upon thousands;
The Lord is among them as at Sinai, in holiness.
18   You have ascended on high, You have led captive Your captives;

You have received gifts among men,
Even among the rebellious also, that the LORD God may dwell there.

19   Blessed be the Lord, who daily bears our burden,
The God who is our salvation.   Selah.
20   God is to us a God of deliverances;
And to GOD the Lord belong escapes from death.
21   Surely God will shatter the head of His enemies,
The hairy crown of him who goes on in his guilty deeds.
22   The Lord said, "I will bring them back from Bashan.
I will bring them back from the depths of the sea;
23   That your foot may shatter them in blood,
The tongue of your dogs may have its portion from your enemies."

24   They have seen Your procession, O God,
The procession of my God, my King, into the sanctuary.
25   The singers went on, the musicians after them,
In the midst of the maidens beating tambourines.
26   Bless God in the congregations,
Even the LORD, you who are of the fountain of Israel.
27   There is Benjamin, the youngest, ruling them,
The princes of Judah in their throng,
The princes of Zebulun, the princes of Naphtali.

28   Your God has commanded your strength;
Show Yourself strong, O God, who have acted on our behalf.
29   Because of Your temple at Jerusalem
Kings will bring gifts to You.
30   Rebuke the beasts in the reeds,
The herd of bulls with the calves of the peoples,
Trampling under foot the pieces of silver;
He has scattered the peoples who delight in war.
31   Envoys will come out of Egypt;
Ethiopia will quickly stretch out her hands to God.

32   Sing to God, O kingdoms of the earth,
Sing praises to the Lord,   Selah.
33   To Him who rides upon the highest heavens, which are from ancient times;
Behold, He speaks forth with His voice, a mighty voice.
34   Ascribe strength to God;
His majesty is over Israel
And His strength is in the skies.
35   O God, You are awesome from Your sanctuary.
The God of Israel Himself gives strength and power to the people.
Blessed be God!

from PSALM 68
especially verses 5 and 6 and 19

I don't have someone to play catch with me.
I don't have someone to watch me play.
I don't have someone to take me to a ball game.
I don't have someone to take me fishing.
I don't have someone to listen to me.
I don't have someone to be like.
I don't have someone to beat at basketball.

I don't have someone to follow.
I don't have someone to set me right when I'm wrong.
I don't have someone to teach me.
I don't have someone to show me how to be a man.
I don't have someone to talk to me.
I don't have someone who's always there for me.
I don't have someone to love me.

I don't have a father.

Once I did. He was strong, but he was mean. And when he wasn't, he wasn't there for me. He never hugged me or kissed me or even wrestled with me.

Then he left me.

I'm so lonely sometimes. There's a big hole in my life. I try to fill it with friends, games, possessions, sports, and movies.
But only a real father can fill that hole.

But now I have a real Father. He's stronger than strong. He can make the earth shake. But He's gentle. He comforted me and lifted me up when I was down. Again and again, He let me know He loved me.

And He came into my life.

And He always has time for me.
He is always watching me and is always for me.
He shows me things no one else can show me.
He will take me places no one else can take me.

He listens to me.
He is the One I want to be like.
He is the One I aim for.

He is the One I follow.
He is the One who gently sets me right when I'm wrong.
He teaches me how to live.
He showed me, and still shows me, how to be a man.
He talks to me.
He is always there for me.
He will always love me.

I have the best Father.

And He will never leave me.

Psalm 69

For the choir director; according to Shoshannim. A Psalm of David.

1   Save me, O God,
For the waters have threatened my life.
2   I have sunk in deep mire, and there is no foothold;
I have come into deep waters, and a flood overflows me.
3   I am weary with my crying; my throat is parched;
My eyes fail while I wait for my God.
4   Those who hate me without a cause are more than the hairs of my head;
Those who would destroy me are powerful, being wrongfully my en-   emies;
What I did not steal, I then have to restore.

5   O God, it is You who knows my folly,
And my wrongs are not hidden from You.
6   May those who wait for You not be ashamed through me, O Lord GOD   of
hosts;
May those who seek You not be dishonored through me, O God of Israel,
7   Because for Your sake I have borne reproach;
Dishonor has covered my face.
8   I have become estranged from my brothers
And an alien to my mother's sons.
9   For zeal for Your house has consumed me,
And the reproaches of those who reproach You have fallen on me.
10   When I wept in my soul with fasting,
It became my reproach.
11   When I made sackcloth my clothing,
I became a byword to them.
12   Those who sit in the gate talk about me,
And I am the song of the drunkards.

13   But as for me, my prayer is to You, O LORD, at an acceptable time;
O God, in the greatness of Your lovingkindness,

Answer me with Your saving truth.
14   Deliver me from the mire and do not let me sink;
May I be delivered from my foes and from the deep waters.
15   May the flood of water not overflow me
Nor the deep swallow me up,
Nor the pit shut its mouth on me.

16   Answer me, O LORD, for Your lovingkindness is good;
According to the greatness of Your compassion, turn to me,
17   And do not hide Your face from Your servant,
For I am in distress; answer me quickly.
18   Oh draw near to my soul and redeem it;
Ransom me because of my enemies!
19   You know my reproach and my shame and my dishonor;
All my adversaries are before You.

20   Reproach has broken my heart and I am so sick.
And I looked for sympathy, but there was none,
And for comforters, but I found none.
21   They also gave me gall for my food
And for my thirst they gave me vinegar to drink.

22   May their table before them become a snare;
And when they are in peace, may it become a trap.
23   May their eyes grow dim so that they cannot see,
And make their loins shake continually.
24   Pour out Your indignation on them,
And may Your burning anger overtake them.
25   May their camp be desolate;
May none dwell in their tents.
26   For they have persecuted him whom You Yourself have smitten,
And they tell of the pain of those whom You have wounded.
27   Add iniquity to their iniquity,
And may they not come into Your righteousness.
28   May they be blotted out of the book of life
And may they not be recorded with the righteous.

29   But I am afflicted and in pain;
May Your salvation, O God, set me securely on high.
30   I will praise the name of God with song
And magnify Him with thanksgiving.
31   And it will please the LORD better than an ox
Or a young bull with horns and hoofs.
32   The humble have seen it and are glad;
You who seek God, let your heart revive.
33   For the LORD hears the needy
And does not despise His who are prisoners.

34   Let heaven and earth praise Him,
The seas and everything that moves in them.
35   For God will save Zion and build the cities of Judah,
That they may dwell there and possess it.
36   The descendants of His servants will inherit it,
And those who love His name will dwell in it.

And it's not your fault but tell me what can you do
When things fall apart and everyone's at you

John Reuben "No Regrets"
from *Are We There Yet?*

from PSALM 69

God, everyone's on my case. No matter what I do or where I go, somebody's on me. Everyday I'm talked about and treated like scum, like I was some kind of low-life.

It's all for stuff I didn't do or for stuff that's good. They're making me pay anyway. Then they still hate and bad-mouth me for no reason. There's no pleasing them.

A lot of it's because I try to follow You and am serious about it. I've become an easy target for those who hate You. Those who like to dis Thee are dissing me.

I don't get a break from it when I get home either, because my family is always on me, too. I think they also resent my commitment to You.

And when I'm down about all this, that just makes people talk more.

It's all gotten to me, Lord. I'm so down in it. And like being stuck in deep mud, I can see no way I can pull myself out.

All the things said about me, both to my face and behind my back -- they tear me up inside. I'm hurting, Lord. I feel sick all the time, worse than just a physical sickness. I wish I did have a virus so I could stay in my room, so people would just leave me alone. As it is, I spend a lot of time in my room, crying on my bed until I'm worn out.

Lord, only You can pull me out of this deep pit. If You don't, I may never get out. Would You help me soon before I sink any deeper? I know You care about me, even if no one else does. You know what I'm going through, even better than I do.

What's more important, I pray nobody who seeks You gets discouraged because of what I'm going through or what I do or say. I pray no one thinks being a Christian isn't worth it because of me. No matter how bad things get, I don't want to blow my witness. If instead, I stay true and You pull me up out of this in a way that shows people You're for real, then all this will be worth it. I want those who know me who are seeking You to be encouraged because of what You do in my life.

Will I thank You then! I just pray then comes soon.

Psalm 70

For the choir director. A Psalm of David; for a memorial.

1   O God, hasten to deliver me;
     O LORD, hasten to my help!
2   Let those be ashamed and humiliated
     Who seek my life;
     Let those be turned back and dishonored
     Who delight in my hurt.
3   Let those be turned back because of their shame
     Who say, "Aha, aha!"

4   Let all who seek You rejoice and be glad in You;
     And let those who love Your salvation say continually,
     "Let God be magnified."
5   But I am afflicted and needy;
     Hasten to me, O God!
     You are my help and my deliverer;
     O LORD, do not delay.

Carry me,
Your love is wider than my need could ever be.

Jars of Clay "River Constantine"
from *If I Left the Zoo*

from PSALM 70

Oh Lord, I'm seeking You. You're my help and my God. I know I have life only because of You.

But when I'm down like I am now, it seems You're far away. Please come near. Let me be glad about You and about life again. I still love it that You've saved me and given me life with You forever. And I always will. I will always love You.

But I want You close now, not just some time way in the future. I want to see more of You in my life today and everyday. I need You now. So please come to me soon. I'm tired of being all down and afflicted. Instead, get me excited about You again. I want to be so hyped about You, I won't be able to stay quiet about it.

I'm seeking You, God. Oh Lord, please come close.

Psalm 71

1   In You, O LORD, I have taken refuge;
Let me never be ashamed.
2   In Your righteousness deliver me and rescue me;
Incline Your ear to me and save me.
3   Be to me a rock of habitation to which I may continually come;
You have given commandment to save me,
For You are my rock and my fortress.
4   Rescue me, O my God, out of the hand of the wicked,
Out of the grasp of the wrongdoer and ruthless man,
5   For You are my hope;
O Lord GOD, You are my confidence from my youth.
6   By You I have been sustained from my birth;
You are He who took me from my mother's womb;
My praise is continually of You.

7   I have become a marvel to many,
For You are my strong refuge.
8   My mouth is filled with Your praise
And with Your glory all day long.
9   Do not cast me off in the time of old age;
Do not forsake me when my strength fails.
10   For my enemies have spoken against me;
And those who watch for my life have consulted together,
11   Saying, "God has forsaken him;
Pursue and seize him, for there is no one to deliver."

12   O God, do not be far from me;
O my God, hasten to my help!
13   Let those who are adversaries of my soul be ashamed and consumed;
Let them be covered with reproach and dishonor, who seek to injure me.
14   But as for me, I will hope continually,
And will praise You yet more and more.
15   My mouth shall tell of Your righteousness
And of Your salvation all day long;
For I do not know the sum of them.
16   I will come with the mighty deeds of the Lord GOD;
I will make mention of Your righteousness, Yours alone.

17   O God, You have taught me from my youth,
And I still declare Your wondrous deeds.
18   And even when I am old and gray, O God, do not forsake me,
Until I declare Your strength to this generation,
Your power to all who are to come.
19   For Your righteousness, O God, reaches to the heavens,
You who have done great things;
O God, who is like You?
20   You who have shown me many troubles and distresses
Will revive me again,
And will bring me up again from the depths of the earth.
21   May You increase my greatness
And turn to comfort me.

22   I will also praise You with a harp,
Even Your truth, O my God;
To You I will sing praises with the lyre,
O Holy One of Israel.
23   My lips will shout for joy when I sing praises to You;
And my soul, which You have redeemed.
24   My tongue also will utter Your righteousness all day long;
For they are ashamed, for they are humiliated who seek my hurt.

And will we change at all when we get old?

MxPx "Teenage Politics"

from PSALMS 70 and 71

Sometimes when I'm sitting in church, I look around at all the adults. Last Sunday I was doing that. And I decided I don't want to ever be like them. It's not just getting fat and bald and growing ear hair. Most adults just aren't real about God.

God is great and righteous. The things He's done in history and does today are incredible. He's so good to us, though we don't deserve it at all. But how do a lot of adults respond? They sit on their fat rears in church one hour a week, if even that, then worship the holy dollar and act like He hardly exists the rest of the week.

I hope I never get like that.

There are exceptions though. Like there's this cool old guy at church. He likes to talk and joke around with me. I can tell him what's happening. He always listens and a lot of times says something from the Bible that really goes with my life and helps me.

I like hanging with him. If I ever get old, I hope I'm like him.

I don't want to become just another boring adult. I will never wimp out and be ashamed of either You or myself. I won't ignore You as soon as church lets out. I'm going to pray and praise You every day. I'm going to tell others about You, and about how You save people. I'm not going to act self-righteous when I talk about You, like some of those adults I see, because You're the one who's righteous, not me. But I'm not going to wimp out on You or on my friends. Because they need You as much as I do.

I want to be excited about You my whole life. I don't want to be one of those who are excited about You and about life when they're young, then get bored and boring when they're older. I want to be confident, committed, and strong in You my whole life. I want to make a difference, not just make money.

And when I'm an old geezer, I want to finish strong. I want people to look at me and marvel, "That oldster's still going for

God." Then, I want to teach kids and teenagers like me about You. I want to pass on what has been passed on to me.

Then when I die, I don't want to be driving 45 in a 65 zone. I want to die knowing I gave life all I've got -- knowing I gave You all I've got.

And I'll know death may be a finish line, but it won't be the end. It will be a beginning instead, because You will raise me up to live with You forever.

I hope we'll both be happy then with the life I lived down here.

Psalm 72
A Psalm of Solomon.

1   Give the king Your judgments, O God,
And Your righteousness to the king's son.
2   May he judge Your people with righteousness
And Your afflicted with justice.
3   Let the mountains bring peace to the people,
And the hills, in righteousness.
4   May he vindicate the afflicted of the people,
Save the children of the needy
And crush the oppressor.

5   Let them fear You while the sun endures,
And as long as the moon, throughout all generations.
6   May he come down like rain upon the mown grass,
Like showers that water the earth.
7   In his days may the righteous flourish,
And abundance of peace till the moon is no more.
8   May he also rule from sea to sea
And from the River to the ends of the earth.
9   Let the nomads of the desert bow before him,
And his enemies lick the dust.
10   Let the kings of Tarshish and of the islands bring presents;
The kings of Sheba and Seba offer gifts.
11   And let all kings bow down before him,
All nations serve him.

12   For he will deliver the needy when he cries for help,
The afflicted also, and him who has no helper.
13   He will have compassion on the poor and needy,
And the lives of the needy he will save.
14   He will rescue their life from oppression and violence,
And their blood will be precious in his sight;
15   So may he live, and may the gold of Sheba be given to him;
And let them pray for him continually;
Let them bless him all day long.

16   May there be abundance of grain in the earth on top of the mountains;
   Its fruit will wave like the cedars of Lebanon;
   And may those from the city flourish like vegetation of the earth.
17   May his name endure forever;
   May his name increase as long as the sun shines;
   And let men bless themselves by him;
   Let all nations call him blessed.

18   Blessed be the LORD God, the God of Israel,
   Who alone works wonders.
19   And blessed be His glorious name forever;
   And may the whole earth be filled with His glory.
   Amen, and Amen.

20   The prayers of David the son of Jesse are ended.

from PSALM 72

Man, do I want Jesus to come back and take over. Then there will be real peace on Earth. Not just these fake peaces that are only breaks between wars. He will bring an abundance of peace everyone can chill out in and enjoy. And it will last until the moon falls out of the sky.

There will be real justice for everyone, because Jesus will judge. He will put evil men in their place. Everything will be made right. Jesus will do it! What politicians just promise, King Jesus will do.

He'll rule for everybody, not just for those who have money or power. Those who are poor or weak and in need -- whom politicians only pretend to help -- Jesus will listen to them, help them, and protect them.

I'm glad He's in control today, too. He helps me, even when no one else will. He gives me peace, even when everything is going crazy.

But it's really going to be something when He comes back and rules. I can hardly begin to imagine how cool it will be. Jesus right down here among us. Jesus governing instead of a bunch of power-hungry politicians. Those stuffed suits will bow down to Him instead. Jesus ruling the whole earth! And His greatness and glory -- the whole world won't have enough room for it. His greatness will be everywhere. It will even make the weather better.

It blows my mind trying to think about it. I can hardly wait. Come soon, Jesus!

Psalm 73
A Psalm of Asaph.

1   Surely God is good to Israel,
   To those who are pure in heart!
2   But as for me, my feet came close to stumbling,
   My steps had almost slipped.
3   For I was envious of the arrogant
   As I saw the prosperity of the wicked.
4   For there are no pains in their death,
   And their body is fat.
5   They are not in trouble as other men,
   Nor are they plagued like mankind.
6   Therefore pride is their necklace;
   The garment of violence covers them.
7   Their eye bulges from fatness;
   The imaginations of their heart run riot.
8   They mock and wickedly speak of oppression;
   They speak from on high.
9   They have set their mouth against the heavens,
   And their tongue parades through the earth.

10   Therefore his people return to this place,
   And waters of abundance are drunk by them.
11   They say, "How does God know?
   And is there knowledge with the Most High?"
12   Behold, these are the wicked;
   And always at ease, they have increased in wealth.
13   Surely in vain I have kept my heart pure
   And washed my hands in innocence;
14   For I have been stricken all day long
   And chastened every morning.

15   If I had said, "I will speak thus,"
   Behold, I would have betrayed the generation of Your children.
16   When I pondered to understand this,
   It was troublesome in my sight
17   Until I came into the sanctuary of God;
   Then I perceived their end.
18   Surely You set them in slippery places;
   You cast them down to destruction.
19   How they are destroyed in a moment!
   They are utterly swept away by sudden terrors!
20   Like a dream when one awakes,
   O Lord, when aroused, You will despise their form.

21   When my heart was embittered
   And I was pierced within,

22   Then I was senseless and ignorant;
   I was like a beast before You.
23   Nevertheless I am continually with You;
   You have taken hold of my right hand.
24   With Your counsel You will guide me,
   And afterward receive me to glory.

25   Whom have I in heaven but You?
   And besides You, I desire nothing on earth.
26   My flesh and my heart may fail,
   But God is the strength of my heart and my portion forever.
27   For, behold, those who are far from You will perish;
   You have destroyed all those who are unfaithful to You.
28   But as for me, the nearness of God is my good;
   I have made the Lord GOD my refuge,
   That I may tell of all Your works.

from PSALM 73

Surely God is good to those who trust in Him and love Him with a pure heart.

But there have been times I've wondered about that.

There have been times when I thought my life sucked. I didn't think God was all that good to me. And I looked at others whose lives seemed to be great, and I envied them.

They are popular and have lots of friends, even though they're jerks. They have hot dates every week, even two or more a week! They've got money and hot cars. They cause big problems for others, but nothing ever seems to go wrong for them. They get away with everything. They act and talk like they're gods or something. And as far as the school is concerned, they are.

They blow off God, except to use Him as a cuss word. Yet look how good their lives are.

I thought, Why am I trying to stick with God and live right? What good does it do me? Popularity? At lunch time, I have to search for a table where I'm even allowed to sit. Dates? Oh, yeah. I've had one of those -- last year. Money? It's probably a good thing I don't have a date, because I don't even have enough net worth for one. Getting away with stuff? Are you kidding? I can't even pick my nose and get away with it. I get punished just for going to school. The popular crowd makes sure of that. I get put down all day long, starting with my caffeine-deprived arrival too early in the morning. Yep, that's me. Cars? Maybe I have my uncle's junker 1974 pickup to look forward to. It puts more gas into pollution than into acceleration. I can hardly wait. Problems? You don't want to hear them all.

I thought about all this, as I often do, and I nearly slipped in my faith. I nearly walked away from God. For there always seems to be an easier path than the one God has chosen for you. And I could think of a lot of different paths I would rather take than the one I found myself on.

If I had done that, if with my life and words I had said, "Following God isn't worth it" -- then I would have failed God; I would have failed my friends and family; I would have failed all who God wants me to impact. That would be the worst, worse than all the stuff I complain about combined.

Still I couldn't understand why my life was so sorry while sorry people's lives were so good. And it bothered me.

Then God helped me see the big picture. Those I was jealous of, who were blowing off God -- no matter how good their lives may seem, if they don't turn to God, they're toast. They're a heartbeat away from  hell. All it can take is a car crash -- and the way they drive, that can easily happen -- and they'll never be cool again. So I was stupid to envy them. I actually should feel sorry for them.

As for me, I have God. And though I had an ignorant, bad attitude toward Him for a while, He is always with me. He takes hold of my hand and guides me. He gives me the strength I need. He gives me Himself.

And He'll make my life right, even if He doesn't make life easy. And when I die, I'll get to be in His presence forever.

What's more important than having God? Can popularity, cars, money, or anything measure up to Him? My life might get seriously bad, and I might even get sick or get in an accident and die, but I'll still have God. And nothing and no one can take that away from me. Popularity, money, dates and all can and will be taken away from those I envied. But no one can take Jesus away from me.

So let others think getting things and living wrong can make them happy. Let sorry people get their jollies for a while. God's love and closeness is my good, and always will be. And nothing can beat that.

WATCH OUT FOR GOD'S TIMING

There have been times when I've been amazed at God's timing in teaching me from the Bible. Just the fact He's given us His word is incredible enough. But there have been more than a few times when God arranged things so that I heard a word exactly when I needed to hear it.

I put this section here because of an experience with Psalm 73. Recently, I was down about how my life was going. It bugged me that I was faithful and had put a lot of work into my writing, among other things, but had little to show for it, still being unpublished at the time -- after over ten years of writing.

But right at that time, I heard my pastor, Tommy Nelson, teach from Luke 6: 17 - 26 and Psalm 73. Among other things, he taught that things will get rough in life, but that "the returns aren't in" yet and that God will reward the faithfulness of His people. So if we're faithful, we shouldn't be deceived or discouraged by those times when things don't seem to be going right.

I needed to hear that. That message really encouraged me and set my attitude right. And I knew the timing of the message wasn't just coincidence. It was God's timing.

Years earlier, I had an even more serious problem with trusting God, but wasn't even aware of it. God used Psalm 37 to help open my eyes and to help me trust Him in my life. And more than once, He has pointed me back to that psalm when I needed to be reminded to trust Him and live like it.

I could go on about other times and God's timing in encouraging me and teaching me from His word. I will say God knows exactly what's going on in your life. And He knows exactly what part of the Bible you're going to check out. And He can bring the two together to speak to you, right where you are in your life.

It's exciting when God does that. And it's important to listen and respond to Him when He does that. So get into the Bible. Then watch out for God's timing in teaching you from His word. One day, you might be surprised.

M. M.

Psalm 74

A Maskil of Asaph.

1   O God, why have You rejected us forever?
Why does Your anger smoke against the sheep of Your pasture?
2   Remember Your congregation, which You have purchased of old,
Which You have redeemed to be the tribe of Your inheritance;
And this Mount Zion, where You have dwelt.
3   Turn Your footsteps toward the perpetual ruins;
The enemy has damaged everything within the sanctuary.
4   Your adversaries have roared in the midst of Your meeting place;
They have set up their own standards for signs.
5   It seems as if one had lifted up
His axe in a forest of trees.
6   And now all its carved work
They smash with hatchet and hammers.

7   They have burned Your sanctuary to the ground;
They have defiled the dwelling place of Your name.
8   They said in their heart, "Let us completely subdue them."
They have burned all the meeting places of God in the land.
9   We do not see our signs;
There is no longer any prophet,
Nor is there any among us who knows how long.
10   How long, O God, will the adversary revile,
And the enemy spurn Your name forever?
11   Why do You withdraw Your hand, even Your right hand?
From within Your bosom, destroy them!
12   Yet God is my king from of old,
Who works deeds of deliverance in the midst of the earth.
13   You divided the sea by Your strength;
You broke the heads of the sea monsters in the waters.
14   You crushed the heads of Leviathan;
You gave him as food for the creatures of the wilderness.
15   You broke open springs and torrents;
You dried up ever-flowing streams.
16   Yours is the day, Yours also is the night;
You have prepared the light and the sun.
17   You have established all the boundaries of the earth;
You have made summer and winter.

18   Remember this, O LORD, that the enemy has reviled,
And a foolish people has spurned Your name.
19   Do not deliver the soul of Your turtledove to the wild beast;
Do not forget the life of Your afflicted forever.
20   Consider the covenant;
For the dark places of the land are full of the habitations of violence.
21   Let not the oppressed return dishonored;
Let the afflicted and needy praise Your name.

22   Arise, O God, and plead Your own cause;
   Remember how the foolish man reproaches You all day long.
23   Do not forget the voice of Your adversaries,
   The uproar of those who rise against You which ascends continually.

from PSALM 74

God, have You rejected me? Are You angry with me about something? It sure seems that way. Jesus, I know You've said You'll never reject those who come to You, but -- I don't know. If You still love me, I can't understand why You let my life get this bad.

Everything that's important to me is falling apart. All I put a lot of time, effort, and prayer into is being smashed into pieces. I've put a lot into trying to live a good life. And I've trusted You to make my life good. Even when things have been rough, I've trusted in You and was glad You're my God. Yet all I have to show for it now is devastation. What's the point anymore?

Lord, I belong to You. What glory or joy does it bring to You for my life to fall apart? I know some of those who dis You are enjoying my suffering. They love it because it makes You look weak or not even there, Lord. They're laughing not just at me, but at You. Are You just going to do nothing? How long before You help Me and show them? I've prayed and done all I know to do. Where are You?

Yet You're still my God. And I know You help and rescue people. You've done it countless times in countless ways. You're strong, You can do anything, and already have. Like creating the universe for starters.

Is it too much to ask while You're doing all these great things, that You don't forget me and my suffering? If you don't remember me, then I'll be torn apart for good. I'm already torn up inside. I can't handle all I'm going through. I have no idea what to do. I see no good in my future.

I need You to help me. Don't let me continue discouraged and put down. Instead, from Your heart, remember me so, with a real smile (I've forgotten what one feels like), I can thank You for what You've done and praise You for who You are.

Please don't delay any longer. I don't know how long I can take all this. And if I fall and give up on life and lose hope in You, and if others see and dishonor You, what good would that do?

Psalm 75

For the choir director; set to Al-tashheth. A Psalm of Asaph, a Song.

1   We give thanks to You, O God, we give thanks,
For Your name is near;
Men declare Your wondrous works.
2   "When I select an appointed time,
It is I who judge with equity.
3   "The earth and all who dwell in it melt;
It is I who have firmly set its pillars.   Selah.
4   "I said to the boastful, 'Do not boast,'
And to the wicked, 'Do not lift up the horn;
5   Do not lift up your horn on high,
Do not speak with insolent pride.'"

6   For not from the east, nor from the west,
Nor from the desert comes exaltation;
7   But God is the Judge;
He puts down one and exalts another.
8   For a cup is in the hand of the LORD, and the wine foams;
It is well mixed, and He pours out of this;
Surely all the wicked of the earth must drain and drink down its dregs.

9   But as for me, I will declare it forever;
I will sing praises to the God of Jacob.
10   And all the horns of the wicked He will cut off,
But the horns of the righteous will be lifted up.

from PSALM 75

Thank You, God. Thanks that You are near. You're always there for me. Thanks for doing mind-blowing things that just gotta be told.

Thanks You're in control, even though I don't always act like it and trust You like I should. Sometimes, I think it's the jerks who rule everything, through popularity, sports, or beating up people. Looking at them, it's hard to believe You really are in control and that Your ways are the best ways to live. But it's not dates, parties, money, success, or school domination that makes a life good. You're the One who gives life and can make it great.

You put down and lift up whoever You please. The big jerks may seem to be having a great time. They sure do brag about what they do. But, like their highs from drugs and alcohol, it won't last.

You're kind and patient, so You give them plenty of chances, and You warn them what's coming. You warn them to quit being so arrogant and stupid, and to quit bragging about it. You tell them plenty of times to turn away from their evil and to turn to You. But if they don't listen, You put them in their place whenever You choose. Instead of being stupid-drunk from beer, they'll be reeling from Your judgment.

Those who try to live right, to live by Your ways, they may be put down now. Don't I know that. But if they stick with You, You will lift them up and give them a life so awesome, they can't even imagine it.

So I'm going to keep thanking You. Those who lift themselves up through evil, You will put down. And those who love You and live right even if it means being put down now, You will lift up. In Your perfect timing, You will do it.

Psalm 76
For the choir director; on stringed instruments.
A Psalm of Asaph, a Song.

1   God is known in Judah;
His name is great in Israel.
2   His tabernacle is in Salem;
His dwelling place also is in Zion.
3   There He broke the flaming arrows,
The shield and the sword and the weapons of war.   Selah.

4   You are resplendent,
More majestic than the mountains of prey.
5   The stouthearted were plundered,
They sank into sleep;
And none of the warriors could use his hands.
6   At Your rebuke, O God of Jacob,
Both rider and horse were cast into a dead sleep.
7   You, even You, are to be feared;
And who may stand in Your presence when once You are angry?

8   You caused judgment to be heard from heaven;
The earth feared and was still
9   When God arose to judgment,
To save all the humble of the earth.   Selah.
10   For the wrath of man shall praise You;
With a remnant of wrath You will gird Yourself.

11   Make vows to the LORD your God and fulfill them;
Let all who are around Him bring gifts to Him who is to be feared.
12   He will cut off the spirit of princes;
He is feared by the kings of the earth.

To see you!

from PSALM 76

God, Your name is great. You are majestic and strong, more than the tallest mountains. Lord, You created them and the universe. How much more awesome in power You must be.

And You have made Yourself known. You dwell with Your people.

What can stand against You? All the armies of the earth could come against You, but all You have to do is appear, and they all wet their pants. And their weapons, even the missiles, You'd break like toothpicks.

Yet the world is full of men stupid enough to try to stand up against You. Arrogant rulers do so every day, speaking and acting like they're gods. They use their power to loot and steal, to oppress and even kill the innocent.

But the time will come when You'll stand up and say, "That's enough. It's Judgment Day." And all the evil men of this earth will be so scared, they'll shut up for a change.

It will be so awesome when You appear on that day. To see Your power. To see You!

What's maybe best of all is You'll be coming to save the poor, the weak, the humble from the evil of this world. You are great and powerful far beyond what I can understand. Yet You care that much about people who are without power, who this world doesn't care much about.

But those who are arrogant against Him, He will put down. So wise up, you people who think you rule. Trust Him who really rules instead of trusting in yourself and your own power. You better be sure things are right between You and God. 'Cause if you don't fear His judgment now, you will fear it later.

Psalm 77

For the choir director; according to Jeduthun. A Psalm of Asaph.

1   My voice rises to God, and I will cry aloud;
    My voice rises to God, and He will hear me.
2   In the day of my trouble I sought the Lord;
    In the night my hand was stretched out without weariness;
    My soul refused to be comforted.

3   When I remember God, then I am disturbed;
When I sigh, then my spirit grows faint.   Selah.
4   You have held my eyelids open;
I am so troubled that I cannot speak.
5   I have considered the days of old,
The years of long ago.
6   I will remember my song in the night;
I will meditate with my heart,
And my spirit ponders:

7   Will the Lord reject forever?
And will He never be favorable again?
8   Has His lovingkindness ceased forever?
Has His promise come to an end forever?
9   Has God forgotten to be gracious,
Or has He in anger withdrawn His compassion?   Selah.
10   Then I said, "It is my grief,
That the right hand of the Most High has changed."

11   I shall remember the deeds of the LORD;
Surely I will remember Your wonders of old.
12   I will meditate on all Your work
And muse on Your deeds.
13   Your way, O God, is holy;
What god is great like our God?
14   You are the God who works wonders;
You have made known Your strength among the peoples.
15   You have by Your power redeemed Your people,
The sons of Jacob and Joseph.   Selah.
16   The waters saw You, O God;
The waters saw You, they were in anguish;
The deeps also trembled.
17   The clouds poured out water;
The skies gave forth a sound;
Your arrows flashed here and there.
18   The sound of Your thunder was in the whirlwind;
The lightnings lit up the world;
The earth trembled and shook.
19   Your way was in the sea
And Your paths in the mighty waters,
And Your footprints may not be known.
20   You led Your people like a flock
By the hand of Moses and Aaron.

from PSALM 77
especially verse 19

I just don't get it. I pray and pray to You, God, and still my life is going bad. I know You'll answer me, but how much longer do I have to wait and be miserable? I can't understand why You let things get so bad in the first place. Don't You care about me anymore?

It used to be when I thought about You, it brought me joy. Now when I think about You, it disturbs me.

I'm so troubled I can't sleep. And I hardly know what to say to You anymore. I just lay back on my bed and think. I remember the way things used to be. I remember placing my trust in You and asking You into my life. I remember You seeming so close. I could feel Your love for me. I remember great answers to prayer. But now? I'm losing hope You'll help me again. It seems like You've changed toward me.

But I know You are great and perfect. Your ways are the best ways, though lately I wonder. You are powerful, doing great things for people, especially saving them like You've saved me.

But I don't know You as well as I once thought I did. I still know You love me, even if I barely know that now. But I don't get how You can love me and let me go through all this.

I keep thinking and pondering. And there are no easy answers, just tough questions.

It really shouldn't surprise me when I don't understand You. Man still doesn't understand a lot of things about even Your creation. We are still caught by surprise by earthquakes and storms. Who can comprehend the power of a tornado, much less predict one? So how can we understand You, the Creator? You've revealed a lot about Yourself. But the things we don't know about You are infinite.

We cannot understand all Your ways. I can't even come close. Like footsteps in the ocean, Your ways, Your steps, are hidden and deep. We cannot comprehend them. Your footsteps are in the deepest water and in the farthest space. They can not be known.

But You can be trusted. But it's tough, Lord, when my life is like this. It's tough to trust You when I don't understand what You're doing, when I can't understand You.

Psalm 78
A Maskil of Asaph.

1   Listen, O my people, to my instruction;
Incline your ears to the words of my mouth.
2   I will open my mouth in a parable;
I will utter dark sayings of old,
3   Which we have heard and known,
And our fathers have told us.
4   We will not conceal them from their children,
But tell to the generation to come the praises of the LORD,
And His strength and His wondrous works that He has done.

5   For He established a testimony in Jacob
And appointed a law in Israel,
Which He commanded our fathers
That they should teach them to their children,
6   That the generation to come might know, even the children yet to be
born,
That they may arise and tell them to their children,
7   That they should put their confidence in God
And not forget the works of God,
But keep His commandments,
8   And not be like their fathers,
A stubborn and rebellious generation,
A generation that did not prepare its heart
And whose spirit was not faithful to God.

9   The sons of Ephraim were archers equipped with bows,
Yet they turned back in the day of battle.
10   They did not keep the covenant of God
And refused to walk in His law;
11   They forgot His deeds
And His miracles that He had shown them.
12   He wrought wonders before their fathers
In the land of Egypt, in the field of Zoan.
13   He divided the sea and caused them to pass through,
And He made the waters stand up like a heap.
14   Then He led them with the cloud by day
And all the night with a light of fire.
15   He split the rocks in the wilderness
And gave them abundant drink like the ocean depths.
16   He brought forth streams also from the rock
And caused waters to run down like rivers.

17   Yet they still continued to sin against Him,
To rebel against the Most High in the desert.
18   And in their heart they put God to the test
By asking food according to their desire.

19   Then they spoke against God;
They said, "Can God prepare a table in the wilderness?
20   "Behold, He struck the rock so that waters gushed out,
And streams were overflowing;
Can He give bread also?
Will He provide meat for His people?"

21   Therefore the LORD heard and was full of wrath;
And a fire was kindled against Jacob
And anger also mounted against Israel,
22   Because they did not believe in God
And did not trust in His salvation.
23   Yet He commanded the clouds above
And opened the doors of heaven;
24   He rained down manna upon them to eat
And gave them food from heaven.
25   Man did eat the bread of angels;
He sent them food in abundance.
26   He caused the east wind to blow in the heavens
And by His power He directed the south wind.
27   When He rained meat upon them like the dust,
Even winged fowl like the sand of the seas,
28   Then He let them fall in the midst of their camp,
Round about their dwellings.
29   So they ate and were well filled,
And their desire He gave to them.
30   Before they had satisfied their desire,
While their food was in their mouths,
31   The anger of God rose against them
And killed some of their stoutest ones,
And subdued the choice men of Israel.
32   In spite of all this they still sinned
And did not believe in His wonderful works.
33   So He brought their days to an end in futility
And their years in sudden terror.

34   When He killed them, then they sought Him,
And returned and searched diligently for God;
35   And they remembered that God was their rock,
And the Most High God their Redeemer.
36   But they deceived Him with their mouth
And lied to Him with their tongue.
37   For their heart was not steadfast toward Him,
Nor were they faithful in His covenant.
38   But He, being compassionate, forgave their iniquity and did not
destroy them;
And often He restrained His anger
And did not arouse all His wrath.

39   Thus He remembered that they were but flesh,
    A wind that passes and does not return.

40   How often they rebelled against Him in the wilderness
    And grieved Him in the desert!
41   Again and again they tempted God,
    And pained the Holy One of Israel.
42   They did not remember His power,
    The day when He redeemed them from the adversary,
43   When He performed His signs in Egypt
    And His marvels in the field of Zoan,
44   And turned their rivers to blood,
    And their streams, they could not drink.
45   He sent among them swarms of flies which devoured them,
    And frogs which destroyed them.
46   He gave also their crops to the grasshopper
    And the product of their labor to the locust.
47   He destroyed their vines with hailstones
    And their sycamore trees with frost.
48   He gave over their cattle also to the hailstones
    And their herds to bolts of lightning.
49   He sent upon them His burning anger,
    Fury and indignation and trouble,
    A band of destroying angels.
50   He leveled a path for His anger;
    He did not spare their soul from death,
    But gave over their life to the plague,
51   And smote all the firstborn in Egypt,
    The first issue of their virility in the tents of Ham.
52   But He led forth His own people like sheep
    And guided them in the wilderness like a flock;
53   He led them safely, so that they did not fear;
    But the sea engulfed their enemies.
54   So He brought them to His holy land,
    To this hill country which His right hand had gained.
55   He also drove out the nations before them
    And apportioned them for an inheritance by measurement,
    And made the tribes of Israel dwell in their tents.
56   Yet they tempted and rebelled against the Most High God
    And did not keep His testimonies,
57   But turned back and acted treacherously like their fathers;
    They turned aside like a treacherous bow.
58   For they provoked Him with their high places
    And aroused His jealousy with their graven images.
59   When God heard, He was filled with wrath
    And greatly abhorred Israel;
60   So that He abandoned the dwelling place at Shiloh,
    The tent which He had pitched among men,

61   And gave up His strength to captivity
      And His glory into the hand of the adversary.
62   He also delivered His people to the sword,
      And was filled with wrath at His inheritance.
63   Fire devoured His young men,
      And His virgins had no wedding songs.
64   His priests fell by the sword,
      And His widows could not weep.

65   Then the Lord awoke as if from sleep,
      Like a warrior overcome by wine.
66   He drove His adversaries backward;
      He put on them an everlasting reproach.
67   He also rejected the tent of Joseph,
      And did not choose the tribe of Ephraim,
68   But chose the tribe of Judah,
      Mount Zion which He loved.
69   And He built His sanctuary like the heights,
      Like the earth which He has founded forever.
70   He also chose David His servant
      And took him from the sheepfolds;
71   From the care of the ewes with suckling lambs He brought him
      To shepherd Jacob His people,
      And Israel His inheritance.
72   So he shepherded them according to the integrity of his heart,
      And guided them with his skillful hands.

**No, I'll never be like you. I'll never ever be like you.
Oh no! I'm just like you!**
                    MxPx "Teenage Politics"

from PSALM 78

When I read about the Israelites and how they were constantly disobeying, distrusting, and just plain dissing God, I think they were real stupid. They saw God do so many incredible things, like all the weird plagues on Egypt and splitting the Red Sea, then the manna in the wilderness and water from the rock and everything else. Yet they were always moaning and groaning and whining and doubting God. Stupid!

Then I think some more and wonder if I would have acted like those whiners. And at first I think, "No!"

Then I'm not so sure.

I've seen God do awesome things. I've seen some cool answers to prayer. And I know what God has done through history because I have the Bible. The Hebrews didn't have that. Best of all, I know Jesus died for me, rose again, and gives me life.

Yet so many times I don't trust God. I'm afraid He won't come through for me. It's like I forget all those times He already has come through for me. I even get afraid He'll make my life sorry or something. Like I know what's best for me better than God does. Yeah, right. So instead of trusting Him, I do things my way and disobey Him.

Then there's all the times I ignore God by blowing off prayer and the Bible. I mean, God saved my life and is so good to me, and He just wants me to talk to Him and listen to Him. I should be excited about that. But too often I'm not. A lot of times I'm not excited about Him either, even though I have every reason to.

So I can be pretty stupid, too. It's a good thing God forgives me and loves me anyway. With love and skill He guides me through life -- and it takes skill to guide me! Just like He was with the Israelites, God remains faithful and trustworthy to me, even when I'm not to Him.

God is so patient and faithful to me. I want to be faithful to Him. When He thinks about me, I want Him to not be mad or sad, like He was about the Israelites, but glad.

Psalm 79
A Psalm of Asaph.

1   O God, the nations have invaded Your inheritance;
They have defiled Your holy temple;
They have laid Jerusalem in ruins.
2   They have given the dead bodies of Your servants for food to the birds of the heavens,
The flesh of Your godly ones to the beasts of the earth.
3   They have poured out their blood like water round about Jerusalem;
And there was no one to bury them.
4   We have become a reproach to our neighbors,
A scoffing and derision to those around us.
5   How long, O LORD? Will You be angry forever?
Will Your jealousy burn like fire?
6   Pour out Your wrath upon the nations which do not know You,
And upon the kingdoms which do not call upon Your name.
7   For they have devoured Jacob
And laid waste his habitation.

8   Do not remember the iniquities of our forefathers against us;
Let Your compassion come quickly to meet us,

For we are brought very low.
9   Help us, O God of our salvation, for the glory of Your name;
And deliver us and forgive our sins for Your name's sake.
10   Why should the nations say, "Where is their God?"
Let there be known among the nations in our sight,
Vengeance for the blood of Your servants which has been shed.
11   Let the groaning of the prisoner come before You;
According to the greatness of Your power preserve those who are
doomed to die.
12   And return to our neighbors sevenfold into their bosom
The reproach with which they have reproached You, O Lord.
13   So we Your people and the sheep of Your pasture
Will give thanks to You forever;
To all generations we will tell of Your praise.

With two fingers pointed screamin' get it together
But who's in the mix to show me any better
So whatever I'm runnin' on my own solo
Tryin' to make things happen off the little bit I know
And I guess I'll get what I get
But yet I don't want to live my life full of regrets.

John Reuben "No Regrets"
from *Are We There Yet?*

from PSALM 79
especially verses 8 and 9

God, it's hard being stuck in this family. I wonder why You put me in it.

I hate being home. I try to be out as much as I can. Even then, I suffer from being part of this family. I can't escape from being my father's kid. "Is that what-his-name's kid?" "Yeah, that kid will probably end up being good-for-nothing, too." At school and around town, I'm always mistrusted and looked down on because of who my parents are and who my older brothers are.

That's still better than being home. The drinking. The anger. The yelling. And worse. I just stay in my room and hope I can shut the rest of the family out. But I never can. And I have the bruises outside and the scars inside to prove it.

What ticks me even more are the times I find myself acting like my parents, especially when I'm angry. It's hard to be a good person when I don't have a good example. It's hard to not follow a bad example. Sometimes I feel myself becoming what I hate.

Oh God, please don't let me suffer all my life for the sins of my family. My home and my life are sorry. I feel trapped. I think about running away, but that will probably make things worse. I don't see any good way out. Please have compassion on me and help me.

And please forgive me for my sins and give me the strength to toss them away. I don't want to become like my parents. I want to be more like Jesus. I want my life to bring honor to You, instead of more dishonor to myself.

Please break the chains of my parents' sin.

Psalm 80
For the choir director; set to El Shoshannim; Eduth. A Psalm of Asaph.

1   Oh, give ear, Shepherd of Israel,
You who lead Joseph like a flock;
You who are enthroned above the cherubim, shine forth!
2   Before Ephraim and Benjamin and Manasseh, stir up Your power
And come to save us!
3   O God, restore us
And cause Your face to shine upon us, and we will be saved.

4   O LORD God of hosts,
How long will You be angry with the prayer of Your people?
5   You have fed them with the bread of tears,
And You have made them to drink tears in large measure.
6   You make us an object of contention to our neighbors,
And our enemies laugh among themselves.
7   O God of hosts, restore us
And cause Your face to shine upon us, and we will be saved.
8   You removed a vine from Egypt;
You drove out the nations and planted it.
9   You cleared the ground before it,
And it took deep root and filled the land.
10   The mountains were covered with its shadow,
And the cedars of God with its boughs.
11   It was sending out its branches to the sea
And its shoots to the River.
12   Why have You broken down its hedges,
So that all who pass that way pick its fruit?
13   A boar from the forest eats it away
And whatever moves in the field feeds on it.

14   O God of hosts, turn again now, we beseech You;
Look down from heaven and see, and take care of this vine,
15   Even the shoot which Your right hand has planted,
And on the son whom You have strengthened for Yourself.

16   It is burned with fire, it is cut down;
They perish at the rebuke of Your countenance.
17   Let Your hand be upon the man of Your right hand,
Upon the son of man whom You made strong for Yourself.
18   Then we shall not turn back from You;
Revive us, and we will call upon Your name.
19   O LORD God of hosts, restore us;
Cause Your face to shine upon us, and we will be saved.

I just don't get it.

from PSALM 80

Oh God, please listen to my prayer.

You shine on Your throne up above. How great Your glory and power must be.

But the way my life is, it's hard for me to get real excited about that. I need You to shine on me down here.

The way my life is going, I'm thinking You're angry with me about something instead. I'm wondering if even my prayers tick You. Because it seems You've been ignoring my prayers -- or even doing the opposite of what I pray for. Instead of giving me answers to my prayers, You give me more tears to cry. Instead of giving me peace and lifting me up, You give me the laughs of those who put me down. How long will You reject my prayers this way? How long will my life be this way?

But, God, I know You're powerful. All You have to do is shine Your smile upon me, and my life will be all right.

I'm not asking too much, am I? You've done so much for me in the past. You saved me and took me and placed me in Your family. You watched over me, protected me, and helped me grow. Because of You, I was living large. My life was going places. You brought me a long way, Lord. Why then are You now allowing my life to fall apart? I just don't get it.

God, I'm Your child. You made me and grew me, and I belong to You. Look down and see my hurting. Listen to my prayer. Take care of me and restore me. Make my life right again. I need You, Father.

Things are bad, and I'm real down. But shine Your smile upon me, and my life will be all right.

Psalm 81

For the choir director; on the Gittith. A Psalm of Asaph.

1   Sing for joy to God our strength;
Shout joyfully to the God of Jacob.
2   Raise a song, strike the timbrel,
The sweet sounding lyre with the harp.
3   Blow the trumpet at the new moon,
At the full moon, on our feast day.
4   For it is a statute for Israel,
An ordinance of the God of Jacob.
5   He established it for a testimony in Joseph
When he went throughout the land of Egypt.
I heard a language that I did not know:

6   "I relieved his shoulder of the burden,
His hands were freed from the basket.
7   "You called in trouble and I rescued you;
I answered you in the hiding place of thunder;
I proved you at the waters of Meribah.   Selah.
8   "Hear, O My people, and I will admonish you;
O Israel, if you would listen to Me!
9   "Let there be no strange god among you;
Nor shall you worship any foreign god.
10   "I, the LORD, am your God,
Who brought you up from the land of Egypt;
Open your mouth wide and I will fill it.

11   "But My people did not listen to My voice,
And Israel did not obey Me.
12   "So I gave them over to the stubbornness of their heart,
To walk in their own devices.
13   "Oh that My people would listen to Me,
That Israel would walk in My ways!
14   "I would quickly subdue their enemies
And turn My hand against their adversaries.
15   "Those who hate the LORD would pretend obedience to Him,
And their time of punishment would be forever.
16   "But I would feed you with the finest of the wheat,
And with honey from the rock I would satisfy you."

from PSALM 81

I'm glad God hears me when I call. I'm really happy He answered when I asked Him to come into my life. He forgave me, lifting that heavy weight of guilt off me. He freed me from being in bondage to sin forever. And He's responded to me and helped me since then.

I still have some tough times. Sometimes God allows them to strengthen my character. Other times, it's so God can show His love and power, and increase my trust by helping me out, kinda like He did with the Hebrews when they had all their trouble with Pharaoh and with going through the wilderness. Then there are tough times I just don't understand at all. Maybe those are to teach me to trust God anyway.

But a lot of times, it's just my own fault. God wants good for me, not bad. He wants my life to be the best. But I mess things up with my actions and attitudes.

Something I'm learning is I need to be ready and have a right mind to handle good that comes along. A couple of times lately I wasn't ready, and it was a bummer. My grandparents gave me more than the usual amount of money for my birthday. Yeah! But then I had no self-control and blew it off on things I don't care about much now. And the money's gone. And right after that, I got a nice girl friend. Double yeah! But I was clueless and didn't know how to treat her right. So that lasted about three days.

I've always wondered if God is good and loves me so much, why does He keep good things from me? Now I'm thinking one reason is I'm not ready to handle a lot of the good God would like to do for me. Good doesn't do you much good if you don't have the right attitude and can't handle it right. Like I found out. So I need to get smarter.

And I need to go after good the right way. There's been times I've gone after it the wrong way, like when I try to deceive my mom into letting me do what I want. Or like when something I want becomes too important to me, and I make an idol out of it. God's not going to reward that stuff.

Now about not so good things. There's times when I get into a mess because I make bad choices. Too many times, I think I know everything, especially about how to live my life. So I don't listen to my parents. I don't even listen to God (especially when He says, "Listen to your parents."). There's so much smart stuff in His word about how to live. But I forget it or blow it off, especially when I'm slack about getting into the word. And I end up doing other stupid things, which leads to more stupidity.

Sooner or later, I end up paying for it. It can be something like the time I broke an arm jumping off a roof I was supposed to stay off of. Hey, I jumped off roofs dozens of times with nooo problem. Or it can be like the time I hurt a friend and harmed a friendship by saying dumb stuff about him. Every time, it's because I thought I was so stinking smart. I thought I knew how to have fun and live. And I had the stupid idea that God wanted to make my life boring. So I didn't listen to Him and did things my way instead of His way.

God's cool, so He doesn't zap me when I'm like that. Otherwise, I'd be crispy-fried by now. He lets me go my own way and find out for myself how stupid it is. I guess that's the only way I learn sometimes.

Wouldn't it be a lot smarter to listen to God and do things His way the first time? Things would go a lot better. I'd be more prepared to handle both the good and bad of life. I'd make better decisions. Life is tough enough without causing bad because of my own stupidity.

So I'm going to stop slacking about getting into His word. I'm going to stop slacking about doing His word, doing what's He says. From now on, when He says, "Listen to me," I'm listening!

I know now God wants me to listen to Him and open up to Him, not because He wants to be bossy or make my life boring, but because He wants my life to be the best.

Psalm 82
A Psalm of Asaph.

1   God takes His stand in His own congregation;
He judges in the midst of the rulers.
2   How long will you judge unjustly
And show partiality to the wicked?   Selah.
3   Vindicate the weak and fatherless;
Do justice to the afflicted and destitute.
4   Rescue the weak and needy;
Deliver them out of the hand of the wicked.
5   They do not know nor do they understand;
They walk about in darkness;
All the foundations of the earth are shaken.
6   I said, "You are gods,
And all of you are sons of the Most High.
7   "Nevertheless you will die like men
And fall like any one of the princes."
8   Arise, O God, judge the earth!
For it is You who possesses all the nations.

from PSALM 82

I've had it with politicians and bad judges. They pass bad laws, and twist and mangle good ones. They kiss up to crooks and kick around good people. Many of them are crooks themselves. If you don't have power or money, you can forget about getting a fair shake from them. If you're weak or poor, or are a overworked tax slave or a crime victim, forget about help from them. They'll probably jack up your taxes and let the criminal loose instead.

They eagerly lie every time their mouth is open. They call good evil and evil good, and with a straight oh-so-sincere face, too.

They are so clueless. They've been crooked liars for so long, they hardly know what truth and lies and good and evil are anymore. And because of them and rulers like them around the world, this earth is royally messed up.

They act like they're gods or something. With the evil they inflict on people, they're as powerful as gods. And with their fat egos in fancy suits, they think they'll rule forever.

They've got another thing coming.

First, they will die like anyone else and maybe worse.

Then the One who really rules will come and judge the judges. He will take His stand, and no one will be able to stand against Him. He will rule over the rulers and over the whole earth. He will say how things are going to be. He will do justice for the weak, the hurting, and the poor. And He will put evil judges and politicians where they belong. For He is the righteous Judge and King.

Oh Lord, may it be soon. You own the whole earth. Come, take possession of it and rule!

Psalm 83

A Song, a Psalm of Asaph.

1   O God, do not remain quiet;
Do not be silent and, O God, do not be still.
2   For behold, Your enemies make an uproar,
And those who hate You have exalted themselves.
3   They make shrewd plans against Your people,
And conspire together against Your treasured ones.
4   They have said, "Come, and let us wipe them out as a nation,
That the name of Israel be remembered no more."

5   For they have conspired together with one mind;
Against You they make a covenant:
6   The tents of Edom and the Ishmaelites,
Moab and the Hagrites;
7   Gebal and Ammon and Amalek,
Philistia with the inhabitants of Tyre;
8   Assyria also has joined with them;
They have become a help to the children of Lot.   Selah.

9   Deal with them as with Midian,
As with Sisera and Jabin at the torrent of Kishon,
10   Who were destroyed at En-dor,
Who became as dung for the ground.
11   Make their nobles like Oreb and Zeeb
And all their princes like Zebah and Zalmunna,
12   Who said, "Let us possess for ourselves
The pastures of God."
13   O my God, make them like the whirling dust,
Like chaff before the wind.
14   Like fire that burns the forest
And like a flame that sets the mountains on fire,
15   So pursue them with Your tempest
And terrify them with Your storm.
16   Fill their faces with dishonor,
That they may seek Your name, O LORD.
17   Let them be ashamed and dismayed forever,
And let them be humiliated and perish,
18   That they may know that You alone, whose name is the LORD,
Are the Most High over all the earth.

I don't understand hate.

from PSALM 83

When you look back through history, it seems somebody was always trying to wipe out the nation of Israel. There was Pharaoh. Then when Israel took the Promised Land, there were all those nations with strange names surrounding them. Then there was Haman in the Book of Esther. And on and on through history all the way up to Hitler.

After the Holocaust, you'd think the world would be sorry and give Jewish people a break. But right after Israel became a nation with land again, the countries surrounding her tried to wipe her off the map. And they tried again in 1967. Today terrorists are still trying. There are still groups of people that hate and kill Jews because they're Jews. I don't understand hate like that. But these anti-Semites hate God, and that's a big reason why they hate God's people.

With all the nations and people that have tried to wipe out the people of Israel through the centuries, you'd think someone would have succeeded. But no one has. Instead most of them are dead, just strange names on the pages of history.

God has allowed Israel to go through some awful persecutions, but every time He brought the nation through it. Man has attempted genocide against Israel time and time again, but every time God foiled them.

That encourages me because it shows God is there, that He's strong and He cares. No one can stop His good plans for His people. And if He can bring Israel through all their troubles and ordeals, He certainly can and will bring me through all mine.

Lord, do protect Israel.

It's not nearly as bad as what Israel has gone through, but right now there are people who are trying to blow me away, because they hate me and don't care about You either.   Come upon them like a sudden storm, blow them away, and humiliate them. So they may know You are God; so they may humble themselves and seek You -- instead of seeking me.

Psalm 84
For the choir director; on the Gittith.
A Psalm of the sons of Korah.

1   How lovely are Your dwelling places,
O LORD of hosts!
2   My soul longed and even yearned for the courts of the LORD;
My heart and my flesh sing for joy to the living God.
3   The bird also has found a house,
And the swallow a nest for herself, where she may lay her young,
Even Your altars, O LORD of hosts,
My King and my God.
4   How blessed are those who dwell in Your house!
They are ever praising You.   Selah.

5   How blessed is the man whose strength is in You,
In whose heart are the highways to Zion!
6   Passing through the valley of Baca they make it a spring;
The early rain also covers it with blessings.
7   They go from strength to strength,
Every one of them appears before God in Zion.

8   O LORD God of hosts, hear my prayer;
     Give ear, O God of Jacob!   Selah.
9   Behold our shield, O God,
     And look upon the face of Your anointed.
10   For a day in Your courts is better than a thousand outside.
     I would rather stand at the threshold of the house of my God
     Than dwell in the tents of wickedness.
11   For the LORD God is a sun and shield;
     The LORD gives grace and glory;
     No good thing does He withhold from those who walk uprightly.
12   O LORD of hosts,
     How blessed is the man who trusts in You!

I want to be where you are.

from PSALM 84

NOTE: You might be looking at the title of this psalm and thinking, "Here comes those sons of Korah again. Who are they?"

You can find out about Korah in Numbers, chapter 16. Korah was jealous of Moses' power and authority, so he led a rebellion against him. This ticked off God so much that the earth opened up and swallowed Korah and the rebels alive.

Yet God later used a number of Korah's descendants to write part of His word, to write some of the Psalms.

So if you come from a "bad" family, don't think God won't accept and use you greatly.

Lord, I want to be where You are. There's no better place. I'm hyped that You have lots of room at Your place for everyone who comes to You -- including me.

I want to be closer to You. There's been a part of me that's always discontent, that's never at peace. It's seems there's always something missing. And I've been searching and reaching for it, without knowing what it is.

Now I know. What's missing is being close to You.

If I have to walk a long, tough road to get close to You, I'll do it. Thanks, Jesus, for already showing me the way, and for paving it with Your life and Your blood. You are the Way. You gave Yourself, even Your life, to become my way.

You said Your way isn't easy. But it's the best. And I know You'll strengthen me for the road You've laid out for me. I know You'll use the road ahead to strengthen me more and more. And You'll walk beside me. Just knowing You're there for me keeps me going.

I hear about the parties and everything going on, and it

sounds like fun. But a day with You dogs a thousand nights any-where else. So I'm not taking those other roads. For You are brighter than the sun. It's You who makes my days bright and my nights starry. It's You, my shield, who protects me and leads me. You are so good to me although I don't deserve it at all. Everything that's good and awesome comes from You. And You don't hold back.

You even give Your glory and Your self.

Oh Lord, You are so awesome. I want You with all I am.

I trust You to lead me to where You are.

Psalm 85
For the choir director. A Psalm of the sons of Korah.

1   O LORD, You showed favor to Your land;
You restored the captivity of Jacob.

2   You forgave the iniquity of Your people;
You covered all their sin.   Selah.

3   You withdrew all Your fury;
You turned away from Your burning anger.

4   Restore us, O God of our salvation,
And cause Your indignation toward us to cease.

5   Will You be angry with us forever?
Will You prolong Your anger to all generations?

6   Will You not Yourself revive us again,
That Your people may rejoice in You?

7   Show us Your lovingkindness, O LORD,
And grant us Your salvation.

8   I will hear what God the LORD will say;
For He will speak peace to His people, to His godly ones;
But let them not turn back to folly.

9   Surely His salvation is near to those who fear Him,
That glory may dwell in our land.

10   Lovingkindness and truth have met together;
Righteousness and peace have kissed each other.

11   Truth springs from the earth,
And righteousness looks down from heaven.

12   Indeed, the LORD will give what is good,
And our land will yield its produce.

13   Righteousness will go before Him
And will make His footsteps into a way.

from PSALM 85
especially verses 10 and 13

"Righteousness and peace have kissed each other." (verse 10) I bet you didn't think you'd see kissing in the Psalms. Well, there you go.

Seriously, this verse is a gold nugget that points to what God was going to do through Jesus.

You might have figured out that this psalm is about salvation. God forgiving sin is mentioned in verse 2. "Salvation" comes up repeatedly, along with the concept of God turning His anger away from men.

So what does that have to do with kissing?

This is going to get heavy so hold on.

God is perfectly just and holy. He will punish all evil and allow no sin into His heaven. Otherwise, heaven wouldn't be heaven. God is also perfectly loving and desires all people come to Him and have peace with Him.

But since all have sinned and done wrong, how can anyone have peace with a just and holy God and get into heaven? How can God be both 100% just and 100% loving toward us? For Him to be 100% loving, it seems He would have to compromise His justice and holiness, ignore our sin, and let us into heaven like a wimp judge who let's criminals off. To be 100% just, it seems He would have to forget His love for us and the peace He desires for us and punish all our wrong, letting us all go to hell.

But God won't settle for anything less than both perfect justice and perfect love. That's why Jesus came and died for us. When Jesus died on the cross, God's justice and love met. Or as this psalm says, God's righteousness and peace "kissed." Jesus gave His life because of His and the Father's great love for us, because He desired forgiveness, life, and peace for us. Jesus also died to satisfy God's righteous justice. For He took the punishment for our sin. (To get an idea of the agony Jesus went through for us, see Psalm 22.) Jesus would not slack on either God's love for us or on God's justice. So He loved us by taking our punishment that God's justice demanded and died for us.

At no other time in history have God's peace and righteousness met and showed themselves more clearly than in the life and death of Jesus. In Jesus, God broke through history and walked as a man -- the Man who lived out and brought together God's holiness, righteous, justice, love, and peace perfectly so we can experience peace with God and the awesome love of God forever.

The last verse of Psalm 85 is right on target. Jesus' righteous life and death has provided the way to God for us. Since both God's just righteousness and peaceful love came together and were satisfied in Jesus, He became the Way for us. (John 14:6)

We can't satisfy God's righteous standards. We can't deserve His peace and love. But Jesus has done that for us. So we need to simply trust Him and start down the way He's made for us -- the way where righteousness and the peace of forgiveness and love come together. He is the Way.

M. M.

Psalm 86
A Prayer of David.

1   Incline Your ear, O LORD, and answer me;
     For I am afflicted and needy.
2   Preserve my soul, for I am a godly man;
     O You my God, save Your servant who trusts in You.
3   Be gracious to me, O Lord,
     For to You I cry all day long.
4   Make glad the soul of Your servant,
     For to You, O Lord, I lift up my soul.
5   For You, Lord, are good, and ready to forgive,
     And abundant in lovingkindness to all who call upon You.
6   Give ear, O LORD, to my prayer;
     And give heed to the voice of my supplications!
7   In the day of my trouble I shall call upon You,
     For You will answer me.
8   There is no one like You among the gods, O Lord,
     Nor are there any works like Yours.
9   All nations whom You have made shall come and worship before You,
O Lord,
     And they shall glorify Your name.
10   For You are great and do wondrous deeds;
     You alone are God.
11   Teach me Your way, O LORD;
     I will walk in Your truth;
     Unite my heart to fear Your name.
12   I will give thanks to You, O Lord my God, with all my heart,
     And will glorify Your name forever.
13   For Your lovingkindness toward me is great,
     And You have delivered my soul from the depths of Sheol.

14   O God, arrogant men have risen up against me,
     And a band of violent men have sought my life,
     And they have not set You before them.

15   But You, O Lord, are a God merciful and gracious,
  Slow to anger and abundant in lovingkindness and truth.
16   Turn to me, and be gracious to me;
  Oh grant Your strength to Your servant,
  And save the son of Your handmaid.
17   Show me a sign for good,
  That those who hate me may see it and be ashamed,
  Because You, O LORD, have helped me and comforted me.

I'm pulled a hundred different ways.

from PSALM 86

Oh Lord, I'm glad I can come and pray to You, especially when I'm down. I can come to You and pray with confidence because of who You are. For You are good and loving and faithful. I can trust You.

I can pray with confidence because You hear and answer prayer. You sure answered when I asked for forgiveness. Thanks for saving me from hell. I once thought You're ready to zap me. Now I know You're ready to forgive me and anyone who sincerely comes to You. You are big good to anyone who calls to You. So I'm calling! -- through the day, every day.

Oh Lord, there is no one like You. No one does great things that make me wonder and make me happy like you do. No one can answer prayer like You.

You are great to me. Your forgiveness, Your kindness, Your patience, Your love toward me is huge.

You are so awesome to me. I want to be as faithful to You as You are to me.

But I don't come close, and I don't understand why. It's like I'm pulled a hundred different ways. So many things want me, but they don't want the best for me. But they attract me anyway. And my mind shoots off in a thousand different directions. I can get so confused, pulled and distracted I don't know who I am, why I'm here, or what I want to do. Part of me gets excited about You. But another part of me just wants to blow You off.

You deserve better than that, Lord. You deserve all of me, not just a part. Help me to pull away from all the worthless distractions pulling at me. Help me to give my focus and energy to what's important -You. Unite my divided heart to love and serve You with all I am, with all of my heart, all of my mind, soul, and strength.

Teach me Your way, Lord, and I will follow. I want my life to glorify You -- forever.

Psalm 87
A Psalm of the sons of Korah. A Song.

1   His foundation is in the holy mountains.
2   The LORD loves the gates of Zion
More than all the other dwelling places of Jacob.
3   Glorious things are spoken of you,
O city of God.   Selah.
4   "I shall mention Rahab and Babylon among those who know Me;
Behold, Philistia and Tyre with Ethiopia:
'This one was born there.'"
5   But of Zion it shall be said, "This one and that one were born in her";
And the Most High Himself will establish her.
6   The LORD will count when He registers the peoples,
"This one was born there."   Selah.
7   Then those who sing as well as those who play the flutes shall say,
"All my springs of joy are in you."

I'll always count with God.

from PSALM 87
especially verse 6
When it's Registration Day for heaven, God will be in charge of it. And it's a good thing. He won't miscount. He won't assign anyone to the wrong place -- thank God! There won't be any paperwork screw-ups or lost data -- though there will be a lot of forgiven data. People won't be hassled or treated differently because of their age, skin color, hair, money, appearance, or clothes.

Legalistic people and stuck-up cliques look down on me because of my clothes and hair, because I don't meet their dress code, because my music's different, because I'm different, because I'm not boring like them. If they were in charge like they act like they are, they'd probably leave me out of heaven. They sure don't think I'm headed there.

They are in for a surprise. God won't leave me out. When I come up, He'll say, "This one trusted in Me and was born again -- and is cool with me. Welcome to my kingdom."

I'll always count with God.

Psalm 88

A Song. A Psalm of the sons of Korah. For the choir director; according to
Mahalath Leannoth. A Maskil of Heman the Ezrahite.

1   O LORD, the God of my salvation,
 I have cried out by day and in the night before You.
2   Let my prayer come before You;
 Incline Your ear to my cry!
3   For my soul has had enough troubles,
 And my life has drawn near to Sheol.
4   I am reckoned among those who go down to the pit;
 I have become like a man without strength,
5   Forsaken among the dead,
 Like the slain who lie in the grave,
 Whom You remember no more,
 And they are cut off from Your hand.
6   You have put me in the lowest pit,
 In dark places, in the depths.
7   Your wrath has rested upon me,
 And You have afflicted me with all Your waves.   Selah.
8   You have removed my acquaintances far from me;
 You have made me an object of loathing to them;
 I am shut up and cannot go out.
9   My eye has wasted away because of affliction;
 I have called upon You every day, O LORD;
 I have spread out my hands to You.

10   Will You perform wonders for the dead?
 Will the departed spirits rise and praise You?   Selah.
11   Will Your lovingkindness be declared in the grave,
 Your faithfulness in Abaddon?
12   Will Your wonders be made known in the darkness?
 And Your righteousness in the land of forgetfulness?

13   But I, O LORD, have cried out to You for help,
 And in the morning my prayer comes before You.
14   O LORD, why do You reject my soul?
 Why do You hide Your face from me?
15   I was afflicted and about to die from my youth on;
 I suffer Your terrors; I am overcome.
16   Your burning anger has passed over me;
 Your terrors have destroyed me.
17   They have surrounded me like water all day long;
 They have encompassed me altogether.
18   You have removed lover and friend far from me;
 My acquaintances are in darkness.

Empty again
Sunken down so far   *So scared to fall*
Might not get up again   *So I lay at Your feet*
All my brokenness   I carry all of my burdens to You

Jars of Clay "Much Afraid"

from PSALM 88

NOTE: I think ol' Heman the Ezrahite was having a bad day. I'll talk more about Heman and bad days in the next psalm. But this psalm just being here shows God can take even our worst days and use them for good.

Oh Lord, how long before You respond to my prayers? I pray and pray, but there's no answer.

Haven't I suffered enough? I've had enough trouble for a whole lifetime already. I can't remember the last time I was really happy. I've been depressed for so long. I am weak from it. I can hardly get out of bed in the morning. Sometimes I don't.

Sometimes, all I can do when I get home is throw myself on my bed and cry and pray. I'm the same way at night. My eyes are red from crying. Don't You hear my prayers? Or are You just going to ignore my prayers and tears?

I'm afraid You'll never answer. But I keep praying. Who else can help me?

Can my friends help me? What friends? I hardly have any friends any more. When things got bad for me, when I really needed friends, they got lost. Even the one who I thought loved me found an excuse to dump me. That helped.

Are you rejecting me, too, God? You say You accept and will never reject anyone who sincerely comes to You, but can You blame me for asking? The way my life is going, I don't feel very accepted. I pray and pray to You, but what good does it do? If You haven't rejected me, You have a funny way of showing it. Why are You this way toward me?

I'm a teenager, yet I feel like I'm about to die. What good would that do? But I hardly want to live any more. I don't if my life is going to keep on being like this. I'm overcome with fear of what my life is becoming. I'm so down in it, I don't know what up is anymore. Life has become a living death for me. Even the brightest day is darkness to me.

And nobody cares.

Do You care?

Psalm 89
A Maskil of Ethan the Ezrahite.

1   I will sing of the lovingkindness of the LORD forever;
    To all generations I will make known Your faithfulness with my mouth.
2   For I have said, "Lovingkindness will be built up forever;
    In the heavens You will establish Your faithfulness."
3   "I have made a covenant with My chosen;
    I have sworn to David My servant,
4   I will establish your seed forever
    And build up your throne to all generations."   Selah.

5   The heavens will praise Your wonders, O LORD;
    Your faithfulness also in the assembly of the holy ones.
6   For who in the skies is comparable to the LORD?
    Who among the sons of the mighty is like the LORD,
7   A God greatly feared in the council of the holy ones,
    And awesome above all those who are around Him?
8   O LORD God of hosts, who is like You, O mighty LORD?
    Your faithfulness also surrounds You.
9   You rule the swelling of the sea;
    When its waves rise, You still them.
10   You Yourself crushed Rahab like one who is slain;
    You scattered Your enemies with Your mighty arm.

11   The heavens are Yours, the earth also is Yours;
    The world and all it contains, You have founded them.
12   The north and the south, You have created them;
    Tabor and Hermon shout for joy at Your name.
13   You have a strong arm;
    Your hand is mighty, Your right hand is exalted.
14   Righteousness and justice are the foundation of Your throne;
    Lovingkindness and truth go before You.
15   How blessed are the people who know the joyful sound!
    O LORD, they walk in the light of Your countenance.
16   In Your name they rejoice all the day,
    And by Your righteousness they are exalted.
17   For You are the glory of their strength,
    And by Your favor our horn is exalted.
18   For our shield belongs to the LORD,
    And our king to the Holy One of Israel.

19   Once You spoke in vision to Your godly ones,
    And said, "I have given help to one who is mighty;
    I have exalted one chosen from the people.
20   "I have found David My servant;
    With My holy oil I have anointed him,
21   With whom My hand will be established;

My arm also will strengthen him.
22   "The enemy will not deceive him,
   Nor the son of wickedness afflict him.
23   "But I shall crush his adversaries before him,
   And strike those who hate him.
24   "My faithfulness and My lovingkindness will be with him,
   And in My name his horn will be exalted.
25   "I shall also set his hand on the sea
   And his right hand on the rivers.
26   "He will cry to Me, 'You are my Father,
   My God, and the rock of my salvation.'
27   "I also shall make him My firstborn,
   The highest of the kings of the earth.
28   "My lovingkindness I will keep for him forever,
   And My covenant shall be confirmed to him.
29   "So I will establish his descendants forever
   And his throne as the days of heaven.

30   "If his sons forsake My law
   And do not walk in My judgments,
31   If they violate My statutes
   And do not keep My commandments,
32   Then I will punish their transgression with the rod
   And their iniquity with stripes.
33   "But I will not break off My lovingkindness from him,
   Nor deal falsely in My faithfulness.
34   "My covenant I will not violate,
   Nor will I alter the utterance of My lips.
35   "Once I have sworn by My holiness;
   I will not lie to David.
36   "His descendants shall endure forever
   And his throne as the sun before Me.
37   "It shall be established forever like the moon,
   And the witness in the sky is faithful."   Selah.

38   But You have cast off and rejected,
   You have been full of wrath against Your anointed.
39   You have spurned the covenant of Your servant;
   You have profaned his crown in the dust.
40   You have broken down all his walls;
   You have brought his strongholds to ruin.
41   All who pass along the way plunder him;
   He has become a reproach to his neighbors.
42   You have exalted the right hand of his adversaries;
   You have made all his enemies rejoice.
43   You also turn back the edge of his sword
   And have not made him stand in battle.
44   You have made his splendor to cease

And cast his throne to the ground.
45   You have shortened the days of his youth;
You have covered him with shame.   Selah.

46   How long, O LORD?
Will You hide Yourself forever?
Will Your wrath burn like fire?
47   Remember what my span of life is;
For what vanity You have created all the sons of men!
48   What man can live and not see death?
Can he deliver his soul from the power of Sheol?   Selah.

49   Where are Your former lovingkindnesses, O Lord,
Which You swore to David in Your faithfulness?
50   Remember, O Lord, the reproach of Your servants;
How I bear in my bosom the reproach of all the many peoples,
51   With which Your enemies have reproached, O LORD,
With which they have reproached the footsteps of Your anointed.
52   Blessed be the LORD forever!
Amen and Amen.

from PSALM 89

This psalm seems a little long, but it's definitely worth digging into.

Something interesting here -- if you read only the first thirty-seven verses, you'd think Ethan the Ezrahite was having a good day, unlike Heman the Ezrahite of Psalm 88. Ethan is singing and psyched about who God is and how good He is.

Then you get to the rest of the psalm, and you see Ethan is not having such a good day. Life's been real tough instead, for both him and the people of Israel. He senses even his youth slipping away. That makes me appreciate the first part of the psalm even more. His circumstances aren't the best, but he doesn't let that give him a negative attitude toward God. Have you noticed that a lot of the psalms are that way? The writers are going though rough times and may be frustrated, even frustrated with God. But they still see God as great. Even Heman's Psalm 88, probably the most depressing psalm in the Bible, starts by acknowledging God as "Lord, the God of my salvation."

Keeping a positive view of God when your life seems negative can be tough to do. Bad circumstances can be like a dirty car windshield that makes the whole world and even God look sorry , especially if we focus on the gunk and smashed bugs of our windshield of circumstances right in front of us, instead of looking beyond and focusing on Him. Remembering who God is and trusting Him can make those difficult times easier. It helps us look beyond the immediate gunk of our circumstances. Then, like in verse 16, we can be glad inside about who God is and how He treats us right, even when life isn't right. But if we focus only on our own difficulties instead of on God, we'll just get more and more down.

Two qualities of God Ethan focuses on in the midst of his difficulties are God's faithfulness and lovingkindness. Because of His faithfulness, we can trust Him to keep His promises to us even when circumstances make it look like He's not. Lovingkindness is a great quality to remember, too. You might remember from Psalm 48 that the Hebrew word for lovingkindness roughly means faithful, loyal love. God is faithful and loving toward us even when we are not, when all we deserve is a good whipping. (verses 30-34). And God's love for us is there when life has us whipped. I don't know about you, but it still blows me away that God is loving, faithful, and even loyal toward us.

Incidentally, one advantage of getting older is you can look back on times when God showed you how great He is by doing great things in your life. That includes times when God took your bad, maybe tragic, circumstances and brought you through them and even used them for good. Remembering times like that can help keep your hope in God up when things get rough.

One other thing -- you might be saying, "That's cool and all, but what's all this about David. What does he have to do with anything?"

One of the most important ways God is faithful is His faithfulness to carry out the Davidic Covenant, or His promise to David. It's in 2 Samuel 7 : 12 - 16. There God promises King David that one of His descendants would rule forever. God has kept that promise, even though most of the kings descending from David seriously dissed God. God was faithful even though the kings and people coming after David usually were not. And it's a good thing. Because the descendant of David who will rule forever is -- Jesus.

M. M.

Psalm 90

A Prayer of Moses, the man of God.

1   Lord, You have been our dwelling place in all generations.
2   Before the mountains were born
    Or You gave birth to the earth and the world,
    Even from everlasting to everlasting, You are God.

3   You turn man back into dust
    And say, "Return, O children of men."
4   For a thousand years in Your sight
    Are like yesterday when it passes by,
    Or as a watch in the night.
5   You have swept them away like a flood, they fall asleep;
    In the morning they are like grass which sprouts anew.
6   In the morning it flourishes and sprouts anew;
    Toward evening it fades and withers away.

7   For we have been consumed by Your anger
    And by Your wrath we have been dismayed.
8   You have placed our iniquities before You,
    Our secret sins in the light of Your presence.
9   For all our days have declined in Your fury;
    We have finished our years like a sigh.
10   As for the days of our life, they contain seventy years,
    Or if due to strength, eighty years,
    Yet their pride is but labor and sorrow;
    For soon it is gone and we fly away.
11   Who understands the power of Your anger
    And Your fury, according to the fear that is due You?
12   So teach us to number our days,
    That we may present to You a heart of wisdom.

13   Do return, O LORD; how long will it be?
    And be sorry for Your servants.
14   O satisfy us in the morning with Your lovingkindness,
    That we may sing for joy and be glad all our days.
15   Make us glad according to the days You have afflicted us,
    And the years we have seen evil.
16   Let Your work appear to Your servants
    And Your majesty to their children.
17   Let the favor of the Lord our God be upon us;
    And confirm for us the work of our hands;
    Yes, confirm the work of our hands.

*I don't want to let my life fly by
Did you ever stop to wonder why?*
MxPx "Tomorrow's Another Day"
from *Slowly Going the Way of the Buffalo*

from PSALM 90

Time sure goes faster than it used to.

When I was little, I thought it would take forever to get older --
and it did. When I finally turned 13, I felt like I'd be a teenager
forever. Now I'm already years older, and I see I'm not going to
be a teenager anywhere close to forever. I'm not even going to
live forever.

When I would hear, "Life is short," I'd think, "Yeah, right." But
life is short -- and it seems to be getting shorter.

In Your eyes, a life must really be short, like just a day. Because You are forever.

When I think about it a while, it makes me feel small. And I ask
hard questions. Will my life count for something? Will it really be
worth living? Or will it end up just work and tears? Will it end a
sigh soon forgotten?

Lord, I don't want to just use up space, water, and air, and get
old, die, turn to dust and take up space at Restland. I want my
life to be more than that.

Help me to make the most of this life. Instead of me wasting
the time You give me like I used to -- when I thought my time
would never run out -- help me to make the most of each day.
Teach me to remember I don't have an unlimited supply of days -
- when a day is past, it's gone and won't come back. That way,
I'll remember to take each day You give me and live it smart and,
at the end of it, present to You a day used wisely.

I want this life to count for something, not just be a boring walk
to death. I want to have an impact, Lord. But I won't -- I can't --
if You don't help me, if Your love and goodness isn't upon me. I
need You, Lord. I need You working in my life. Without You, my
life won't be worth even the short time I have.

Lord, I pray You'd smile upon my life. And, yeah, make me
smile again. I want to see You working in my life. I want to see
You.

Cause my life to count, to make a difference. Yes, cause my
life to make a difference that lasts.

Psalm 91

1   He who dwells in the shelter of the Most High
Will abide in the shadow of the Almighty.
2   I will say to the LORD, "My refuge and my fortress,
My God, in whom I trust!"
3   For it is He who delivers you from the snare of the trapper
And from the deadly pestilence.
4   He will cover you with His pinions,
And under His wings you may seek refuge;
His faithfulness is a shield and bulwark.

5   You will not be afraid of the terror by night,
Or of the arrow that flies by day;
6   Of the pestilence that stalks in darkness,
Or of the destruction that lays waste at noon.
7   A thousand may fall at your side
And ten thousand at your right hand,
But it shall not approach you.
8   You will only look on with your eyes
And see the recompense of the wicked.
9   For you have made the LORD, my refuge,
Even the Most High, your dwelling place.
10   No evil will befall you,
Nor will any plague come near your tent.

11   For He will give His angels charge concerning you,
To guard you in all your ways.
12   They will bear you up in their hands,
That you do not strike your foot against a stone.
13   You will tread upon the lion and cobra,
The young lion and the serpent you will trample down.
14   "Because he has loved Me, therefore I will deliver him;
I will set him securely on high, because he has known My name.
15   "He will call upon Me, and I will answer him;
I will be with him in trouble;
I will rescue him and honor him.
16   "With a long life I will satisfy him
And let him see My salvation."

from PSALM 91

God is my shelter. In the shadow of the Almighty is my peace. He's always there for me. I can always run to Him.

The world out there is more than I can handle sometimes. Life can overwhelm me. But under His wings, I won't fear anything. He shelters me. He protects me. He's the One I trust. I'll stay close to Him.

For His love and faithfulness are stronger than anything the world can throw at me. His love and faithfulness toward me are all I need. God's love is enough for me.

Yet He also sends angels to look out for me. With all the slips and accidents I've had, and with all the close calls I've had, they must be pretty busy. When I look back on it, it's only because of God and His angels looking out for me that I haven't broken every bone in my body -- and it's only because of Him tough times haven't broken my spirit.

But, unlike my parents, I'm not going to worry. Because if any trouble comes, it has to get through Jesus first. And if He does let it through, I know He'll do it for good reason from His love. And I know I won't have to face it alone. When I call for help, He'll be there for me. He'll stay with me no matter how bad things get. And He'll bring me through it and out of it into His peace.

He gives me security no one else can give me. He is my security. By His side is peace and protection. Underneath His arms is love.

He'll put His arm around me and lead me through life. And it will be a full life He shows me. For His presence makes it full.

Then He'll carry me into the perfect peace and awesome joy that only He can give. I'll get to experience heaven -- I'll get to see Him.

Psalm 92
A Psalm, a Song for the Sabbath day.

1 It is good to give thanks to the LORD
And to sing praises to Your name, O Most High;
2 To declare Your lovingkindness in the morning
And Your faithfulness by night,
3 With the ten-stringed lute and with the harp,
With resounding music upon the lyre.
4 For You, O LORD, have made me glad by what You have done,
I will sing for joy at the works of Your hands.
5 How great are Your works, O LORD!
Your thoughts are very deep.
6 A senseless man has no knowledge,
Nor does a stupid man understand this:
7 That when the wicked sprouted up like grass
And all who did iniquity flourished,
It was only that they might be destroyed forevermore.
8 But You, O LORD, are on high forever.

9   For, behold, Your enemies, O LORD,
     For, behold, Your enemies will perish;
     All who do iniquity will be scattered.

10   But You have exalted my horn like that of the wild ox;
     I have been anointed with fresh oil.
11   And my eye has looked exultantly upon my foes,
     My ears hear of the evildoers who rise up against me.
12   The righteous man will flourish like the palm tree,
     He will grow like a cedar in Lebanon.
13   Planted in the house of the LORD,
     They will flourish in the courts of our God.
14   They will still yield fruit in old age;
     They shall be full of sap and very green,
15   To declare that the LORD is upright;
     He is my rock, and there is no unrighteousness in Him.

from PSALM 92

Lord, it is so good You are who You are. You are the highest forever! It's awesome to be under Your rule and to belong to You. For You have raised me up high, too. You have made me big happy by what You have done and by just being who You are. You make me want to jam on my guitar, crank up my music, and bounce off the walls.

I want to get up in the morning (And that by itself is a miraculous work of God.) and say "Good morning!" to You and tell You how much I love You and how much I appreciate Your love. When I go to bed at night, I want to thank You for Your loving faithfulness in leading me through another day.

How great are Your works, Lord! I don't know what's greater -- Your big works like creating the universe or the zillions of smaller things You do every day, like hearing and answering millions of prayers, or like watching out for me and making my life good and growing. How infinite Your love, power, and mind must be. It makes my brain hurt to think about all the things You do and all Your deep thoughts and purposes behind them.

It makes me want to thank You and tell people about You, today and tomorrow, and next year, and when I'm old. You rock, and there's nothing about You that isn't the best!

Psalm 93

1   The LORD reigns, He is clothed with majesty;
The LORD has clothed and girded Himself with strength;
Indeed, the world is firmly established, it will not be moved.
2   Your throne is established from of old;
You are from everlasting.

3   The floods have lifted up, O LORD,
The floods have lifted up their voice,
The floods lift up their pounding waves.
4   More than the sounds of many waters,
Than the mighty breakers of the sea,
The LORD on high is mighty.
5   Your testimonies are fully confirmed;
Holiness befits Your house,
O LORD, forevermore.

Come to me, and I will walk along Your shore
Feel Your crashing waves sing in time
with the music of my heart.

Jars of Clay "River Constantine"
from If I Left the Zoo

from PSALM 93

The Lord reigns. He must be awesome to see sitting on His throne. His majesty is great. So much of this world He created is majestic. How much more majestic He, the Creator, must be. It would blow me away to just see Him. I can hardly take it in

how exalted and awesome He must be in His shining glory.

I can barely comprehend that He and His rule go back infinitely in time. Before there was a universe, He was there.

Once I stood on an ocean cliff when a storm was coming in. I watched the waves. They were massive. Nearing the edge of the raging ocean, they swelled up and rose higher and higher until they seemed almost as high as the cliffs. Then they would slowly turn over and turn white and smash the rocks and face of the land. The waves pounding the cliffs seemed to make the whole world shake. And the cool, clean spray would fill the air.

I don't know how long I stood there watching and listening in awe.

It will be like that and more to see the God who created the oceans and the waves and the storms. His might and His majesty are great. His presence is pure and refreshing. And like an endless ocean, He is so much more than anyone can comprehend, can take in. I could spend an eternity gazing upon Him and experiencing Him, and I still wouldn't be able to take it in -- not even a small part of who He is.

God is holy and infinite -- forever.

Psalm 94

1   O LORD, God of vengeance,
    God of vengeance, shine forth!
2   Rise up, O Judge of the earth,
    Render recompense to the proud.
3   How long shall the wicked, O LORD,
    How long shall the wicked exult?
4   They pour forth words, they speak arrogantly;
    All who do wickedness vaunt themselves.
5   They crush Your people, O LORD,
    And afflict Your heritage.
6   They slay the widow and the stranger
    And murder the orphans.
7   They have said, "The LORD does not see,
    Nor does the God of Jacob pay heed."

8   Pay heed, you senseless among the people;
    And when will you understand, stupid ones?
9   He who planted the ear, does He not hear?
    He who formed the eye, does He not see?
10   He who chastens the nations, will He not rebuke,
    Even He who teaches man knowledge?
11   The LORD knows the thoughts of man,
    That they are a mere breath.

12   Blessed is the man whom You chasten, O LORD,
    And whom You teach out of Your law;
13   That You may grant him relief from the days of adversity,
    Until a pit is dug for the wicked.

14   For the LORD will not abandon His people,
      Nor will He forsake His inheritance.
15   For judgment will again be righteous,
      And all the upright in heart will follow it.
16   Who will stand up for me against evildoers?
      Who will take his stand for me against those who do wickedness?

17   If the LORD had not been my help,
      My soul would soon have dwelt in the abode of silence.
18   If I should say, "My foot has slipped,"
      Your lovingkindness, O LORD, will hold me up.
19   When my anxious thoughts multiply within me,
      Your consolations delight my soul.
20   Can a throne of destruction be allied with You,
      One which devises mischief by decree?
21   They band themselves together against the life of the righteous
      And condemn the innocent to death.
22   But the LORD has been my stronghold,
      And my God the rock of my refuge.
23   He has brought back their wickedness upon them
      And will destroy them in their evil;
      The LORD our God will destroy them.

from PSALM 94

(NOTE: Another good passage on revenge is Romans 12: 17 - 21.)

Lord, I'm glad You're the God of love and forgiveness. But there are times when I'm even more glad You're the God of vengeance, and now is one of those times.

There's these evil scum who strut around the school, so proud of themselves and their sleaziness. They are always getting their jollies making life miserable for someone. And now they're making life miserable for me.

I want to get back at them bad. I know if I tried to, it would probably make things worse. But I think it would be worth it, I want pay-back against them so bad. Then I remember You're the One in charge of vengeance, and You want me to leave it to You. Besides, You're better at pay-back than me or anyone. You'll be sure to get it done right.

I just wish You'd be faster about it. They're not letting up with their evil. They're making life tough for me and my friends. They get worse and worse because they think You don't see or don't care, that You'll let them get away with it. Show them different.

Lord, I have to admit I'm scared sometimes. My head gets full of anxious thoughts. Sometimes, just the thought of going to school in the morning where those goons are waiting for me -- it makes me so anxious I feel sick in my stomach.

Then I remember You will never abandon me. You show me from Your word that You'll always look out for me and be there for me. You'll be there to take hold of me and pull me up when I'm going down. I remember when You've helped me in the past. Oh man, where would I be without Your help?

Your presence and promises calm me. I have peace because You are my peace and my strength. You'll protect me. And You'll make things right again.

Who will stand up for me? Who will take his stand for me against those who do me wrong?

God will.

Psalm 95

1   O come, let us sing for joy to the LORD,
  Let us shout joyfully to the rock of our salvation.
2   Let us come before His presence with thanksgiving,
  Let us shout joyfully to Him with psalms.
3   For the LORD is a great God
  And a great King above all gods,
4   In whose hand are the depths of the earth,
  The peaks of the mountains are His also.
5   The sea is His, for it was He who made it,
  And His hands formed the dry land.

6   Come, let us worship and bow down,
  Let us kneel before the LORD our Maker.
7   For He is our God,
  And we are the people of His pasture and the sheep of His hand.
  Today, if you would hear His voice,
8   Do not harden your hearts, as at Meribah,
  As in the day of Massah in the wilderness,
9   "When your fathers tested Me,
  They tried Me, though they had seen My work.
10   "For forty years I loathed that generation,
  And said they are a people who err in their heart,
  And they do not know My ways.
11   "Therefore I swore in My anger,
  Truly they shall not enter into My rest."

Lord, the feelings are not the same.

I guess I'm older...I guess I've changed.
Keith Green "Grace By Which I Stand"
from *So You Wanna Go Back to Egypt*

from PSALM 95

God is so great. He rules like nobody else. Sometimes I get so hyped about Him, I feel like shouting, "Yea, Lord!"

He deserves all my worship, all my thanks, all I am. The peaks of the mountains and the depths of the ocean were created by Him and belong to Him. I'm created by Him and belong to Him, too.

Yet there are times, too many times, when I get bored about Him or even have doubts about Him. I doubt whether He's really there for me and cares about me, even though He's shown me again and again that He does. I doubt whether He listens to me and will answer my prayers, even though He has in the past. He's in the business of hearing and answering prayer. And the competition is all sorry. Yet even when He does good things for me, a lot of times I'm not very excited about Him.

There are times I even doubt His love for me, though He proved His love once and for all on the cross. Yet, though He died for me, I get cold-hearted toward Him.

I want to stop doubting God. He deserves trust, not doubt. And I want to stop being ho-hum and hard-hearted toward Him. I don't want to be like the Hebrews who were constantly doubting and dissing God even though they had seen Him do great things. God gave them chance after chance to trust Him and open their hearts and minds to Him. But they ended up missing out on the good God had prepared for them, because they closed and hardened their hearts and kept grumbling and doubt-ing instead. They died in the wilderness and only their children got the land.

Lord, I don't want to miss out on Your best for me. I don't want to miss out on experiencing You. Help me with my doubts. Help me to trust You, and not begrudgingly, but with joy. Help me to stay excited about You and to love You with a whole heart the way You want me to -- the way I want to. Because that's the kind of trust You deserve. That's the kind of love You deserve.

If I give You any less, I'm just cheating myself.

Psalm 96

1   Sing to the LORD a new song;
    Sing to the LORD, all the earth.
2   Sing to the LORD, bless His name;
    Proclaim good tidings of His salvation from day to day.
3   Tell of His glory among the nations,
    His wonderful deeds among all the peoples.
4   For great is the LORD and greatly to be praised;
    He is to be feared above all gods.
5   For all the gods of the peoples are idols,
    But the LORD made the heavens.
6   Splendor and majesty are before Him,
    Strength and beauty are in His sanctuary.

7   Ascribe to the LORD, O families of the peoples,
    Ascribe to the LORD glory and strength.
8   Ascribe to the LORD the glory of His name;
    Bring an offering and come into His courts.
9   Worship the LORD in holy attire;
    Tremble before Him, all the earth.
10 Say among the nations, "The LORD reigns;
    Indeed, the world is firmly established, it will not be moved;
    He will judge the peoples with equity."

11 Let the heavens be glad, and let the earth rejoice;
    Let the sea roar, and all it contains;
12 Let the field exult, and all that is in it.
    Then all the trees of the forest will sing for joy
13 Before the LORD, for He is coming,
    For He is coming to judge the earth.
    He will judge the world in righteousness
    And the peoples in His faithfulness.

Why am I so afraid to tell people about Him?

from PSALM 96

God is the best. He is strong, beautiful, and majestic like nothing else. He reigns with all power, righteous justice, perfect wisdom, and incredible love toward all people -- toward me!

So why am I so afraid to tell people about Him, about Jesus and what He's done for us? I've tried all sorts of crazy things and had all sorts of accidents, and God's protected me. Yet I'm scared something awful is going to happen if I share about Him? In my youth group I get all hyped, and I decide I'm going to go and tell my friends about Jesus. But when the time comes at school or wherever, I wimp out.

I guess I'm afraid about what people will think of me, that they'll think I'm some religious nut or something. But what's more important -- what people think about me or their relationship with God? If I really care about my friends, I'll care more about where they're going than about what they think about me.

I need to make telling people about Jesus an every day part of my life. After all, God is good to me every day. I don't have to be obnoxious or beat them up with a Bible. With God's help -- and I will need His help -- I can talk like I would when talking about something that's important or awesome. I tell people about what CDs or movies are good. But I don't tell them about how good Jesus is? I need to get a grip and stop wimping out on Jesus and on my friends.

Maybe I will feel a little funny talking about Jesus. That will be nothing compared to the joy of seeing someone come to Him and of knowing I was faithful to Jesus and to my friends.

And when Jesus comes to judge the earth and rule, it will be so cool to take friends into His kingdom with me. Then we'll get to hang and enjoy God forever!

Jesus is awesome, and He's given me life! It's time to stop keeping it to myself. It's time to stop keeping Jesus to myself.

Psalm 97

1   The LORD reigns, let the earth rejoice;
Let the many islands be glad.
2   Clouds and thick darkness surround Him;
Righteousness and justice are the foundation of His throne.
3   Fire goes before Him
And burns up His adversaries round about.
4   His lightnings lit up the world;
The earth saw and trembled.
5   The mountains melted like wax at the presence of the LORD,
At the presence of the Lord of the whole earth.
6   The heavens declare His righteousness,
And all the peoples have seen His glory.

7   Let all those be ashamed who serve graven images,
Who boast themselves of idols;
Worship Him, all you gods.

8   Zion heard this and was glad,
And the daughters of Judah have rejoiced

Because of Your judgments, O LORD.
9   For You are the LORD Most High over all the earth;
You are exalted far above all gods.

10   Hate evil, you who love the LORD,
Who preserves the souls of His godly ones;
He delivers them from the hand of the wicked.
11   Light is sown like seed for the righteous
And gladness for the upright in heart.
12   Be glad in the LORD, you righteous ones,
And give thanks to His holy name.

Only He deserves first place in my life.

from PSALM 97

The Lord rules! The earth had best rejoice. Because nobody tops God. It doesn't pay to mess with Him.

Just His presence is enough to make a mountain melt. Why do Satan and the rest of God's enemies even think they stand a chance? Whenever God wants, His fire will go out and crispy-fry those idiots.

God's presence is so pure, powerful, and bright, it would probably melt any of us in our present state. Look how powerful one bolt of lightning He creates can be. Being directly with God would probably be like being on the surface of the sun. We couldn't handle it. I don't think even the holiest man on earth could handle God's presence without an infinitely strong Sonscreen. So He surrounds Himself with a thick, cloudy darkness so His brightness doesn't overwhelm us. And if we trust Him, He'll transform us so one day we can be with Him and enjoy Him and not become toast.

What we can see of Him is still mind-blowing. Think about all the trillions of stars and planets and everything else in the sky He's created. The universe says there is a God, and He is awesome!

God could rule just by His power if He wanted. Like anyone could stop Him. A lot of evil human rulers rule by raw power. But not God. Righteousness and justice are the foundation of His throne. He rules to make everything right and just in the end. He doesn't have to grasp for power like a politician. He already has it. And His love and holiness is as strong as His power.

God is so awesome, I'll never be able to get a grip on it. He makes my life bright. I'm so glad He's my God. Yet I blow Him off sometimes. I don't understand why.

How stupid it is to put anything in God's place, either by worshipping some idol or Satan, or by just making something more important to you than God. Everyone who does that should feel dumb and ashamed -- including me. I know I feel funny when I catch myself making a sport or hobby or whatever so important to me that it crowds out time for God.

The Lord is Most High way over everything. Only He deserves to be worshipped. And only He deserves first place in my life. I am psyched about Him, and I will worship Him and thank Him for all He is -- and not just with words -- with my life.

Psalm 98
A Psalm.

1   O sing to the LORD a new song,
  For He has done wonderful things,
  His right hand and His holy arm have gained the victory for Him.
2   The LORD has made known His salvation;
  He has revealed His righteousness in the sight of the nations.
3   He has remembered His lovingkindness and His faithfulness to the
  house of Israel;
  All the ends of the earth have seen the salvation of our God.

4   Shout joyfully to the LORD, all the earth;
  Break forth and sing for joy and sing praises.
5   Sing praises to the LORD with the lyre,
  With the lyre and the sound of melody.
6   With trumpets and the sound of the horn
  Shout joyfully before the King, the LORD.

7   Let the sea roar and all it contains,
  The world and those who dwell in it.
8   Let the rivers clap their hands,
  Let the mountains sing together for joy
9   Before the LORD, for He is coming to judge the earth;
  He will judge the world with righteousness
  And the peoples with equity.

from PSALM 98

God has done such great things. And He hasn't just done them off somewhere in heaven where nobody can see them. He's done them in history -- and even in my life.

He's given the Way for people to come to Him and be with Him forever, and He's made Him well known. He came down to earth and lived a life of perfect righteousness before hundreds of thousands of people. He fulfilled Old Testament prophesies about Himself, showing God is faithful and that He keeps His promises. Finally, during the Passover when people from all nations converged on Jerusalem, He died on the cross in front of them all. Then He rose again. And before going back to heaven, He visited hundreds. In His dying and rising again, He showed the salvation of God for all to see.

Then He showed the salvation of God to me.

When I think about it, it makes me quiet, kind of pondering and peaceful.

Then there are other times when what God has done hypes me so much I feel like shouting, singing, jamming and bouncing off everything. Jesus makes me want to mosh.

One day, Jesus is going to make the whole world mosh and jam. Because He is coming back to rule. And He will do it right! It will be even more impossible to miss this time.

Psalm 99

1   The LORD reigns, let the peoples tremble;
He is enthroned above the cherubim, let the earth shake!
2   The LORD is great in Zion,
And He is exalted above all the peoples.
3   Let them praise Your great and awesome name;
Holy is He.
4   The strength of the King loves justice;
You have established equity;
You have executed justice and righteousness in Jacob.
5   Exalt the LORD our God
And worship at His footstool;
Holy is He.

6   Moses and Aaron were among His priests,
And Samuel was among those who called on His name;
They called upon the LORD and He answered them.
7   He spoke to them in the pillar of cloud;
They kept His testimonies
And the statute that He gave them.
8   O LORD our God, You answered them;
You were a forgiving God to them,
And yet an avenger of their evil deeds.
9   Exalt the LORD our God
And worship at His holy hill,
For holy is the LORD our God.

He really listens to me.

from PSALM 99

God rules. Everybody else, bow down! He sits on His throne of justice and power. And He will make the world shake!

God is great! Nobody else comes close. He is high above what anyone can even imagine. His name and everything that's behind it is great and awesome. His name is holy.

And He is strong, just, and righteous. He will rule and bring about perfect justice on the earth -- no matter who tries to stop Him.

So I'm going to worship God. I suggest You do likewise. He deserves our worship. For He is great and holy.

He is so high above us, it makes you wonder why He has anything to do with us down here. Yet He's always involved in people's lives. He's spoken to us again and again and has given us His word. He helps us out again and again. He is holy and hates our wrong. Yet He's a loving and forgiving God toward us. He even came down here and lived with us and died to forgive us.

And He listens to us. All through history, people have prayed to Him, and He answered them. I've prayed to Him, and He answered me. He even wants us to pray and talk to Him. He really listens to us.   ▼

He really listens to me.

God is so high, exalted and holy, so high above us. Yet He forgives us and listens to us -- He loves us.

This is the One I can worship and love my whole life.

Psalm 100
A Psalm for Thanksgiving.

1   Shout joyfully to the LORD, all the earth.
2   Serve the LORD with gladness;
Come before Him with joyful singing.
3   Know that the LORD Himself is God;
It is He who has made us, and not we ourselves;
We are His people and the sheep of His pasture.
4   Enter His gates with thanksgiving
And His courts with praise.
Give thanks to Him, bless His name.
5   For the LORD is good;
His lovingkindness is everlasting
And His faithfulness to all generations.

from **PSALM 100**

I used to think going to church was seriously boring. I've slept through a lot of long sermons.

Then I thought about how good God is to me, and not just one day a week, but all the time. He loves me forever. He even gave His Son for me so I can be with Him forever. And in my life every day, He is faithful to me, always providing for me, guiding me, and watching out for me. What did I ever do to deserve that?

He's made me, and I belong to Him. And He is good. Surely, I should be glad to worship Him.

Then I actually wanted to go to church and thank Him for being awesome to me, and for being who He is.

And before I knew it, I wanted to thank Him every day.

I still have trouble staying awake when the pastor talks too long, though. I wish he could be shorter like this psalm.

Psalm 101
A Psalm of David.

1   I will sing of lovingkindness and justice,
To You, O LORD, I will sing praises.
2   I will give heed to the blameless way.
When will You come to me?
I will walk within my house in the integrity of my heart.
3   I will set no worthless thing before my eyes;
I hate the work of those who fall away;
It shall not fasten its grip on me.
4   A perverse heart shall depart from me;
I will know no evil.
5   Whoever secretly slanders his neighbor, him I will destroy;
No one who has a haughty look and an arrogant heart will I endure.
6   My eyes shall be upon the faithful of the land, that they may dwell with me;
He who walks in a blameless way is the one who will minister to me.
7   He who practices deceit shall not dwell within my house;
He who speaks falsehood shall not maintain his position before me.
8   Every morning I will destroy all the wicked of the land,
So as to cut off from the city of the LORD all those who do iniquity.

I will stop playing games with God

from PSALM 101

(NOTE: Before verses 5 and 8 make you decide to get up tomorrow morning and "destroy all the wicked of the land," remember David was king. It was his duty as king to be sure justice was carried out. Unless you're a king somewhere, destroying the wicked is not your duty. Sorry.)

I will stop playing games with God. I'm going to get real and start walking the walk. I will walk in God's ways. So help me God (I'm going to need it).

I will stop being two-faced, acting one way at church, another way at home, and still another way with my friends -- that's three faces. Anyway, I will stop being a hypocrite.

I will stop watching things I shouldn't be watching and letting garbage attach to my mind. I'm better than that. I won't let any evil or addiction get a grip on me.

I will stop letting others drag me down. I'm going to love those around me, but not the wrong things they do. I'm not going to let myself be dragged into doing them myself. If that means I have to stop hanging with certain people, then I stop hanging with them.

I will dig into the Bible. Being a Christian who doesn't listen to God's word is like being an MxPx fan who doesn't listen to their music -- except it's even more stupid. So I will stop slacking on getting into the word. I'm studying it everyday -- and I'm doing it everyday.

I will talk the talk. I'm not going to be afraid anymore to talk Jesus. And I will watch what I say. And if one of my friends is saying smack, like spreading bad rumors about someone, instead of joining in, I'll end that conversation.

I will hang with friends who will help me live right, friends I can trust who will be there for me. Friends who will set a good example for me and pull me in the right direction. Friends who aren't afraid to get on me if I'm doing wrong and who will encourage me to do right.

I will stop playing games with God today. I will walk the walk. I will talk the talk. I know I'm going to need all the help from God and friends that I can get. But I'm going to do it -- every day.

Psalm 102

A Prayer of the Afflicted when he is faint and
pours out his complaint before the LORD.

1   Hear my prayer, O LORD!
And let my cry for help come to You.
2   Do not hide Your face from me in the day of my distress;
Incline Your ear to me;
In the day when I call answer me quickly.
3   For my days have been consumed in smoke,
And my bones have been scorched like a hearth.
4   My heart has been smitten like grass and has withered away,
Indeed, I forget to eat my bread.
5   Because of the loudness of my groaning
My bones cling to my flesh.
6   I resemble a pelican of the wilderness;
I have become like an owl of the waste places.
7   I lie awake,
I have become like a lonely bird on a housetop.

8   My enemies have reproached me all day long;
Those who deride me have used my name as a curse.
9   For I have eaten ashes like bread
And mingled my drink with weeping
10   Because of Your indignation and Your wrath,
For You have lifted me up and cast me away.
11   My days are like a lengthened shadow,
And I wither away like grass.

12   But You, O LORD, abide forever,
And Your name to all generations.
13   You will arise and have compassion on Zion;
For it is time to be gracious to her,
For the appointed time has come.
14   Surely Your servants find pleasure in her stones
And feel pity for her dust.
15   So the nations will fear the name of the LORD
And all the kings of the earth Your glory.
16   For the LORD has built up Zion;
He has appeared in His glory.
17   He has regarded the prayer of the destitute
And has not despised their prayer.

18   This will be written for the generation to come,
That a people yet to be created may praise the LORD.
19   For He looked down from His holy height;
From heaven the LORD gazed upon the earth,
20   To hear the groaning of the prisoner,

To set free those who were doomed to death,
21   That men may tell of the name of the LORD in Zion
And His praise in Jerusalem,
22   When the peoples are gathered together,
And the kingdoms, to serve the LORD.

23   He has weakened my strength in the way;
He has shortened my days.
24   I say, "O my God, do not take me away in the midst of my days,
Your years are throughout all generations.
25   "Of old You founded the earth,
And the heavens are the work of Your hands.
26   "Even they will perish, but You endure;
And all of them will wear out like a garment;
Like clothing You will change them and they will be changed.
27   "But You are the same,
And Your years will not come to an end.
28   "The children of Your servants will continue,
And their descendants will be established before You."

from PSALM 102

I know what you're thinking -- "Oh boy, another one of those psalms from some guy who was having a really bad day." And you're right -- this is a psalm from some guy who was having a really bad day. And we don't even know who it is.

But we all have bad days. And like the other Bad Day psalms (That's a special theological category there.), this one shows us some things to help us handle those bad days.

In case we haven't mentioned it, this guy is having a really bad day. Read the first eleven verses if you don't believe me. But notice, although he is very down about his situation, he doesn't give up on God. Right at the start, he prays. And he prays very honestly. He doesn't plaster on a holy smile or play games to try to manipulate God. He trusts God to understand and respond with compassion.

That goes with another important thing the guy does. He doesn't focus just on His problems. He focuses on God. Starting with verse 12, he makes a point to remember God and what He's like. And doing that encourages him.

It's important for us to focus on God, too. When we're down, it is too easy to focus only on our problems -- which makes us more down. We need to look at the big picture, both the good and the bad. Most of all, we need to look to God, who is always bigger than our problems.

And this psalm has some good things to remember about God

when we're down (or any time).

First off, God doesn't change, no matter how bad things get (verses 12, 26, and 27). He's cares. He hears and responds to the prayers of those who are down (verses 17, 19, and 20). No matter how down you are, His ear and His love are never too far.

Because of who God is, there is a great future coming (verses 18, 26-28). If you trust God, life will not always be a bummer. You can be confident about the future like the guy who wrote this psalm.

Something cool about this psalm is the writer, even in the middle of his difficult time, looks way into the future and makes an amazing prophesy in verses 25 and 26. He tells of the day God will bring in a new creation. Read Revelation 21 if you want to find out more about that. If he was just having a big pity party and was focusing only on how bad his life is, he probably would have missed this awesome thing God showed him about the future.

I don't know how many times I've been down about life. And during my frequent pity parties, I've thought my life will always be bad. We need to ditch that attitude and be like the guy who wrote this psalm. No matter how bad things get, we can be like him and look to the future with confidence -- and NOT because we've called the Psychic Hot Line -- but because we have an awesome God who loves us. He's in control of our present and our future.

M. M.

Psalm 103
A Psalm of David.

1   Bless the LORD, O my soul,
And all that is within me, bless His holy name.
2   Bless the LORD, O my soul,
And forget none of His benefits;
3   Who pardons all your iniquities,
Who heals all your diseases;
4   Who redeems your life from the pit,
Who crowns you with lovingkindness and compassion;
5   Who satisfies your years with good things,
So that your youth is renewed like the eagle.

6   The LORD performs righteous deeds
And judgments for all who are oppressed.
7   He made known His ways to Moses,
His acts to the sons of Israel.

8   The LORD is compassionate and gracious,
     Slow to anger and abounding in lovingkindness.
9   He will not always strive with us,
     Nor will He keep His anger forever.
10   He has not dealt with us according to our sins,
     Nor rewarded us according to our iniquities.
11   For as high as the heavens are above the earth,
     So great is His lovingkindness toward those who fear Him.
12   As far as the east is from the west,
     So far has He removed our transgressions from us.
13   Just as a father has compassion on his children,
     So the LORD has compassion on those who fear Him.
14   For He Himself knows our frame;
     He is mindful that we are but dust.

15   As for man, his days are like grass;
     As a flower of the field, so he flourishes.
16   When the wind has passed over it, it is no more,
     And its place acknowledges it no longer.
17   But the lovingkindness of the LORD is from everlasting to everlasting
on those who fear Him,
     And His righteousness to children's children,
18   To those who keep His covenant
     And remember His precepts to do them.

19   The LORD has established His throne in the heavens,
     And His sovereignty rules over all.
20   Bless the LORD, you His angels,
     Mighty in strength, who perform His word,
     Obeying the voice of His word!
21   Bless the LORD, all you His hosts,
     You who serve Him, doing His will.
22   Bless the LORD, all you works of His,
     In all places of His dominion;
     Bless the LORD, O my soul!

I take Him for granted.

from PSALM 103

I go along in my life day to day, doing this and doing that. And I get so into myself and whatever I'm doing, I forget all the things God does for me. A lot of times I take Him for granted.

I shouldn't. He does so many cool things for me. Because of Jesus, He forgives me completely. He takes all the things I've felt guilty about and throws them far away, far beyond the horizon. If, instead, He gave me all the punishment I deserve, I'd be in BIG trouble.

But instead of giving me what I deserve, He loves me and cares about me. He pulls me out of the pits even if I'm the one who put me in them.

Then there's all the times I've been sick, and He's helped me get well. I don't think much about it when I'm feeling good; but my mom and I sure do think about it when I'm not.

Even my youth -- I don't think much about it because I've always been young, but my youth is a gift from God. I've always been in such a hurry to get older. Maybe I should appreciate more being the teenager God's made me. I certainly have more energy, fun, and good looks than most of the older people I know. And it's cool to be able to go all out all day and all night, then sleep all I want at weird hours, then be able to go all out again. I never thought much about it until my folks told me that's not normal.

I could probably go on all day about the ways God is good to me, and I'd only have part of it. His rule is beyond awesome and generous. His love toward me and all His children is bigger than the sky. That's how He is.

God loves me and is so good to me in so many ways. I want to remember and appreciate Him more. Not only that -- He makes me so happy -- I want my life to make Him happy.

Psalm 104

1   Bless the LORD, O my soul!
O LORD my God, You are very great;
You are clothed with splendor and majesty,
2   Covering Yourself with light as with a cloak,
Stretching out heaven like a tent curtain.
3   He lays the beams of His upper chambers in the waters;
He makes the clouds His chariot;
He walks upon the wings of the wind;
4   He makes the winds His messengers,
Flaming fire His ministers.

5   He established the earth upon its foundations,
So that it will not totter forever and ever.
6   You covered it with the deep as with a garment;
The waters were standing above the mountains.
7   At Your rebuke they fled,
At the sound of Your thunder they hurried away.
8   The mountains rose; the valleys sank down
To the place which You established for them.

9   You set a boundary that they may not pass over,
      So that they will not return to cover the earth.

10   He sends forth springs in the valleys;
      They flow between the mountains;
11   They give drink to every beast of the field;
      The wild donkeys quench their thirst.
12   Beside them the birds of the heavens dwell;
      They lift up their voices among the branches.
13   He waters the mountains from His upper chambers;
      The earth is satisfied with the fruit of His works.

14   He causes the grass to grow for the cattle,
      And vegetation for the labor of man,
      So that he may bring forth food from the earth,
15   And wine which makes man's heart glad,
      So that he may make his face glisten with oil,
      And food which sustains man's heart.
16   The trees of the LORD drink their fill,
      The cedars of Lebanon which He planted,
17   Where the birds build their nests,
      And the stork, whose home is the fir trees.

18   The high mountains are for the wild goats;
      The cliffs are a refuge for the shephanim.
19   He made the moon for the seasons;
      The sun knows the place of its setting.
20   You appoint darkness and it becomes night,
      In which all the beasts of the forest prowl about.
21   The young lions roar after their prey
      And seek their food from God.
22   When the sun rises they withdraw
      And lie down in their dens.
23   Man goes forth to his work
      And to his labor until evening.

24   O LORD, how many are Your works!
      In wisdom You have made them all;
      The earth is full of Your possessions.
25   There is the sea, great and broad,
      In which are swarms without number,
      Animals both small and great.
26   There the ships move along,
      And Leviathan, which You have formed to sport in it.

27   They all wait for You
      To give them their food in due season.
28   You give to them, they gather it up;
      You open Your hand, they are satisfied with good.

29   You hide Your face, they are dismayed;
  You take away their spirit, they expire
  And return to their dust.
30   You send forth Your Spirit, they are created;
  And You renew the face of the ground.

31   Let the glory of the LORD endure forever;
  Let the LORD be glad in His works;
32   He looks at the earth, and it trembles;
  He touches the mountains, and they smoke.
33   I will sing to the LORD as long as I live;
  I will sing praise to my God while I have my being.
34   Let my meditation be pleasing to Him;
  As for me, I shall be glad in the LORD.
35   Let sinners be consumed from the earth
  And let the wicked be no more.
  Bless the LORD, O my soul.
  Praise the LORD!

from PSALM 104

The way God created the earth and everything that lives on it is pretty mind-blowing when you think about it.

He made the earth in a way so it would support all sorts of life. He gave it lots of water and an atmosphere of air. He gave it an orbit so it would be just the right distance from the sun.

Then he created a zillion different kinds of creatures, a lot of them really weird or remote or both. Biologists are still discovering new species God made but we haven't found until now.

He could have created the earth boring if He wanted to. But He isn't boring, so He didn't.

Instead, He created cheetahs that can go 70 miles an hour, hummingbirds that flap their wings faster than you can see and hover better than a helicopter, birds with all sorts of bright colors, penguins, birds and animals that can make just about every noise imaginable -- and mockingbirds that can imitate them. He created carnivorous plants that can eat hamburgers, lizards that can change color, bizarre fish that look weirder than a heavy metal poster, and duck-billed platypuses that no one can figure out.

And that's not even talking about all the insects He's made -- all million-plus species. I see a lot of weird ones just around where I live. No telling how weird they get around the Amazon or in the Congo.

I have no idea why God created a lot of these creatures, except He wanted to. He is creative like nobody else -- and it looks like He enjoys being that way.

He could keep His splendor, His majesty and wonder in heav-

en, high away from us. Instead, He lets us enjoy it everyday in His creation.

And He provides for all these creatures, giving them air, water, and all sorts of different food. He provides for species I wish He didn't provide for, like fire ants, wasps, and gnats.

If God cares so much for all these creatures -- donkeys, goats, badgers, cows, whales, minnows, tigers, kitties, big beasts, small beasts, big birds, little birds, cool bugs, bad bugs -- creating so many different kinds of them, then providing for them -- then think how much He cares for people. Think how much He cares for me.

I'm glad God is my God.

Psalm 105

1   Oh give thanks to the LORD, call upon His name;
Make known His deeds among the peoples.
2   Sing to Him, sing praises to Him;
Speak of all His wonders.
3   Glory in His holy name;
Let the heart of those who seek the LORD be glad.
4   Seek the LORD and His strength;
Seek His face continually.
5   Remember His wonders which He has done,
His marvels and the judgments uttered by His mouth,
6   O seed of Abraham, His servant,
O sons of Jacob, His chosen ones!
7   He is the LORD our God;
His judgments are in all the earth.

8   He has remembered His covenant forever,
The word which He commanded to a thousand generations,
9   The covenant which He made with Abraham,
And His oath to Isaac.
10   Then He confirmed it to Jacob for a statute,
To Israel as an everlasting covenant,

11   Saying, "To you I will give the land of Canaan
    As the portion of your inheritance,"
12   When they were only a few men in number,
    Very few, and strangers in it.
13   And they wandered about from nation to nation,
    From one kingdom to another people.
14   He permitted no man to oppress them,
    And He reproved kings for their sakes:
15   "Do not touch My anointed ones,
    And do My prophets no harm."

16   And He called for a famine upon the land;
    He broke the whole staff of bread.
17   He sent a man before them,
    Joseph, who was sold as a slave.
18   They afflicted his feet with fetters,
    He himself was laid in irons;
19   Until the time that his word came to pass,
    The word of the LORD tested him.
20   The king sent and released him,
    The ruler of peoples, and set him free.
21   He made him lord of his house
    And ruler over all his possessions,
22   To imprison his princes at will,
    That he might teach his elders wisdom.
23   Israel also came into Egypt;
    Thus Jacob sojourned in the land of Ham.
24   And He caused His people to be very fruitful,
    And made them stronger than their adversaries.

25   He turned their heart to hate His people,
    To deal craftily with His servants.
26   He sent Moses His servant,
    And Aaron, whom He had chosen.
27   They performed His wondrous acts among them,
    And miracles in the land of Ham.
28   He sent darkness and made it dark;
    And they did not rebel against His words.
29   He turned their waters into blood
    And caused their fish to die.
30   Their land swarmed with frogs
    Even in the chambers of their kings.
31   He spoke, and there came a swarm of flies
    And gnats in all their territory.
32   He gave them hail for rain,
    And flaming fire in their land.
33   He struck down their vines also and their fig trees,
    And shattered the trees of their territory.
34   He spoke, and locusts came,

And young locusts, even without number,
35   And ate up all vegetation in their land,
And ate up the fruit of their ground.
36   He also struck down all the firstborn in their land,
The first fruits of all their vigor.

37   Then He brought them out with silver and gold,
And among His tribes there was not one who stumbled.
38   Egypt was glad when they departed,
For the dread of them had fallen upon them.
39   He spread a cloud for a covering,
And fire to illumine by night.
40   They asked, and He brought quail,
And satisfied them with the bread of heaven.
41   He opened the rock and water flowed out;
It ran in the dry places like a river.
42   For He remembered His holy word
With Abraham His servant;
43   And He brought forth His people with joy,
His chosen ones with a joyful shout.
44   He gave them also the lands of the nations,
That they might take possession of the fruit of the peoples' labor,
45   So that they might keep His statutes
And observe His laws,
Praise the LORD!

I can trust Him.

from PSALM 105

(NOTE: Sometime, also check out Romans 8:28 and the story of Joseph in Genesis.)

God is awesome. He desires people to seek Him and pray.
Because He loves them and wants to hear from them. Because
He likes to answer people's prayers in excellent ways.

He does great things for His people, including for me. And His
word and His promises to me are good and faithful. I can trust
Him.

Sometimes I have to be reminded of that. Because life can get
a little cra-zy. God promises to cause all the things that happen
in my life to work together for good. But stuff happens that
makes me wonder or forget that. And I need to be reminded.

Even when I remember His word and His promises to me, it
can be tough to really believe them. Because there are times
God says one thing, but circumstances seem to say the opposite. And I have to decide what I'm going to trust: God, who I
can't see, or circumstances, which I can see all too well.

It helps to know I'm not the first one to face that choice. Look at Abraham. God promised to make a nation of people out of his family. But there was a slight problem -- family? What family? Abe and his wife Sarah were old, and I don't mean thirty-old. I mean OLD. And they didn't have any kids. Sarah even laughed at God's promise. But she had a kid anyway, and now Abraham's descendants are all over the place.

Or Joseph: when he was a teenager, God showed him in a dream he was gonna rule. "Yeeah. Riight," his brothers said, then sold him into slavery.

As if that wasn't bad enough, he later went to prison on a false charge. God's word to him years back that he was going to rule must have seriously tested him: whether he was going to be true to God and keep trusting Him, or look at where he was and give up on God. He definitely had to choose whether he was going to trust God and His word when circumstances said the opposite. And he had a lot of time in prison to think about it. To be honest, I would have been seriously tempted to dis God. But Joseph didn't. And God didn't let him down. Practically overnight, Joseph did rule -- and not just any place. He ruled Egypt!

All over the Bible, in history, and also in people's lives today, God promised things that seemed impossible. But He came through, kept His word, and did it. The difficulties didn't stop God. They just made His acts that much more awesome.

All those acts of God are there to remind me I can trust Him and His word. When He promises something, it's as good as done -- no matter what the circumstances. God will not be stopped from keeping His word.

Nothing can stop Him from keeping His word to me.

Psalm 106

1   Praise the LORD!
Oh give thanks to the LORD, for He is good;
For His lovingkindness is everlasting.
2   Who can speak of the mighty deeds of the LORD,
Or can show forth all His praise?
3   How blessed are those who keep justice,
Who practice righteousness at all times!

4   Remember me, O LORD, in Your favor toward Your people;
Visit me with Your salvation,
5   That I may see the prosperity of Your chosen ones,

That I may rejoice in the gladness of Your nation,
That I may glory with Your inheritance.

6   We have sinned like our fathers,
    We have committed iniquity, we have behaved wickedly.
7   Our fathers in Egypt did not understand Your wonders;
    They did not remember Your abundant kindnesses,
    But rebelled by the sea, at the Red Sea.
8   Nevertheless He saved them for the sake of His name,
    That He might make His power known.
9   Thus He rebuked the Red Sea and it dried up,
    And He led them through the deeps, as through the wilderness.
10   So He saved them from the hand of the one who hated them,
    And redeemed them from the hand of the enemy.
11   The waters covered their adversaries;
    Not one of them was left.
12   Then they believed His words;
    They sang His praise.

13   They quickly forgot His works;
    They did not wait for His counsel,
14   But craved intensely in the wilderness,
    And tempted God in the desert.
15   So He gave them their request,
    But sent a wasting disease among them.

16   When they became envious of Moses in the camp,
    And of Aaron, the holy one of the LORD,
17   The earth opened and swallowed up Dathan,
    And engulfed the company of Abiram.
18   And a fire blazed up in their company;
    The flame consumed the wicked.

19   They made a calf in Horeb
    And worshiped a molten image.
20   Thus they exchanged their glory
    For the image of an ox that eats grass.
21   They forgot God their Savior,
    Who had done great things in Egypt,
22   Wonders in the land of Ham
    And awesome things by the Red Sea.
23   Therefore He said that He would destroy them,
    Had not Moses His chosen one stood in the breach before Him,
    To turn away His wrath from destroying them.
24   Then they despised the pleasant land;
    They did not believe in His word,
25   But grumbled in their tents;
    They did not listen to the voice of the LORD.

26   Therefore He swore to them
That He would cast them down in the wilderness,
27   And that He would cast their seed among the nations
And scatter them in the lands.

28   They joined themselves also to Baal-peor,
And ate sacrifices offered to the dead.
29   Thus they provoked Him to anger with their deeds,
And the plague broke out among them.
30   Then Phinehas stood up and interposed,
And so the plague was stayed.
31   And it was reckoned to him for righteousness,
To all generations forever.

32   They also provoked Him to wrath at the waters of Meribah,
So that it went hard with Moses on their account;
33   Because they were rebellious against His Spirit,
He spoke rashly with his lips.

34   They did not destroy the peoples,
As the LORD commanded them,
35   But they mingled with the nations
And learned their practices,
36   And served their idols,
Which became a snare to them.
37   They even sacrificed their sons and their daughters to the demons,
38   And shed innocent blood,
The blood of their sons and their daughters,
Whom they sacrificed to the idols of Canaan;
And the land was polluted with the blood.
39   Thus they became unclean in their practices,
And played the harlot in their deeds.

40   Therefore the anger of the LORD was kindled against His people
And He abhorred His inheritance.
41   Then He gave them into the hand of the nations,
And those who hated them ruled over them.
42   Their enemies also oppressed them,
And they were subdued under their power.
43   Many times He would deliver them;
They, however, were rebellious in their counsel,
And so sank down in their iniquity.

44   Nevertheless He looked upon their distress
When He heard their cry;
45   And He remembered His covenant for their sake,
And relented according to the greatness of His lovingkindness.
46   He also made them objects of compassion
In the presence of all their captors.

47   Save us, O LORD our God,
   And gather us from among the nations,
   To give thanks to Your holy name
   And glory in Your praise.
48   Blessed be the LORD, the God of Israel,
   From everlasting even to everlasting.
   And let all the people say, "Amen."
   Praise the LORD!

So why am I sorry to Him?

from PSALM 106

God is so good to me. His love for me lasts forever.

He is incredible. Who could say all the great things He has done? You could try to praise Him for all His mighty acts, and wear yourself out praising Him until you fall over, and You still would have just started. God is that great.

And He's saved me and been cool to me.

So why am I sorry to Him?

When I read about how the nation of Israel was constantly doing wrong and dissing God, I think, "How could they be so stupid when God had done so many awesome things for them?"

But when I really think about it, I'm stupid, too.

I'm always forgetting the good things God does for me. Like when I pray for something, and God answers. And I don't even think to thank God. I don't even remember praying for it. Or there's the times when things aren't going exactly the way I like so I get the attitude that God isn't good to me. Get real!

A lot of times, I just forget God completely. I live my life like He's not there. I go through a whole day or even a week with hardly a thought about Him, not even thanking Him or thinking about what He'd want me to do.

Of course, sooner or later, forgetting God causes things to start going bad. **Then** I start thinking about God. You'd think I'd figure out by now that living life as if God isn't there or doesn't care doesn't work. But, like I said, I'm stupid.

Then there's all the times I don't listen to God. I don't read His word because I'm too busy doing more important things, like video games, talking on the phone, and watching T.V. When I have a decision to make about something, I don't ask God for guidance. Or I know what God would want me to do or that I should at least ask Him, but I know how to live my life better than God does. After all, it's my life, right? Of course, I eventually find out who really knows better -- the hard way. Why the hard way? Because I'm **stupid**.

There's all the times I forget to thank God for all the cool things He does for me. That's sorry. And why am I sorry like that? A lot of times it's because I'm too busy envying the cool things God does for someone else. Stupid!

But, I'm not so stupid that I'd get into idolatry like the Israelites, right? They bowed down to images they made like I focus on the images on a T.V. . . . . Well, I don't worship the stuff on T. V. I just spend several more hours a day watching it than I do reading the Bible or praying or . . . next question?

What's worse is when my stupidity -- yeah, my sin -- hurts not just myself. It hurts others, too. There's the people I've let down. The people I've put down. The people I've used. Yeah -- sometimes I'm worse than stupid.

Yet when I pray and fess up, God forgives me.   And He doesn't discipline me near as bad as I deserve. Instead, He has compassion and understanding toward me and helps me do better next time. He's so cool to me, even when I'm not to Him. He even paid for all my sin on the cross so I'll get to go to heaven and be with Him -- no matter how stupid I get before then.

There's one way I'm not stupid any more. I used to think I'd go to heaven if I were good. Now I know there's no way I can be that good. Now I know there's one big reason I'm going to heaven -- because He is good.

He is good to me, not according to what I deserve, but according to the infinite greatness of His love.

Praise the Lord for that!

Psalm 107

1   Oh give thanks to the LORD, for He is good,
For His lovingkindness is everlasting.
2   Let the redeemed of the LORD say so,
Whom He has redeemed from the hand of the adversary
3   And gathered from the lands,
From the east and from the west,
From the north and from the south.

4   They wandered in the wilderness in a desert region;
They did not find a way to an inhabited city.
5   They were hungry and thirsty;
Their soul fainted within them.

6   Then they cried out to the LORD in their trouble;
    He delivered them out of their distresses.
7   He led them also by a straight way,
    To go to an inhabited city.
8   Let them give thanks to the LORD for His lovingkindness,
    And for His wonders to the sons of men!
9   For He has satisfied the thirsty soul,
    And the hungry soul He has filled with what is good.

10   There were those who dwelt in darkness and in the shadow of death,
    Prisoners in misery and chains,
11   Because they had rebelled against the words of God
    And spurned the counsel of the Most High.
12   Therefore He humbled their heart with labor;
    They stumbled and there was none to help.
13   Then they cried out to the LORD in their trouble;
    He saved them out of their distresses.
14   He brought them out of darkness and the shadow of death
    And broke their bands apart.
15   Let them give thanks to the LORD for His lovingkindness,
    And for His wonders to the sons of men!
16   For He has shattered gates of bronze
    And cut bars of iron asunder.

17   Fools, because of their rebellious way,
    And because of their iniquities, were afflicted.
18   Their soul abhorred all kinds of food,
    And they drew near to the gates of death.
19   Then they cried out to the LORD in their trouble;
    He saved them out of their distresses.
20   He sent His word and healed them,
    And delivered them from their destructions.
21   Let them give thanks to the LORD for His lovingkindness,
    And for His wonders to the sons of men!
22   Let them also offer sacrifices of thanksgiving,
    And tell of His works with joyful singing.

23   Those who go down to the sea in ships,
    Who do business on great waters;
24   They have seen the works of the LORD,
    And His wonders in the deep.
25   For He spoke and raised up a stormy wind,
    Which lifted up the waves of the sea.
26   They rose up to the heavens, they went down to the depths;
    Their soul melted away in their misery.
27   They reeled and staggered like a drunken man,
    And were at their wits' end.
28   Then they cried to the LORD in their trouble,

And He brought them out of their distresses.
29   He caused the storm to be still,
So that the waves of the sea were hushed.
30   Then they were glad because they were quiet,
So He guided them to their desired haven.
31   Let them give thanks to the LORD for His lovingkindness,
And for His wonders to the sons of men!
32   Let them extol Him also in the congregation of the people,
And praise Him at the seat of the elders.

33   He changes rivers into a wilderness
And springs of water into a thirsty ground;
34   A fruitful land into a salt waste,
Because of the wickedness of those who dwell in it.
35   He changes a wilderness into a pool of water
And a dry land into springs of water;
36   And there He makes the hungry to dwell,
So that they may establish an inhabited city,
37   And sow fields and plant vineyards,
And gather a fruitful harvest.
38   Also He blesses them and they multiply greatly,
And He does not let their cattle decrease.

39   When they are diminished and bowed down
Through oppression, misery and sorrow,
40   He pours contempt upon princes
And makes them wander in a pathless waste.
41   But He sets the needy securely on high away from affliction,
And makes his families like a flock.
42   The upright see it and are glad;
But all unrighteousness shuts its mouth.
43   Who is wise? Let him give heed to these things,
And consider the lovingkindnesses of the LORD.

> *tired and cold and empty inside, i'm afraid —*
> *no, terrified of the doubt and the emptiness*
> *and what if i could find faith through this doubt*
> *in myself, and in You*
> *because it's more of a prayer*
> *when i cry out*
>
> joshua stevens, "untitled #465"

from PSALM 107

I'm giving thanks to the Lord. For He is always good; He is always loving, especially to those in trouble who cry out to Him.

Teenagers wander in the wilderness, looking for life, looking for meaning, looking, but never finding what they're looking for. The desert of their lives becomes barren, and they become so hungry and thirsty. They feel like giving up. All they have the strength left to do is to cry out to the Lord.

He hears and leads them out of the desert of their emptiness. And He gives them the real life they were looking for. He fills their lives with meaning. They are satisfied because of Him.

Others dwell in darkness, in living death. They are imprisoned in their misery. They may be imprisoned in jail as well, because they disobeyed God, going into alcohol, drugs, worse. In chains of their own making, they humble themselves to admit their wrong. But they've messed up their lives so much, they're in such bondage and despair, it seems no one can help them. So they cry out to the Lord.

And though it was their own fault, He forgives them and reaches down. He leads them out of the shadows of sin and death. He breaks their bondage. He tears apart their chains.

Fools follow their own ways instead of God's -- because they're fools. They rebel against God and end up afflicted. They end up finding themselves going in a direction they don't want to go and to a place they don't want to be. Finally, they cry out to the Lord.

And out of his love, He forgives them and saves them. He heals their lives and leads them in the right direction.

Teenagers find themselves in the storms of life. The winds and waves blow in suddenly, and they are defenseless. The floods of divorce, death, abuse, rejection -- they're too deep and strong. They're more than teens can handle alone.

Though life once lifted them high, they're now sinking into the depths. They're overwhelmed by the dark waters. It feels like they're going down. And they see nothing to look ahead to, nothing to grab on to. They see nothing they can do -- except to cry out to the Lord.

And the Lord hears their cry. He sees their tears and brings them out of the darkness. He stills the storm and leads them to peace.

He led me to peace.

So give thanks to the Lord for His love and faithfulness. Never forget the wonders He has done for us. You who God has filled, thank Him. You who God has set free, praise Him. Don't keep quiet about it. Tell everyone about His forgiveness and goodness.

For there is nothing God won't do for His teenagers. He'll change a desert into a lake with a beach. He'll turn starving teen hunger into a cook-out or a pizza feast. Those who are down, He'll lift up. Those who are putting them down, He'll put down. He'll give the homeless a home, street kids a warm room. He'll give a family to the lonely. He'll be security for the fearful. He'll give forgiveness and life to whoever trusts Him and just asks. He even gives His Son.

Look at what God has done and be glad. Never forget the Lord and the wonderful things He does. Always remember and ponder the awesome faithful love of the Lord God.

Psalm 108
A Song, a Psalm of David.

1   My heart is steadfast, O God;
      I will sing, I will sing praises, even with my soul.
2   Awake, harp and lyre;
      I will awaken the dawn!
3   I will give thanks to You, O LORD, among the peoples,
      And I will sing praises to You among the nations.
4   For Your lovingkindness is great above the heavens,
      And Your truth reaches to the skies.
5   Be exalted, O God, above the heavens,
      And Your glory above all the earth.
6   That Your beloved may be delivered,
      Save with Your right hand, and answer me!

7   God has spoken in His holiness:
      "I will exult, I will portion out Shechem
      And measure out the valley of Succoth.
8   "Gilead is Mine, Manasseh is Mine;
      Ephraim also is the helmet of My head;
      Judah is My scepter.
9   "Moab is My washbowl;
      Over Edom I shall throw My shoe;
      Over Philistia I will shout aloud."

10   Who will bring me into the besieged city?
       Who will lead me to Edom?

11 Have not You Yourself, O God, rejected us?
And will You not go forth with our armies, O God?
12 Oh give us help against the adversary,
For deliverance by man is in vain.
13 Through God we will do valiantly,
And it is He who shall tread down our adversaries.

There's nothing You and I can't do.

from PSALM 108

Lord, I'm through trying to live life myself. I'm through trying to do things my own way and by my own power.

I thought I was so smart, even smarter than You when it came to living my life. I've found out the hard way I'm not. Duh. When I think about some of the things I've done, I have to admit I've been pretty stupid instead.

Now I see trying to live just my way is dumb. Who knows better how to live, You -- who's been around forever, who's seen it all, whose truth, knowledge and wisdom goes way far beyond what I can ever comprehend -- or me.

Yeah, trying to live life by myself, my own way, is stupid. And, being stupid, it's taken me a while to figure that out.

But now if I live Your way, if I do things with You, Lord -- now that's different. With You, there's no telling what I can do. Because You rule. You can do anything. Your power, wisdom, and love are infinite.

And if there's nothing You can't do, then there's nothing You and I can't do.

So I'm through exalting myself as the boss of my life. Jesus, You said those who exalt themselves will be put down, and haven't I found that out. Now, I'm exalting You as Lord of my life. 'Cause now, I'm humbled enough to know I need You every day, and that Your ways are way better than mine. You rule in my life now. And Your rule wins in the end. So lead me, Lord! Show me the way.

Now my confidence is stronger, because I'm not confident in just myself and my brilliant wisdom. My confidence is in God and in His leadership. I am going to live life right and have an impact -- because, from now on, I'm going to live it with God.

Psalm 109

For the choir director. A Psalm of David.

1   O God of my praise,
Do not be silent!
2   For they have opened the wicked and deceitful mouth against me;
They have spoken against me with a lying tongue.
3   They have also surrounded me with words of hatred,
And fought against me without cause.
4   In return for my love they act as my accusers;
But I am in prayer.
5   Thus they have repaid me evil for good
And hatred for my love.

6   Appoint a wicked man over him,
And let an accuser stand at his right hand.
7   When he is judged, let him come forth guilty,
And let his prayer become sin.
8   Let his days be few;
Let another take his office.
9   Let his children be fatherless
And his wife a widow.
10   Let his children wander about and beg;
And let them seek sustenance far from their ruined homes.
11   Let the creditor seize all that he has,
And let strangers plunder the product of his labor.
12   Let there be none to extend lovingkindness to him,
Nor any to be gracious to his fatherless children.
13   Let his posterity be cut off;
In a following generation let their name be blotted out.

14   Let the iniquity of his fathers be remembered before the LORD,
And do not let the sin of his mother be blotted out.
15   Let them be before the LORD continually,
That He may cut off their memory from the earth;
16   Because he did not remember to show lovingkindness,
But persecuted the afflicted and needy man,
And the despondent in heart, to put them to death.
17   He also loved cursing, so it came to him;
And he did not delight in blessing, so it was far from him.
18   But he clothed himself with cursing as with his garment,
And it entered into his body like water
And like oil into his bones.
19   Let it be to him as a garment with which he covers himself,
And for a belt with which he constantly girds himself.
20   Let this be the reward of my accusers from the LORD,
And of those who speak evil against my soul.
21   But You, O GOD, the Lord, deal kindly with me for Your name's
sake;

Because Your lovingkindness is good, deliver me;
22   For I am afflicted and needy,
And my heart is wounded within me.
23   I am passing like a shadow when it lengthens;
I am shaken off like the locust.
24   My knees are weak from fasting,
And my flesh has grown lean, without fatness.
25   I also have become a reproach to them;
When they see me, they wag their head.

26   Help me, O LORD my God;
Save me according to Your lovingkindness.
27   And let them know that this is Your hand;
You, LORD, have done it.
28   Let them curse, but You bless;
When they arise, they shall be ashamed,
But Your servant shall be glad.
29   Let my accusers be clothed with dishonor,
And let them cover themselves with their own shame as with a robe.

30   With my mouth I will give thanks abundantly to the LORD;
And in the midst of many I will praise Him.
31   For He stands at the right hand of the needy,
To save him from those who judge his soul.

from PSALM 109

It stinks when you try to live right and treat people right -- and you get wrong in return.

There's been times when people tried to make my life miserable for no reason. And I think, "What did I do to deserve that?"

The worst are those who've done me bad when all I've done them is good. They told lies about me even though I've always been honest with them. They bad-mouthed me and cussed me, but I prayed for them. Every chance they got, they acted out their hate against me, even though I showed them nothing but love.

Sometimes it seems life, too, repays me bad for good. When I do right, try my best, and end up with nothing to show for it, or worse. Like the times when I put out for a sport, making every practice, going all out -- and I rode the bench anyway. I hated that. Or that class with the impossible teacher. I work my tail off and still don't make the grade. Or the times I try to please my dad and impress him -- and he doesn't care.

It makes me think, "Why bother?" If I try hard and do something, but I have nothing to show for it, if I do good and get bad in return, why bother even trying?

Then I remember God treats people right. He is loving and just. He stands with those who are wronged and put down. Those who love Him and try to live out their love, He'll cause all things, even the bad things, to work together for their good. God is a rewarder of those who seek Him and who seek to walk in His ways.

I just need to be more patient about it. One time, I was kinda ticked at God because of a bummer situation. But then He used it for greater good than I could imagine. That made me thankful -- and feel kinda funny.

As for those who return hate for love, and evil for good, what goes around comes around. God's justice won't let them get away with it forever. And I've seen God's justice happen. Guys who do nothing but curse, I've seen curses come down upon them. Those who hate good, I've seen good taken away from them. Those who love evil, that's what they got.

So even when for a long time it seems it doesn't make a difference, it does make a difference whether someone loves and does good or evil. It makes a difference when I do good.

God will make sure of that.

Psalm 110
A Psalm of David.

1   The LORD says to my Lord:
"Sit at My right hand
Until I make Your enemies a footstool for Your feet."
2   The LORD will stretch forth Your strong scepter from Zion, saying,
"Rule in the midst of Your enemies."
3   Your people will volunteer freely in the day of Your power;
In holy array, from the womb of the dawn,
Your youth are to You as the dew.

4   The LORD has sworn and will not change His mind,
"You are a priest forever
According to the order of Melchizedek."
5   The Lord is at Your right hand;
He will shatter kings in the day of His wrath.
6   He will judge among the nations,
He will fill them with corpses,
He will shatter the chief men over a broad country.
7   He will drink from the brook by the wayside;
Therefore He will lift up His head.

from PSALM 110

NOTE: This is a real heavy psalm about the Messiah. I don't feel comfortable getting much into the theology of this psalm in this book. But if you want to get into it or if you're wondering, "Who in the world is Melchizedek?", check out Genesis 14: 17 - 20 and Hebrews chapters 5 and 7. Be warned -- this is not a subject for spiritual babies. (Hebrews 5: 11-14)

If you want to read about Jesus coming back, read Revelation 19.

Jesus has been waiting two thousand years.

One day, the Father will say to Him, "It's time."

Then Jesus will call together His armies. And with eyes of fire, He will come.

His face will be brighter than the sun, banishing all darkness. His voice will be like thunder and the crashing ocean waves, breaking all evil. No one will be able to stand against the power of His Word.

But Satan, Antichrist, and their armies of evil will not submit. They will dare to continue to war against the King of Kings. So Jesus, the King, will wage war on them. And He will crush them. With His word of judgment, the Messiah King will shatter the enemies of God. He will fill the countryside of Armageddon with their corpses. And their evil will rule the earth no more.

And I'll get to be there. Because when the call comes, I will volunteer to serve in His army. And not just me. In the uniforms of the Messiah, the youth of His army will spread over the earth, more numerous than beads of water on a dewy morning. And like the dew in the sun, we will shine. Because we will be reflecting the light of the Son.

Darkness? Darkness, which obscured the light for two thousand years, will be no more. In His light the world will finally see: He is the King of Kings. He is the Lord of Lords.

And His head that once hung down from the cross as He died for me -- I'll get to see Him lift up His head high in victory over the enemy. And He will rule -- forever.

Psalm 111

1   Praise the LORD!
   I will give thanks to the LORD with all my heart,
   In the company of the upright and in the assembly.
2   Great are the works of the LORD;
   They are studied by all who delight in them.
3   Splendid and majestic is His work,
   And His righteousness endures forever.
4   He has made His wonders to be remembered;
   The LORD is gracious and compassionate.
5   He has given food to those who fear Him;
   He will remember His covenant forever.
6   He has made known to His people the power of His works,
   In giving them the heritage of the nations.

7   The works of His hands are truth and justice;
   All His precepts are sure.
8   They are upheld forever and ever;
   They are performed in truth and uprightness.
9   He has sent redemption to His people;
   He has ordained His covenant forever;
   Holy and awesome is His name.
10   The fear of the LORD is the beginning of wisdom;
   A good understanding have all those who do His commandments;
   His praise endures forever.

from PSALM 111

I will give thanks to the Lord with all I've got, because the works He does are great.

He has done so many awesome things in history and today. And He's really going to shake the world in the future. The more I check out what He has done and will do, the more I learn what He is like -- and the more I appreciate Him. His works are majestic, like creating the universe just for starters. How majestic He must be!

He has done awesome acts to show us and help us remember what He is like. He has shown He's powerful. He has shown He cares and would even stop the world for His people. He has shown His love in the life and death of His Son.

He has shown His word to be 100% trustworthy. Again and again, He has demonstrated through history He keeps His word. His promises, His guidance -- all His word -- can be relied on, no matter what. People forget their promises, but God never forgets His word. He keeps His word forever.

The name of God is holy and awesome. And He has proven it! Being in awe of Him is the beginning of living smart. And the smart guy studies His word -- and lives it.

God's not just up there somewhere; He acts down here in people's lives, and in my life. I get to experience Him now and forever. That is so great, I'm going to thank and praise Him forever.

An afterword to PSALM 111

I write the first draft from Psalm 111 three days after attending the Stand in the Gap Solemn Assembly in Washington, D.C. on October 4, 1997, along with perhaps a million other men, including a lot of teenagers.

The first three verses of this psalm remind me very much of this event. It was a great and powerful work of God in history and in the lives of many, including me. And I was definitely giving thanks "to the Lord with all my heart . . . in the assembly." Reflecting on it now only increases my gratitude and awe.

I don't know for sure what God is doing, but Stand in the Gap shows He is definitely doing something big! And, like the psalm says, we should study what God is doing (verses 2 and 4) and get with the program. As for me, I don't want to be on the sidelines. I am striving to get ready for whatever God is going to do.

I pray it is a Great Awakening.

M. M. , October 7, 1997

Psalm 112

1   Praise the LORD!
How blessed is the man who fears the LORD,
Who greatly delights in His commandments.
2   His descendants will be mighty on earth;
The generation of the upright will be blessed.
3   Wealth and riches are in his house,
And his righteousness endures forever.
4   Light arises in the darkness for the upright;
He is gracious and compassionate and righteous.
5   It is well with the man who is gracious and lends;
He will maintain his cause in judgment.
6   For he will never be shaken;
The righteous will be remembered forever.
7   He will not fear evil tidings;
His heart is steadfast, trusting in the LORD.
8   His heart is upheld, he will not fear,
Until he looks with satisfaction on his adversaries.

9   He has given freely to the poor,
     His righteousness endures forever;
     His horn will be exalted in honor.
10   The wicked will see it and be vexed,
     He will gnash his teeth and melt away;
     The desire of the wicked will perish.

**See, through the years I've now come to understand
That no one can make it happen better for me than God can
So I'll wait on no man, only you God.**

John Reuben "Rest Easy"
from *Are We There Yet?*

from PSALM 112
especially verses 4 (a favorite memory verse of mine), 7 and 8

It's not easy being a teenager. When I was a little kid, it seemed I didn't have any worries. Not anymore. Now it seems there's always things coming at me. And life can get dark, from bad happening or from just being down. A couple of times, it's gotten real dark.

But I'm learning not to worry or fear life like I have at times. Because I've seen God take bad things and use them for good. I've seen Him take something evil throws at me and use it for the very opposite that evil intended. Now I know, no matter how bad things get, God is in control, and He's not going to drop the ball on me. He'll take care of me.

Even when things are dark, so dark I can hardly see any good, I can trust God. Because He causes light to arise in the darkness. And light is brightest when it pierces the dark. When Jesus shines into my darkness is when I see Him best.

If God allows dark times in my life, it's only to help me see Him better and to draw me closer to the light of His presence. He will never abandon me or take that light away from me.

So I will not fear. If bad happens, it's only so God can turn it into good. Yeah, I don't know what the future holds. But I know who holds the future. And He's got a strong grip. I can trust Him.

And he's got an awesome future for all who love Him and His word. So yeah, my trust isn't in myself or in luck or anything else. My trust is in the Lord. So there'll be no fear here.

Psalm 113

1   Praise the LORD!
Praise, O servants of the LORD,
Praise the name of the LORD.
2   Blessed be the name of the LORD
From this time forth and forever.
3   From the rising of the sun to its setting
The name of the LORD is to be praised.
4   The LORD is high above all nations;
His glory is above the heavens.

5   Who is like the LORD our God,
Who is enthroned on high,
6   Who humbles Himself to behold
The things that are in heaven and in the earth?
7   He raises the poor from the dust
And lifts the needy from the ash heap,
8   To make them sit with princes,
With the princes of His people.
9   He makes the barren woman abide in the house
As a joyful mother of children.
Praise the LORD!

*No one loves me like you
No one loves me the way you do*
Jars of Clay "No One Loves Me Like You"
from *If I Left the Zoo*

from PSALM 113

NOTE: Just a reminder: in Jewish thought, a "name" referred to one's character.

I can't get over how God is the best. About all I can do sometimes is cut loose and praise Him. Nothing and nobody touches Him.

He is perfect. He is beyond perfect. Think up the best, most beautiful, most awesome thing you can think of -- and God is way beyond that. I can't even think about Him too much before it gives me a headache. He is so high above us. He is so high above anything we can even imagine.

The Lord is so holy. His name is holy. His name is great. Everywhere, all the time, from East to West, from the rising of the sun to it's going down, the Lord's name deserves to be praised.

Who rules like the Lord? High above any other authority, high above all of man's lame governments, high above the earth, high even above the heavens, God rules.

But that's not what gets me the most about God. What really blows my mind is, though He is so high above us, even though He is so BIG, He stoops way down to be concerned about us down here, to look out for us.

He even looks out for me.

He protects me. He provides for me. He listens to me. Even though He has a zillion other prayers coming up to Him, He listens to me. When I'm down, and I pray, He lifts me up. Even when I think I'll never be happy again, He comforts me and makes me smile.

I am glad the Lord is my God. What other king ever loved me like my King does?

I'm just one person among billions. Think of all the others He looks after, too. (I think I'm getting another one of those headaches!) Yet, still, He looks after me, and as an individual -- as I really am. I'm not just another face in the crowd to God.

He is so high above us, He doesn't have to care about us like that. He doesn't have to care about me like that. But He does -- because He wants to.

God is so cool. He's so cool to me. How can I not praise Him?

Psalm 114

1   When Israel went forth from Egypt,
The house of Jacob from a people of strange language,
2   Judah became His sanctuary,
Israel, His dominion.

3   The sea looked and fled;
The Jordan turned back.
4   The mountains skipped like rams,
The hills, like lambs.
5   What ails you, O sea, that you flee?
O Jordan, that you turn back?
6   O mountains, that you skip like rams?
O hills, like lambs?

7 - Tremble, O earth, before the Lord,
Before the God of Jacob,
8   Who turned the rock into a pool of water,
The flint into a fountain of water.

from PSALM 114

NOTE: Psalm 114 is among the most creative and artistic psalms.   I'm not even going to try to write nice poetry like this. But it makes it a little hard to understand. Knowing this psalm is about God leading the nation of Israel out of Egypt and into the Promised Land might help.

In fact, Psalm 114 is one of six psalms, 113 through 118, that were traditionally sung at the Jewish Passover, which celebrates God protecting and delivering Israel from Egypt. These six are called the *Hallel.*

God leads His people with love and power. His love for them is so strong, He would shake the world for them.

When the Lord led Israel out of Egypt, the Red Sea fled because of Him and let His people through. Then God unleashed the sea on the enemies of Israel, on the armies of Pharaoh, and drowned them.

Then in the desert, where there was no water, God caused water to come out of rock to provide for His people. Bringing dryness out of water or water out of dryness -- God did both for His people. Both are easy to Him.

When God came down to Mount Sinai to give guidance to His people, the mountain quaked under the consuming fire and thunder of the Almighty. And the Lord Himself wrote the Law.

And when it was time to enter the Promised Land, God stopped the flow of the Jordan River to let them in. A mere river is not going to stop God. God stops rivers -- stops anything -- for His people whenever He wants.

The walls and armies of the Canaanites, of the enemies of God -- they were but houses of cards and toy soldiers to Him. The walls of Jericho were just the first to fall. Only fools try to stop God. History is full of dead fools.

God's people live on and will live forever. But where are the Pharaohs? Where are the Canaanites? Where are the Assyrians? Where is Hitler?

One day God will shake the earth a final time, and then the world will finally get it -- Heaven and Earth cannot stop the Lord from carrying out His awesome plans for His people.

Nothing can stop the God of Israel from leading His people to the place He has prepared for them.

Psalm 115

1   Not to us, O LORD, not to us,
But to Your name give glory
Because of Your lovingkindness, because of Your truth.
2   Why should the nations say,
"Where, now, is their God?"
3   But our God is in the heavens;
He does whatever He pleases.
4   Their idols are silver and gold,
The work of man's hands.
5   They have mouths, but they cannot speak;
They have eyes, but they cannot see;
6   They have ears, but they cannot hear;
They have noses, but they cannot smell;
7   They have hands, but they cannot feel;
They have feet, but they cannot walk;
They cannot make a sound with their throat.
8   Those who make them will become like them,
Everyone who trusts in them.

9   O Israel, trust in the LORD;
He is their help and their shield.
10   O house of Aaron, trust in the LORD;
He is their help and their shield.
11   You who fear the LORD, trust in the LORD;
He is their help and their shield.
12   The LORD has been mindful of us; He will bless us;
He will bless the house of Israel;
He will bless the house of Aaron.
13   He will bless those who fear the LORD,
The small together with the great.
14   May the LORD give you increase,
You and your children.
15   May you be blessed of the LORD,
Maker of heaven and earth.

16   The heavens are the heavens of the LORD,
But the earth He has given to the sons of men.
17   The dead do not praise the LORD,
Nor do any who go down into silence;
18   But as for us, we will bless the LORD
From this time forth and forever.
Praise the LORD!

Help me to put aside my stupid idols.

from PSALM 115

All the glory belongs to You, Lord, not to me or anyone else. For nobody loves like You. Nobody is true like You.

Yet I have trouble trusting You. I don't know why. I think if I could see You, it would be easy to trust You then. Some of my friends say it's hard to believe in a God we can't see.

If we could see You, would we really trust You the way we should? It would make sense we would, but maybe we give ourselves too much credit. The Israelites saw You a lot. They still distrusted and messed up. Then You came and lived down here, Jesus. And what did we do? We didn't believe in You and trust You. We killed You. And even though You rose from the dead and offered us forgiveness and life anyway, a lot of us use You as a cuss word. I've caught myself doing that although I know better.

But (changing the subject) as I read the Bible about all the idols dumb people worshipped back then, I laugh at them. I think I would never have done anything that stupid -- worshipping gold or wood or stone "gods," trusting in them instead of You. How "duh"! At least I'm better than them.

But maybe I'm giving myself too much credit again. How much do I trust in things to make my life good, like a cool computer, sports, possessions, hot clothes, or a cool car? How much do I give my attention and effort to stuff like that instead of to You? Don't answer that. And do I ever worship gold? No, but don't ask me about green. How often do I seek attention and glory for the brazen idol of Myself instead of You? Is it more important to me to please You or to please Myself? Don't answer that one either.

Do I really make You first place in my life, or me?

I know the answer to that one.

Lord, help me to get things straight. Help me to put aside my stupid idols, including the holy trinity of me, myself and I, and put You first. And help me to really trust You. For no one helps me and protects me like You. You know what's best for me much better than I do. And You will do whatever You please to bring about the best.

So help me, Lord -- You know I need it -- to put You first and trust You, the way You deserve. Because You are lofty and awesome. Yet You are so good to me. I want to be good to You. I want my words, my trust, and my life to make You smile.

Psalm 116

1   I love the LORD, because He hears
My voice and my supplications.
2   Because He has inclined His ear to me,
Therefore I shall call upon Him as long as I live.
3   The cords of death encompassed me
And the terrors of Sheol came upon me;
I found distress and sorrow.
4   Then I called upon the name of the LORD:
"O LORD, I beseech You, save my life!"

5   Gracious is the LORD, and righteous;
Yes, our God is compassionate.
6   The LORD preserves the simple;
I was brought low, and He saved me.
7   Return to your rest, O my soul,
For the LORD has dealt bountifully with you.
8   For You have rescued my soul from death,
My eyes from tears,
My feet from stumbling.
9   I shall walk before the LORD
In the land of the living.
10   I believed when I said,
"I am greatly afflicted."
11   I said in my alarm,
"All men are liars."

12   What shall I render to the LORD
For all His benefits toward me?
13   I shall lift up the cup of salvation
And call upon the name of the LORD.
14   I shall pay my vows to the LORD,
Oh may it be in the presence of all His people.
15   Precious in the sight of the LORD
Is the death of His godly ones.
16   O LORD, surely I am Your servant,
I am Your servant, the son of Your handmaid,
You have loosed my bonds.
17   To You I shall offer a sacrifice of thanksgiving,
And call upon the name of the LORD.
18   I shall pay my vows to the LORD,
Oh may it be in the presence of all His people,
19   In the courts of the LORD'S house,
In the midst of you, O Jerusalem.
Praise the LORD!

He's always there for me.

from PSALM 116

I love the Lord, because He listens to me. I can go and talk to Him any time, and He's always there for me.

He's always ready to listen to me. He even wants me to talk to Him. He wants to listen to me. The Lord Himself likes me to talk to Him!

When I pray and ask Him for something, He doesn't blow me off or forget my prayer, even if it's about something small or is just kinda dumb. Instead, a lot of times, He answers my prayers even better than I was hoping. He surprises me a lot how cool He is to me.

He sure has surprised me when I've been down. One time, I was way low. I thought my life would never be good again. But I called out to Him, and He rescued me and dried my tears and lifted me up. Yeah, He is compassionate and hears the crying of regular people like me.

Even when He doesn't answer the way I like, I know it's because He wants the best for me. Like I said, my prayers are dumb sometimes, and what I want isn't always the best. But He listens anyway.

Because He loves me and listens to me the way He does, I will love Him and serve Him. And I will pray and talk to Him for the rest of my life.

I can lean on Him. I can rest on Him. I know when things get tough, I can trust Him. He is always cool to me. He is always there for me -- even if I just need someone to talk to, someone to really listen to me.

from Psalm 116, verse 15
IN MEMORY OF YOUNG MARTYRS

I studied Psalm 116 and wrote on the final draft of the above piece the morning after seven people were killed in Fort Worth at a church rally celebrating See You at the Pole. The event made verse 15 more meaningful than ever to me: "Precious in the sight of the Lord is the death of His godly ones." And I wrote the first version of the following, which I posted on my web site (www.godknows99.com).

In memory of young martyrs.

On the night of Wednesday, September 15th, 1999, the See You at the Pole movement suffered its first martyrs.

At a rally celebrating See You at the Pole in Fort Worth, Texas at Wedgwood Baptist Church, a gunman wearing black and cursing Jesus burst into the meeting, opened fire with a semi-automatic handgun, and exploded a pipe bomb.

Not far from where the See You at the Pole movement was born, four teens and three adults died for their participation in that movement. Seven others were wounded.

Some may dismiss this tragic event as simply the random act of a deranged gunman. I do not. These deaths have meaning and purpose which one day, perhaps soon, shall be revealed. As I read the following morning, "Precious in the sight of the Lord is the death of His godly ones." (Psalm 116:15)

One meaning may be this being yet another wake-up call that it is no longer "safe" to be a Christian in America. In our complacency, we have thought that persecution and martyrdom is something that happens somewhere else at some other time. If that was ever so, it is so no longer.

Combined with the Columbine shootings and recent court rulings taking away religious freedoms, this event brings home that being a committed Christian anywhere is not risk-free. Whether from Christ-haters wearing black, arrogant judges robed in black, or simply those who's hearts are darkened, there are many with the power of government, or with the power of lies and hate, or even with the power of the gun who would take away your freedoms or even your life.

And Christian teenagers seem to be the main target. Teenagers who are committed to following Jesus are a threat to Satan. And some, including this writer, think the next awakening will start with the youth. So the followers of evil, empowered by Satan, are lashing out.

But who said being a Christian is supposed to be safe? We are to follow Christ, who suffered and died for God and for us. And Christians have been persecuted and martyred again and again through the centuries and today. We still have it easy compared to most. In Sudan, East Timor and elsewhere, claiming the name of Christ is a death sentence. In numerous other countries, it is illegal to be a Christian. Then in countries like China, you can be a Christian, but only if you are a meek member of a state-approved so-called "church". In comparison, most of us haven't come anywhere close to imprisonment or death for our Lord.

But persecution has come and is coming to American teenagers and those who labor with them. So how are we to respond? Are we to timidly keep our faith to ourselves and be closet Christians? Or are we to boldly live for Jesus and pray and tell everyone about Him, no matter who doesn't like it, no matter what the cost?

If we choose to be courageous for Christ, then the deaths of those in Fort Worth and at Columbine will not be in vain.

So with these young martyrs and with martyrs through the centuries, let us put our lives on the line for Jesus. Many have died for proclaiming this truth -- let us proclaim it also:

JESUS is LORD!

M. M., September 17th, 1999

Psalm 117

1   Praise the LORD, all nations;
    Laud Him, all peoples!
2   For His lovingkindness is great toward us,
    And the truth of the LORD is everlasting.
    Praise the LORD!

from PSALM 117
Hallelujah!
For God's love and faithfulness toward us is powerful. Nothing can stop it. And His truth lasts forever.
But this psalm doesn't. It is short -- really, really short.
Hallelujah!

also from PSALM 117
One thing about this psalm that is cool is the call for all nations and peoples to praise God. God loves the whole world, not just some holy clique. He desires people from every nation and background to come to Him. That includes skaters, posers,

bladers, thrashers, surfers, wahines, groms, bikers, rappers, headbangers, hackers, preps, punks, crusties, trends, trads, skins, goths, geeks, freaks, jocks, rednecks, cowboys, rude boys, rejects, mods, hippies, homies, core kids, metalheads, straight edge, ska-punks, nerds, and brains.

God's word and the good news about Jesus are for everyone. His kingdom will have all sorts of different people.

So ⟶ cliques, prejudice, or racism
among His people ⟶ are OUT!   M. M.

Psalm 118

1   Give thanks to the LORD, for He is good;
For His lovingkindness is everlasting.
2   Oh let Israel say,
"His lovingkindness is everlasting."
3   Oh let the house of Aaron say,
"His lovingkindness is everlasting."
4   Oh let those who fear the LORD say,
"His lovingkindness is everlasting."

5   From my distress I called upon the LORD;
The LORD answered me and set me in a large place.
6   The LORD is for me; I will not fear;
What can man do to me?
7   The LORD is for me among those who help me;
Therefore I will look with satisfaction on those who hate me.
8   It is better to take refuge in the LORD
Than to trust in man.
9   It is better to take refuge in the LORD
Than to trust in princes.

10   All nations surrounded me;
In the name of the LORD I will surely cut them off.
11   They surrounded me, yes, they surrounded me;
In the name of the LORD I will surely cut them off.
12   They surrounded me like bees;
They were extinguished as a fire of thorns;
In the name of the LORD I will surely cut them off.
13   You pushed me violently so that I was falling,
But the LORD helped me.
14   The LORD is my strength and song,
And He has become my salvation.
15   The sound of joyful shouting and salvation is in the tents of the righteous;
The right hand of the LORD does valiantly.
16   The right hand of the LORD is exalted;
The right hand of the LORD does valiantly.
17   I will not die, but live,
And tell of the works of the LORD.
18   The LORD has disciplined me severely,
But He has not given me over to death.

19   Open to me the gates of righteousness;
I shall enter through them, I shall give thanks to the LORD.
20   This is the gate of the LORD;
The righteous will enter through it.
21   I shall give thanks to You, for You have answered me,
And You have become my salvation.

22   The stone which the builders rejected
Has become the chief corner stone.
23   This is the LORD'S doing;
It is marvelous in our eyes.
24   This is the day which the LORD has made;
Let us rejoice and be glad in it.
25   O LORD, do save, we beseech You;
O LORD, we beseech You, do send prosperity!
26   Blessed is the one who comes in the name of the LORD;
We have blessed you from the house of the LORD.
27   The LORD is God, and He has given us light;
Bind the festival sacrifice with cords to the horns of the altar.
28   You are my God, and I give thanks to You;
You are my God, I extol You.
29   Give thanks to the LORD, for He is good;
For His lovingkindness is everlasting.

I got rejected again today.

from PSALM 118
especially verse 22
NOTE: Verse 22 prophesies the rejection and exaltation of the Messiah. It is quoted six times in the New Testament by Jesus and others.

I got rejected again today. Just like the other day, and the one before that. Oh well -- just another day.

Every day I face rejection, from the team I want to be on, from the cool crowd, from the friends I wish I had -- from the date I wish I had -- and on and on. It makes me dread things like try-outs and Homecoming. It makes me dread just going to school.

What's worse is when I get rejected at church, too.

It can get me down. But then I remember how rejected Jesus was.

He was rejected at the synagogues. The religious leaders hated Him. Nothing He did pleased them. Living a perfect life, doing miracles, healing people, teaching like nobody ever taught before -- nothing was good enough for them.

It wasn't only the leaders. Crowds tried to stone Him. One time he healed a seriously messed-up, demon-possessed guy and the people in the area asked Him to go away. You're welcome! Even most of His followers rejected Him, leaving Him when they didn't understand Him. Then even Peter rejected Him, denying he ever knew Jesus. A "friend" did me that way once.

As if all that wasn't enough rejection, He was arrested, tortured, and executed like He was some criminal.

Nobody's ever been rejected like Jesus.

But God didn't reject Him. Instead, God raised Him up and made Him the leader, the Lord of His church and the King of His kingdom. The Father has made Him the focus of what He is doing. Like a cornerstone that a building stands on, God is building His kingdom on the name of Jesus. People tried to throw Jesus away like a rock. Instead, He has become the Rock.

God didn't stop there. He takes the rejected, the ones leaders and cool cliques and even church people leave out, and He accepts them. He puts them on His team and uses them in what He is building. Those who others think are useless and uncool, God accepts them as cool with Him.

So, yeah, I'm rejected a lot. So was Jesus. And because I accept Jesus, God accepts me. Jesus accepts me. He knows what it's like to be rejected, and He'll never reject me. People may not let me into their little group; coaches may not want me on their teams. But Jesus wants me. He has put me on His team. And it's the only team that's guaranteed to win in the end. He doesn't stick me on the bench, either. He uses me and puts me in the game if I'm willing to read His Playbook, practice, and get ready.

So I'm rejected. So what? I'm accepted by the One who counts.

All right, did you really think was going to kill a lot of trees by printing Psalm 119? Nope, I'm going to make you lazy people get up, get your Bibles, and read that awesome, slightly long psalm in there. It might take a little while, by the way.

What are you waiting for? Come on. Up with you. Go get your Bibles. Now!

Speaking of the Word...

from PSALM 119

Lord, I am glad You've given us the Bible. It is so cool to have words from You. To open up the Bible and read Your word to me -- that's too wonderful. Digging into Your word is like digging into treasure that never tarnishes and never runs out. Your word is purer than pure and more perfect than perfect. I love it. And I can trust it completely.

For You are always faithful to keep Your word. When You make a promise in Your word, I know You'll do it. That's real good to know a lot of times, especially tough times. Your word and promises encourage me when I'm down. No matter how crazy things get, I can hold on to them and know You'll come through for me. Even when life is stormy, Your word gives me peace.

Oh Lord, Your word is very deep. So open my eyes and my mind to understand it. I don't want to miss a word of what You have to say to me.

Forgive me for those times when I take Your word for granted and blow it off. I don't understand why I'm that way. Your word is so awesome. It's awesome You've spoken to us at all.

And help me to not just read the word, but to do it. You keep Your word; help me to keep it also. Your word shines on me and inside me, showing me the ways I should change. Your word shines ahead, showing me how to live, showing me the way I should go. Help me to go that way. You know I need Your help.

Some people give me a hard time because I get into the word and try to live it. I don't care. I'm going to seek You and Your word no matter what. I'm going to live by Your word. Your ways are the best, no matter what anyone else thinks.

Oh Lord, I love Your word. No other book touches it. Nobody's words touch Your words. No way touches Your ways. I could go on and on about how awesome Your word is -- and the guy who wrote this psalm apparently did. Yet even what he wrote only begins to say how excellent You and Your word is. Thank you so much for giving Your word to me.

Psalm 120
A Song of Ascents.

1   In my trouble I cried to the LORD,
And He answered me.
2   Deliver my soul, O LORD, from lying lips,
From a deceitful tongue.
3   What shall be given to you, and what more shall be done to you,
You deceitful tongue?
4   Sharp arrows of the warrior,
With the burning coals of the broom tree.

5   Woe is me, for I sojourn in Meshech,
For I dwell among the tents of Kedar!
6   Too long has my soul had its dwelling
With those who hate peace.
7   I am for peace, but when I speak,
They are for war.

I wish I could be in a place where I belonged.

from PSALM 120

NOTE: Psalms 120 - 134 are the Psalms of Ascents. They were sung by those going up to Jerusalem for religious observances, especially Passover and Yom Kippur.

Since Jerusalem is on a hill, you literally had to go up to get there, one reason why these are called Psalms of Ascents.

When I'm in trouble, I turn to God and pray hard. And He answers me.

And it's a good thing. Because I'm in the middle of trouble again. Fact is, I'm in the middle of it practically every day -- my new school's a war zone for me. And the war doesn't stop when the bell rings either.

I just want to mind my own business and be cool. But, face it, I don't belong. I tried to fit in. Boy, did I try. It didn't do any good. I might as well be in a foreign, hostile land than to be at school. In fact, that's what school is for me. I don't belong there and never will. So now I try to be invisible, get through the day in one piece, and go home. It gets lonely. But that's all I hope for out of a school day anymore.

But a lot of guys there won't let me have even that, just because I'm different from them. Even though I don't cause trouble for anyone, they aren't interested in peace or in me staying in one piece. I tell them I don't want to cause any trouble. I am for peace, especially when I'm out-numbered and out-muscled. But when I try to talk to them, they use it as an excuse to trash me, threaten me, or beat me up some more. No matter how much I am for peace, they are for war.

I wish I could be in a place where I belonged.

Psalm 121
A Song of Ascents.

1   I will lift up my eyes to the mountains;
From where shall my help come?
2   My help comes from the LORD,
Who made heaven and earth.
3   He will not allow your foot to slip;
He who keeps you will not slumber.
4   Behold, He who keeps Israel
Will neither slumber nor sleep.

5   The LORD is your keeper;
The LORD is your shade on your right hand.
6   The sun will not smite you by day,
Nor the moon by night.
7   The LORD will protect you from all evil;
He will keep your soul.
8   The LORD will guard your going out and your coming in
From this time forth and forever.

from PSALM 121

I will look up. For who helps me out? God does.

He created heaven and earth. He's way more than powerful enough to give me all the help I need. He is love. He cares enough to care about me.

For starters, He watches my steps. He looks out for me. And with all the accidents and near-accidents I've had, it's a good thing. He must be really alert to watch out for me and keep me in one piece, what with all the crazy stuff I get into -- like that time I jumped into a swimming pool from a tree. But God never sleeps or even takes a nap. I don't have to worry about Him ever saying, "Oops, sorry you got hurt. I didn't see that in time. Without my caffeine and sugar, I get sleepy-eyed. Sorry." Sometimes, I don't watch where I'm going or know what's coming, but God always does.

And He always will.

I know stuff happens I wish wouldn't happen. But God will protect me and bring me through it, even if it's a broken leg like last summer -- or a broken heart like last month. He'll protect me and be there beside me all my life, and beyond. And I know if He allows anything bad, it's to bring good out of it and to help me trust Him.

And I can trust Him. I don't have to fear. I can go out and live. Because He will watch out for me -- now and forever.

Psalm 122
A Song of Ascents, of David.

1   I was glad when they said to me,
"Let us go to the house of the LORD."
2   Our feet are standing
Within your gates, O Jerusalem,
3   Jerusalem, that is built
As a city that is compact together;
4   To which the tribes go up, even the tribes of the LORD—
An ordinance for Israel—
To give thanks to the name of the LORD.
5   For there thrones were set for judgment,
The thrones of the house of David.

6   Pray for the peace of Jerusalem:
"May they prosper who love you.
7   "May peace be within your walls,
And prosperity within your palaces."
8   For the sake of my brothers and my friends,
I will now say, "May peace be within you."
9   For the sake of the house of the LORD our God,
I will seek your good.

It's cool caring about something bigger than me.

from PSALM 122

I'm glad when Sunday comes around, and it's time to go to church. My parents used to have to drag me out of bed on Sunday mornings. And church was so boring to me. I slept through half of it a lot of times.

Not anymore. Heck, one morning I shocked my parents by going to church on a Sunday they weren't going.

I guess I'm not totally into myself like I was, practically seeing myself as the center of the universe. Now I know how much I need God. God and faith in Him isn't just a bunch of religion to me anymore. It's reality. It's reality I need to make my life right.

I appreciate more the things He does for me, especially what Jesus did for me. So I want to take time out to thank Him.

And I like hanging with my friends at the youth group. It's more than hanging with friends, though. Having God in common, ...

WORSHIPING HIM

......together, and serving Him and others together gives us a bond that's more than just another friendship. We're real brothers and sisters. There's a real connection there -- I guess God's Spirit connects us.

It's cool caring about something bigger than me. Sometimes, I can almost feel it changing me, like on that mission trip last summer. I've found out nothing beats being a part of what God is doing.

My church used to be a big boring brick building to me. Not anymore. It is being a part of what God is doing with His people, including me.

I still get a little bored during some of the sermons -- my attention span has it's limits. But now I feel if I miss church, I'm missing out -- and I would be.

Psalm 123
A Song of Ascents.

1   To You I lift up my eyes,
  O You who are enthroned in the heavens!
2   Behold, as the eyes of servants look to the hand of their master,
  As the eyes of a maid to the hand of her mistress,

  So our eyes look to the LORD our God,
  Until He is gracious to us.
3   Be gracious to us, O LORD, be gracious to us,
  For we are greatly filled with contempt.
4   Our soul is greatly filled
  With the scoffing of those who are at ease,
  And with the contempt of the proud.

from PSALM 123

Lord, I look up to You and pray. For You are King. You're in control of everything. You have the power to answer my prayer and all the trillion prayers of Your people. I'm praying because I know everything good I have in my life comes from You. You're my Master and Provider. I look to You to guide me and take care of me. You've been good to me in the past, and I'm confident You'll be good to me in the future. I don't deserve Your goodness, but I need it. I'll look to You and pray as long as it takes.

Right now I'm praying about being put down all the time. I've had my fill of it. I know being put down is part of life. Even You have had all sorts of lies told about You. So You know how it is for me, having trash talked about me all the time. It's coming from egotistic jerks who build themselves up by putting others down.

I've got to be honest -- when things get bad like this, it's hard for me to really trust You, Lord. I get afraid You're not going to answer my prayers and come through for me. Because I can see my problems all too well. But I can't see how or when you're going to solve them. I know that's where my faith should come in, to trust in You, Your goodness, and Your timing even when I can't see You and have no idea what You're doing, but...it's not easy.

But even if my faith is weak, I know it's in the right One. So I'm going to keep on trusting You. Lord, would You help me out again? Not because I deserve it -- but because of who You are. You are faithful even when our faith is weak. You are good to those who don't deserve it, but humbly ask anyway. You are good to me. Please stretch Your strong hand down and lift me up.

Psalm 124
A Song of Ascents, of David.

1   "Had it not been the LORD who was on our side,"
Let Israel now say,
2   "Had it not been the LORD who was on our side
When men rose up against us,
3   Then they would have swallowed us alive,
When their anger was kindled against us;
4   Then the waters would have engulfed us,
The stream would have swept over our soul;
5   Then the raging waters would have swept over our soul."

6   Blessed be the LORD,
Who has not given us to be torn by their teeth.
7   Our soul has escaped as a bird out of the snare of the trapper;
The snare is broken and we have escaped.
8   Our help is in the name of the LORD,
Who made heaven and earth.

I'm free forever.

from PSALM 124

If God had not been on my side -- oh, man! If God had not been on my side when things were bad, I don't even want to think about what would have happened. I would have been taken down. The troubled waters of my life would have surrounded me, overwhelmed me, and swept me away. I would have been trapped in currents too powerful for me. The raging dark waters would have pulled me down and rushed over me. I would have drowned, helpless under the flood surging over me.

But I wasn't helpless -- because the Lord is my help. The Lord, who has the power to create heaven and earth, has the power to help me and bring me through anything. And He pulled me out of the dark waters. I thought I was trapped in darkness, but He set me free.

Thank God!

I used to not think much about the freedom God gives me. Not anymore. Life and freedom tastes better than ever now. And now I won't forget where it comes from.

And nobody, especially not Satan, will ever be able to trap me and imprison my soul. I'm free forever. For the Lord is on my side. He is the One who frees me. And if He frees me, then I'm free!

Psalm 125
A Song of Ascents.

1   Those who trust in the LORD
Are as Mount Zion, which cannot be moved but abides forever.
2   As the mountains surround Jerusalem,
So the LORD surrounds His people
From this time forth and forever.
3   For the scepter of wickedness shall not rest upon the land of the right-
eous,
So that the righteous will not put forth their hands to do wrong.

4   Do good, O LORD, to those who are good
And to those who are upright in their hearts.
5   But as for those who turn aside to their crooked ways,
The LORD will lead them away with the doers of iniquity.
Peace be upon Israel.

from PSALM 125

I trust Jesus now.

Now I have peace and security -- peace I didn't have before. I used to be real insecure about who I was. And I was nervous about the future -- when I wasn't dreading the present. But now I'm confident. I'm confident in God. I'm confident about the future because He's in control of it and has a great one for me. I'm confident in who I am because of God's work on me.

Trusting in Jesus has changed my life. I have Someone strong to hold onto who will always hold onto me. He's always right there for me. That gives me a peace and stability that wasn't there before.

I know there will be hassles and hard times that will try to get me down. God is stronger than any of them. He'll bring me through them.

God surrounds me. Jesus puts His strong arms of love around me. In His arms, I have peace -- forever.

Evil may take shots at me. But the Lord guards me. Evil will not rule over me. And I will never give in to it. For only God rules.

I trust in the Lord. I cannot be moved away from Him. I will stick with God, and nothing can get to me. Because God surrounds me. And nothing is stronger than God.

I will trust in Him forever. I will have peace in Him forever. I will live with Him forever.

Psalm 126
A Song of Ascents.

1   When the LORD brought back the captive ones of Zion,
We were like those who dream.
2   Then our mouth was filled with laughter
And our tongue with joyful shouting;
Then they said among the nations,
"The LORD has done great things for them."
3   The LORD has done great things for us;
We are glad.

4   Restore our captivity, O LORD,
As the streams in the South.
5   Those who sow in tears shall reap with joyful shouting.
6   He who goes to and fro weeping, carrying his bag of seed,
Shall indeed come again with a shout of joy, bringing his sheaves with
him.

from PSALM 126

One of the amazing things about God is how in history and in people's lives He takes situations that are the worst and does things with them that are the best. I know. I'm like the guy who wrote this psalm -- God has done things in down times in my life, things that were so awesome, it felt like a dream. In the middle of my worst times, I've seen God do such incredible things it made me laugh and it took a while to sink in that it was for real. God knows how to come out of nowhere to turn my head around and turn my grief into joy.

What happened for the guy who wrote this psalm is the nation of Israel had been taken away from their land and exiled for seventy years. So for most or all of his life, he had not seen his homeland. Then God acts, and, suddenly, he gets to go home! His dream comes true. (If you want to read about it, check out the book of Ezra.)

I've probably said this before, but it's worth saying again -- God's light shines brightest in the darkness. God shows His greatness best in times that are the worst -- even in situations that seem hopeless. The disciples felt hopeless after Jesus was crucified. Yet out of Jesus's death came His resurrection and salvation for hundreds of millions. In modern history, perhaps no time was darker than the Holocaust. Who would have thought any good could come out of such terrible suffering and death. Yet afterwards, the nation of Israel was restored to their land even though they had been exiled for centuries.

And it works that way in the lives of His people today. I know it has in mine. God brings awesome things out of awful times. When He does that, it makes you wanna shout, "The Lord has done great things for me!"

So what should we do when those awful times come around? Should we give up and lose hope? No! Like in verses five and six, we keep on being faithful to God and others. We keep on doing our best. We keep on living out the Word and spreading it like seed. We keep on keeping on.

And you might feel like crying. And wondering when God is going to finally act might drive you crazy. But you stick with God, and He will do things that will amaze you and turn your tears of sadness into shouts of joy. You be faithful during those times when you wonder, "What's the use?" And you'll see for yourself the great things God will do with your life.

M. M.

I'm not satisfied with ordinary life.

also from PSALM 126

I'm not satisfied with ordinary life.

My family and friends call me a dreamer. That's O.K. 'Cause I am one. A lot of times, when I'm laying back in my room or bored in class, I dream about what my life could be.

But I also scheme how to make it that way. I dream about life, but I don't want to just dream it. I want to live it.

I can get pretty excited about life. I love it when things happen that make me laugh or even make me feel like I'm living a dream, especially when God makes it happen. God is cool; sometimes it seems He makes things happen that has me laughing all the time. Some say I laugh too much and that I'm an excitable kid. I don't care. I know God wants life to be exciting and full, even with it's down times.

Yeah, I have my down times, too. Because ordinary life can get old and be a downer. Once I've got a taste of God's best, I don't want to settle for anything less.

And maybe I'm hurting and crying a bit when those times come. But I keep walking and talking with God. I keep striving to make the most of my life. 'Cause I know He'll take my tears and hurting, and He'll take my striving and use it. He'll make me wanna shout!

I know some think I'll get over it, that I'll be satisfied with regular life like other people when I'm older. Maybe they're right.

Maybe I'll be just another boring adult.

Not. I'll never be that way. I'm gonna keep laughing. I'm gonna keep dreaming and scheming. I'm going to keep looking to really live this awesome life God has for me.

Psalm 127
A Song of Ascents, of Solomon.

1   Unless the LORD builds the house,
They labor in vain who build it;
Unless the LORD guards the city,
The watchman keeps awake in vain.
2   It is vain for you to rise up early,
To retire late,
To eat the bread of painful labors;
For He gives to His beloved even in his sleep.

3   Behold, children are a gift of the LORD,
The fruit of the womb is a reward.
4   Like arrows in the hand of a warrior,
So are the children of one's youth.
5   How blessed is the man whose quiver is full of them;
They will not be ashamed
When they speak with their enemies in the gate.

from PSALM 127

Unless the Lord is with me and helps me, anything I do is useless. Unless the Lord protects me, a whole gang as my bodyguard isn't going to be enough.

I used to try to live and do everything my way, with my great wisdom and power. I thought I knew it all and didn't need any help. Well, I found out. I messed up all the time. When I tried to make things better, they got worse. And when I finally did something half-way right, I didn't get much satisfaction out of it.

So from now on, I'm doing things with God. I want Him to be the boss, not me. The more He's the one running things, the better. And the more He's the one working through me, the better. Because the only thing I can do better than God is screw up.

So I'm going to pray for His guidance and help every day. When He says in the Bible to do something, I'm going to do my best to do it with His help. Instead of thinking about just what I want to do, I'm going to think about what would Jesus do. I'm going to rely on Him instead of on just myself.

To get things done right, I need Him. To live right, I need Him.

While I'm at it, I've got to show my parents this psalm. The hours they work are way too long, so they need to read verse two.

And when they hassle me for sleeping in, I can tell them, "The Lord gives to His beloved in his sleep."

And when they're steamed at me and about to go postal, I can remind them that "children are a gift of the Lord."

I'm sure they would appreciate that.

Psalm 128
A Song of Ascents.

1   How blessed is everyone who fears the LORD,
Who walks in His ways.
2   When you shall eat of the fruit of your hands,
You will be happy and it will be well with you.
3   Your wife shall be like a fruitful vine
Within your house,
Your children like olive plants
Around your table.
4   Behold, for thus shall the man be blessed
Who fears the LORD.

5   The LORD bless you from Zion,
And may you see the prosperity of Jerusalem all the days of your life.
6   Indeed, may you see your children's children.
Peace be upon Israel!

His ways really are the best.

from PSALM 128
(NOTE: If you are "like olive plants," that is not a curse. It does not mean you get oily skin.)

I used to think God gave us commandments and told us how to live because He's bossy, or likes being a big cop, or He's a celestial killjoy. Or all of the above. I think different now.

I see and hear about others who are having fun doing things they shouldn't be doing. I have to admit I wish I were them sometimes. But I notice a lot of times, their wrong comes back to them. I hear people talk quietly about the big trouble this guy or that girl got themselves in.

I admit sometimes I've been the one who's doing what I shouldn't be doing. Maybe it's fun, or at least I think so at the time. That's when I don't get busted or worse. I don't want to talk about "worse."

But lately I've been doing more things God's way, especially things for others like helping with little kids at my church, and helping build a house for a poor family. I've noticed the happiness I get from doing things like that is deeper and lasts longer than the jollies I get from the not-so-good things. Like this past summer, I went on a mission trip, and it was the time of my life. Thinking about it still makes me smile.

And in everyday stuff, I'm getting better, like just treating people right. It makes me feel cool to build someone up, even make their day, instead of putting them down. Some days, it makes my day.

I'm doing better about not doing the not-so-good things, too. Besides, I've noticed they can get boring real quick. And who needs the hassles and the worries they cause? Who needs getting grounded for weeks? Or worse? Dumb jollies fade fast; bad consequences don't.

I'm finding out the best happiness really does come from living life God's way. He didn't give us commandments and guidance to take away our joy. He gave them to give us joy, and to protect us from harm or worries that would take it away.

His ways really are the best. His ways give real happiness that lasts.

Psalm 129
A Song of Ascents.

1 "Many times they have persecuted me from my youth up,"
   Let Israel now say,
2 "Many times they have persecuted me from my youth up;
   Yet they have not prevailed against me.
3 "The plowers plowed upon my back;
   They lengthened their furrows."
4 The LORD is righteous;
   He has cut in two the cords of the wicked.

5 May all who hate Zion
   Be put to shame and turned backward;
6 Let them be like grass upon the housetops,
   Which withers before it grows up;
7 With which the reaper does not fill his hand,
   Or the binder of sheaves his bosom;
8 Nor do those who pass by say,
   "The blessing of the LORD be upon you;
   We bless you in the name of the LORD."

from PSALM 129

People get on me all the time. Sometimes it's because of my faith. Sometimes it's because of my background, where I come from, and my ethnicity. Sometimes it's just because I'm different. And maybe some are jealous, I don't know. Whatever it is, people are always on me, trying to make my life miserable.

But they won't win.

Yeah, they might hassle me a lot. They might even beat me up bad. But they won't win. Because the Lord will stop them. The Lord and His people win in the end.

What I go through is nothing compared to what Israel has gone through. The Jewish people have been attacked many times through history. Evil men, from Pharaoh to Haman to Hitler, have tried to wipe them out. At times, it was because of Israel's faith. Often, it was because of their background, their ethnicity. Other times, it was because they were different, worshipping one God and not being like the polytheist peoples around them. And there's been jealousy of what they have, especially their land.

Then there's the fact that Satan simply hates Israel. Jewish people are God's people, and the Messiah comes from them. Satan hates them for that. And as long as he can, he will inspire evil men to hate them.

But Satan and the scum allied with him will all lose. They may all go down into the lake of fire still hating Israel. But they **will** all go down into the lake of fire.

And Israel will still be around.

If God can bring the people of Israel through all they've suffered, and if He can stop all the evil men and powers through history that have tried to do them in, then God can certainly bring me through any trouble evil throws at me.

And He will bring me through.

PRAYER AND FORGIVENESS

The next psalm is one of the many places in the Bible that links prayer and forgiveness together. The psalmist realizes if God holds his sins against him, he doesn't have much hope of having his prayers answered. The one who wrote Psalm 66 also realized unforgiven sin can kill a prayer before it gets past the ceiling. (Psalm 66:18)

But -- good news! -- God does forgive. Anyone who sincerely comes to Jesus, trusting in Him and asking for forgiveness, Jesus will forgive and never reject. (John 6:37) He'll forgive you and accept you -- and listen to you -- when you put your trust in Him and pray.

That annoys some self-righteous people who think God ought to listen only to their prayers, kinda like Jonah was ticked when God listened to the prayers of the super-evil Ninevites. (Jonah chapters 3 and 4) And it really ticks off Satan, who wants everyone to join him in hell. But if you know you're a praying sinner who needs God's forgiveness (like me), it's great news!

And once you're forgiven, not only can you pray with confidence, even boldness (Psalm 66:19-20; Hebrews 4:16), Jesus also prays for you! You heard me right. Check out Hebrews 7:25 and 9:24 near the back of the New Testament and also Romans 8:34. If you've trusted in Jesus, He intercedes --prays -- for you. I can't think of anyone better I want praying for me!

There's a lot more, because the Bible says a lot about how forgiveness and prayer go together. For now, remember: Nothing can stifle prayer like unforgiven sin. But nothing can unleash prayer like trusting in Jesus and receiving His forgiveness.

M. M.

Psalm 130
A Song of Ascents.

1   Out of the depths I have cried to You, O LORD.
2   Lord, hear my voice!
Let Your ears be attentive
To the voice of my supplications.
3   If You, LORD, should mark iniquities,
O Lord, who could stand?
4   But there is forgiveness with You,
That You may be feared.

5   I wait for the LORD, my soul does wait,
And in His word do I hope.
6   My soul waits for the Lord
More than the watchmen for the morning;
Indeed, more than the watchmen for the morning.
7   O Israel, hope in the LORD;
For with the LORD there is lovingkindness,
And with Him is abundant redemption.
8   And He will redeem Israel
From all his iniquities.

I wait here in the dark – waiting for Your light . . .

from PSALM 130

Out of my dark depths, out of this long night, I've prayed hard to You, Lord. Please hear my voice. Please listen and hear my prayers.

I know I've committed darkness, and I don't deserve for You to answer my prayers. If you were to put a mark down against us for every sin we did, who could stand and survive to pray before You for even a minute? I sure couldn't.

But You don't hold my wrong against me. You've forgiven me. Because Jesus died for me and now stands for me before You.

He even brings prayers for me before You.

So Lord, please hear those prayers. Please hear my prayers. I wait and look for You to answer. I hope in You and in Your promises. I wait for You. For You are my only hope.

I wait here in the dark -- waiting for Your light to break through. I wait for You to turn my long night into morning.

And though I can see no light now, I do hope in You. For I know Your light is coming. Because with You, there is massive love, power, and forgiveness.

And You do love me. You do forgive me.

With the power of Your love, You will bring me out of my darkness. You will fill my life with Your light.

Psalm 131
A Song of Ascents, of David.

1   O LORD, my heart is not proud, nor my eyes haughty;
Nor do I involve myself in great matters,
Or in things too difficult for me.
2   Surely I have composed and quieted my soul;
Like a weaned child rests against his mother,
My soul is like a weaned child within me.
3   O Israel, hope in the LORD
From this time forth and forever.

No I'm not mad but I think they forget What It's Like and How Hard It Is to be a Teenager

MxPx "Teenage Politics"

from PSALM 131

Lord, sometimes the world is too crazy. Life gets too complicated for me, and I'm not too proud to know it. I wish I didn't have to deal with things too difficult for me -- like certain relationships and math, for starters. But I know life isn't easy and will just get more complicated as I get older and go out into the real world.

I like being a teenager, and I want to get older. But sometimes, I just want life to be simple and free again. Part of me wishes I could just be a kid.

When it gets too much for me, all I want to do is go to my room and shut out the world.

A lot of times when I'm on my bed, I pray and think about You. Doing that for a while gets me real quiet and a little sleepy -- and it feels like I'm lying against You. Like a child lying against a parent, I'm there resting sleepily against You.

I am Your child. I lean on You for rest, protection, and love. I am Your child, no matter how crazy things get. And I always will be. For You will always be my Father. Forever, You will be there for me. I can run to You. You are my peace in an unpeaceful world.

I am Your child. I trust You and rest on You.

Psalm 132

A Song of Ascents.

1   Remember, O LORD, on David's behalf,
All his affliction;
2   How he swore to the LORD
And vowed to the Mighty One of Jacob,
3   "Surely I will not enter my house,
Nor lie on my bed;
4   I will not give sleep to my eyes
Or slumber to my eyelids,
5   Until I find a place for the LORD,
A dwelling place for the Mighty One of Jacob."

6   Behold, we heard of it in Ephrathah,
We found it in the field of Jaar.
7   Let us go into His dwelling place;
Let us worship at His footstool.
8   Arise, O LORD, to Your resting place,
You and the ark of Your strength.
9   Let Your priests be clothed with righteousness,
And let Your godly ones sing for joy.

10   For the sake of David Your servant,
Do not turn away the face of Your anointed.
11   The LORD has sworn to David
A truth from which He will not turn back:
"Of the fruit of your body I will set upon your throne.
12   "If your sons will keep My covenant
And My testimony which I will teach them,
Their sons also shall sit upon your throne forever."

13   For the LORD has chosen Zion;
He has desired it for His habitation.
14   "This is My resting place forever;
Here I will dwell, for I have desired it.
15   "I will abundantly bless her provision;
I will satisfy her needy with bread.
16   "Her priests also I will clothe with salvation,
And her godly ones will sing aloud for joy.
17   "There I will cause the horn of David to spring forth;
I have prepared a lamp for Mine anointed.
18   "His enemies I will clothe with shame,
But upon himself his crown shall shine."

from PSALMS 131 and 132

One of the cool things about David -- and definitely one of the coolest things in God's eyes -- was his humility. David wrote Psalm 131, and it shows what a humble heart he had.

David also showed his humility by how he put God first, and Psalm 132 talks some about that. Saul, the self-centered king before David, tried to use God by bringing the Ark of the Covenant into battle. He lost the battle and the Ark. David exalted God by bringing the Ark back into Jerusalem. And when he did that, he didn't dress in kingly apparel or the latest designer fashions. He didn't sit on a fancy throne or in a Corvette. Instead, he humbled himself before God and before the people by dressing simply and dancing before the ark with all his might. In fact, one of his wives thought he should have acted more kingly and gave him a hard time about it afterwards. David responded, "Too bad! I will be humble and celebrate the Lord." (2 Samuel 6)

David kept putting God first by seeking to build a temple for Him. (verses 1 - 5) And when God said He appreciated the thought but David's son Solomon would build it instead, David didn't pout about it. Instead, he was thankful. (2 Samuel 7) And later he decided to take on the relatively humble task of gathering the materials needed to build the temple.

How did the Lord remember David? How did God respond to his humility? He exalted him and made him great. (verses 11, 12, 17, 18)

It still works that way today. The way to become truly great is not to seek to become big stuff. The way to real greatness is to humble yourself before God. Check out 1 Peter 5: 5, 6, Luke 9: 46 - 48, and Luke 14 : 7 - 11.

M. M.

Psalm 133
A Song of Ascents, of David.

1   Behold, how good and how pleasant it is
For brothers to dwell together in unity!
2   It is like the precious oil upon the head,
Coming down upon the beard,
Even Aaron's beard,
Coming down upon the edge of his robes.
3   It is like the dew of Hermon
Coming down upon the mountains of Zion;
For there the LORD commanded the blessing—life forever.

from PSALM 133

My close friends are cool. They're like brothers and sisters. They are great to hang with. I like doing everything with them. I like doing nothing with them. And we can talk about everything and nothing all night -- which seriously annoys my parents when I'm on the phone.

When I need to talk, they're there for me. And I can talk to them about anything.

What's the best is the oneness we have. We're relaxed and completely ourselves with each other. The barriers there are with most people aren't there with us. A lot of times we even know what the other's thinking, and we're thinking the same thing, before we even say it. And we stick with each other, no matter how stupid one of us might get.

God is the one who made us one. His Spirit in each other makes us one. When we talk about Him, we're on the same wavelength. We encourage each other to keep running with Him. And that keeps us fresh. It helps keep us pure and real. It's like a still, chilly morning after a long night, with the sun reflecting off the dew, when the air is pure and you can see forever. We help each other see life more clearly. We help each other wake up fresh and see things as they really are.

When I think about it, God has given us close friends to help us really live. Like a land without dew or rain, life would get awfully dry without them. And the dust would obscure the way to go.

But instead God has given me life and friends that are forever.

I take my best friends for granted sometimes, but they really are the best.

Now if only my little brother were that cool. He's more like oily hair you can't get rid of.

Psalm 134
A Song of Ascents.

1 Behold, bless the LORD, all servants of the LORD,
Who serve by night in the house of the LORD!
2 Lift up your hands to the sanctuary
And bless the LORD.
3 May the LORD bless you from Zion,
He who made heaven and earth.

from PSALM 134

This is a short psalm about some obscure people, those who had the night shift in the temple. In this psalm, the religious pilgrims who are getting ready to leave Jerusalem to go back home encourage the temple's night workers and watchmen to serve God and worship Him in their work.

Like I said, these night shift workers are really obscure. They don't get a lot of attention. You probably have never heard any talks on them. If you used to have a children's Bible, I bet you there wasn't any pictures of them in it. And if you weren't reading this, you'd probably just zip right through Psalm 134 -- be honest. And you might be wondering why I'm writing more than a couple of sentences on these night shift people.

But these people are important to God. He values their work. He's even made them and their work the subject of this short, yet important psalm. This is the last Psalm of Ascents, the last of the ones sung during pilgrimages to Jerusalem.

The Bible is full of people few know or appreciate. But God appreciates them. Check out all the people with funny names in Romans 16, for starters. In His word, God honors and remembers a lot of people others forget.

Do you ever feel forgotten? Do you ever feel you and the things you do don't get any recognition or appreciation? Do you ever feel like another face in the crowd that nobody knows? Well, God knows you. And He won't forget you.

And if you're serving God by working in the church nursery, or by visiting the elderly, or by mowing a lawn for free, or by just being nice to people at work as you scoop their ice cream or bag their groceries or sell them a movie ticket, God knows about it. And He'll remember and appreciate it -- even if nobody else does.

He'll remember you.

M. M.

Psalm 135

1   Praise the LORD! Praise the name of the LORD;
Praise Him, O servants of the LORD,
2   You who stand in the house of the LORD,
In the courts of the house of our God!

3   Praise the LORD, for the LORD is good;
Sing praises to His name, for it is lovely.
4   For the LORD has chosen Jacob for Himself,
Israel for His own possession.

5   For I know that the LORD is great
And that our Lord is above all gods.
6   Whatever the LORD pleases, He does,
In heaven and in earth, in the seas and in all deeps.
7   He causes the vapors to ascend from the ends of the earth;
Who makes lightnings for the rain,
Who brings forth the wind from His treasuries.

8   He smote the firstborn of Egypt, Both of man and beast.
9   He sent signs and wonders into your midst, O Egypt,
Upon Pharaoh and all his servants.
10   He smote many nations
And slew mighty kings,
11   Sihon, king of the Amorites, And Og, king of Bashan,
And all the kingdoms of Canaan;
12   And He gave their land as a heritage,
A heritage to Israel His people.
13   Your name, O LORD, is everlasting,
Your remembrance, O LORD, throughout all generations.
14   For the LORD will judge His people
And will have compassion on His servants.
15   The idols of the nations are but silver and gold,
The work of man's hands.
16   They have mouths, but they do not speak;
They have eyes, but they do not see;
17   They have ears, but they do not hear,
Nor is there any breath at all in their mouths.
18   Those who make them will be like them,
Yes, everyone who trusts in them.

19   O house of Israel, bless the LORD;
O house of Aaron, bless the LORD;
20   O house of Levi, bless the LORD;
You who revere the LORD, bless the LORD.
21   Blessed be the LORD from Zion,
Who dwells in Jerusalem.
Praise the LORD!

God is God.

from PSALM 135

I'm going to praise the Lord. I love His name. For I know He is the greatest. I know He is far above any so-called gods.

The Lord does whatever He pleases. He creates storms that can literally blow you away. Way back, He wanted to create the universe. So He just said it, and, boom, there it is. When He wanted to create man, He just took some dust and made him. Later, when He wanted to take Israel out of Egypt, He sent weird plagues until Pharaoh gave in. The fool Pharaoh changed his mind anyway and came after them. But so what? God decided to split the Red Sea to rescue the people of Israel from Pharaoh's army, no problem. When He decided to let the water fall back to snuff out Pharaoh's army, no problem with that either.

Got the picture yet? God does whatever He wants, whenever He wants, wherever He wants. And He does it well. So deal with it.

I don't get people who say they believe in God, but have a problem with Him actually doing anything. They need to get a grip. God is God. God does whatever He wants. What's the problem with that?

Yet people don't have any problem worshipping weak gods. They worship dead people, like Buddha or Elvis. Or they worship images or statues. Or they worship money.

Those fools will become like what they worship. Those who worship Buddha or other dead people will be dead like them. Those who worship statues will end up stiff like them. Those who worship money might end up with a lot of money, but not much of a life. And when they die, they'll be lifeless like money, but not rich anymore.

I'm going to worship the Real Thing, thank you. And I'm going to live forever, like Him.

God's greatness is forever. His name, who He is, is awesome and beautiful. His name will always be awesome.

He and nothing else gets my worship.

Psalm 136

1   Give thanks to the LORD, for He is good,
For His lovingkindness is everlasting.
2   Give thanks to the God of gods,
For His lovingkindness is everlasting.
3   Give thanks to the Lord of lords,
For His lovingkindness is everlasting.
4   To Him who alone does great wonders,
For His lovingkindness is everlasting;
5   To Him who made the heavens with skill,
For His lovingkindness is everlasting;
6   To Him who spread out the earth above the waters,
For His lovingkindness is everlasting;
7   To Him who made the great lights,
For His lovingkindness is everlasting:
8   The sun to rule by day,
For His lovingkindness is everlasting,
9   The moon and stars to rule by night,
For His lovingkindness is everlasting.

10   To Him who smote the Egyptians in their firstborn,
For His lovingkindness is everlasting,
11   And brought Israel out from their midst,
For His lovingkindness is everlasting,
12   With a strong hand and an outstretched arm,
For His lovingkindness is everlasting.
13   To Him who divided the Red Sea asunder,
For His lovingkindness is everlasting,
14   And made Israel pass through the midst of it,
For His lovingkindness is everlasting;
15   But He overthrew Pharaoh and his army in the Red Sea,
For His lovingkindness is everlasting.
16   To Him who led His people through the wilderness,
For His lovingkindness is everlasting;
17   To Him who smote great kings,
For His lovingkindness is everlasting,
18   And slew mighty kings,
For His lovingkindness is everlasting:
19   Sihon, king of the Amorites,
For His lovingkindness is everlasting,
20   And Og, king of Bashan,
For His lovingkindness is everlasting,
21   And gave their land as a heritage,
For His lovingkindness is everlasting,
22   Even a heritage to Israel His servant,
For His lovingkindness is everlasting.

23   Who remembered us in our low estate,
    For His lovingkindness is everlasting,
24   And has rescued us from our adversaries,
    For His lovingkindness is everlasting;
25   Who gives food to all flesh,
    For His lovingkindness is everlasting.
26   Give thanks to the God of heaven,
    For His lovingkindness is everlasting.

from PSALM 136

God's everlasting lovingkindness is better than the best.

I know what you're thinking -- "It had better be for the guy who wrote this psalm to repeat the same thing 26 times."

There are reasons for that. First, the psalms are songs. And songs often repeat themselves. You can probably think of recent songs doing that.

More importantly, the excellence of God's lovingkindness is worth repeating.

Remember that "lovingkindness" roughly means "faithful love." And the faithfulness of God's love toward us is amazing. He loved us long before we were born and will love us long after we die. He keeps loving us even though He knew long ago every bad thing we have done or will ever do. He's faithful to us in spite of all the times we've dissed Him. His awesome love toward us is everlasting -- it never wears out no matter how much time passes and no matter how much stupidity we do that would wear out anyone else's love. He's faithful in His love toward us, who don't deserve it, even when we're not faithful toward Him, who does deserve it. From the beginning, to creating an earth where we can live and enjoy life, to creating us, forgiving us, and providing for us, to coming back for us in the future, to bringing in a perfect new Heaven and Earth, to eternity, He loves us.

And as if that weren't enough, His love toward us is so faithful and strong He endured crucifixion and died for us.

Nobody else has loved us like that. And nobody ever will.

And that's worth repeating.

M. M.

Psalm 137

1   By the rivers of Babylon,
      There we sat down and wept,
      When we remembered Zion.
2   Upon the willows in the midst of it
      We hung our harps.
3   For there our captors demanded of us songs,
      And our tormentors mirth, saying,
      "Sing us one of the songs of Zion."

4   How can we sing the LORD'S song
      In a foreign land?
5   If I forget you, O Jerusalem,
      May my right hand forget her skill.
6   May my tongue cling to the roof of my mouth
      If I do not remember you,
      If I do not exalt Jerusalem
      Above my chief joy.

7   Remember, O LORD, against the sons of Edom
      The day of Jerusalem,
      Who said, "Raze it, raze it
      To its very foundation."
8   O daughter of Babylon, you devastated one,
      How blessed will be the one who repays you
      With the recompense with which you have repaid us.
9   How blessed will be the one who seizes and dashes your little ones
      Against the rock.

from PSALM 137

NOTE: The last verse of this psalm troubles people, so let's deal with it.

The last two verses look forward to Babylon experiencing the same brutal defeat they inflicted on the Jews. (See 2 Kings 25: 6-7 for a sample of the Babylonians' brutality.) So what the end of this psalm is about isn't baby hatred; it is a desire for payback, that Babylon suffer what they inflicted on Israel, a devastating brutal military defeat.

A frequent message of the Bible is sin has consequences. No one can commit the evil the kings and armies of Babylon did and get away with it forever. Babylon eventually was crushed by the Persian Empire. And, yes, innocent people, including babies, suffered when Babylon got theirs. Sin often causes innocent people to suffer -- something to consider when you're tempted to do wrong.

And remember, the psalms are an honest, accurate record of men's thoughts, emotions and prayers before God. Being an honest record, not every thought portrayed is going to be excellent and pure. God's word is perfect and reliable. Men are not, including men portrayed in God's word.

Why did we have to move?

My parents try to cheer me up. They try to make me happy. I know they're tired of seeing me down. It's like they're trying to al-most force me to be happy. But it just makes things worse.

How can I be happy where I don't belong? All my friends, all my favorite hang-outs, they're not here. They're back where we moved from. I don't have any friends here. I don't have any place where I belong.

I especially don't belong at school. There's all these faces I don't know. And nobody knows me. Those who think they know me, to them I'm just that new kid -- that new kid to ignore or put down.

I've never been surrounded by so many people and been so alone at the same time.

Some days, it's all I can do to hold in my tears until after school.

I will never forget my friends. They were the best. But that doesn't help much when they're so far away.

Why did we have to move?

When will I be in a place where I belong?

Psalm 138
A Psalm of David.

1   I will give You thanks with all my heart;
I will sing praises to You before the gods.
2   I will bow down toward Your holy temple
And give thanks to Your name for Your lovingkindness and Your truth;
For You have magnified Your word according to all Your name.
3   On the day I called, You answered me;
You made me bold with strength in my soul.

4   All the kings of the earth will give thanks to You, O LORD,
When they have heard the words of Your mouth.
5   And they will sing of the ways of the LORD,
For great is the glory of the LORD.
6   For though the LORD is exalted,
Yet He regards the lowly,
But the haughty He knows from afar.

7   Though I walk in the midst of trouble, You will revive me;
You will stretch forth Your hand against the wrath of my enemies,
And Your right hand will save me.
8   The LORD will accomplish what concerns me;
Your lovingkindness, O LORD, is everlasting;
Do not forsake the works of Your hands.

Your love is for real.

from PSALM 138

I thank You, Lord, with all I've got. You make me want to sing, which is a scary thing. I thank You for Your incredible love and Your truth.

You have shown me Your word, Your promises, and Your love are for real. You've shown me, not only in the Bible and in other people's lives, but in my life. You showed me in a way so big, I couldn't miss it.

For right after I prayed about what was real important to me. You answered in a way even more awesome than I hoped for. It blew me away. The way You answered made it real clear it was from You. Thanks! What Your word says about prayer and Your answering it isn't just words to me anymore. What Your word says about You isn't just words. For now You let me see it for myself.

Seeing You act in my life like that makes me hyped about You. And it increases my courage to trust You and to live by Your word. My faith is stronger now because of what You've done.

Oh Lord, You are great. For even though You are high and exalted and the King of Kings, yet You are concerned about me. You responded to my prayer in such an awesome way. You didn't have to do that, but You did. Because You're awesome.

Now I am so much more confident about life. I know, even when things get rough. You'll be there for me and will bring me through it all.

You'll take care of me and will accomplish Your good plans for me. And Your plans are the best. I can trust them, though they'll probably turn out different than my plans. All the things about my life and future that I worry and think about a lot, You'll take care of it all in Your perfect timing.

I can rely on Your strong love for me. It is faithful and forever.

Thank you for remembering me and acting in my life the way You have. Now I know You'll never forget me.

Psalm 139
For the choir director. A Psalm of David.

1   O LORD, You have searched me and known me.
2   You know when I sit down and when I rise up;
     You understand my thought from afar.
3   You scrutinize my path and my lying down,
     And are intimately acquainted with all my ways.

4   Even before there is a word on my tongue,
     Behold, O LORD, You know it all.
5   You have enclosed me behind and before,
     And laid Your hand upon me.
6   Such knowledge is too wonderful for me;
     It is too high, I cannot attain to it.

7   Where can I go from Your Spirit?
     Or where can I flee from Your presence?
8   If I ascend to heaven, You are there;
     If I make my bed in Sheol, behold, You are there.
9   If I take the wings of the dawn,
     If I dwell in the remotest part of the sea,
10   Even there Your hand will lead me,
     And Your right hand will lay hold of me.
11   If I say, "Surely the darkness will overwhelm me,
     And the light around me will be night,"
12   Even the darkness is not dark to You,
     And the night is as bright as the day.
     Darkness and light are alike to You.

13   For You formed my inward parts;
     You wove me in my mother's womb.
14   I will give thanks to You, for I am fearfully and wonderfully made;
     Wonderful are Your works,
     And my soul knows it very well.
15   My frame was not hidden from You,
     When I was made in secret,
     And skillfully wrought in the depths of the earth;
16   Your eyes have seen my unformed substance;
     And in Your book were all written
     The days that were ordained for me,
     When as yet there was not one of them.

17   How precious also are Your thoughts to me, O God!
     How vast is the sum of them!
18   If I should count them, they would outnumber the sand.
     When I awake, I am still with You.

19   O that You would slay the wicked, O God;
     Depart from me, therefore, men of bloodshed.
20   For they speak against You wickedly,
     And Your enemies take Your name in vain.
21   Do I not hate those who hate You, O LORD?
     And do I not loathe those who rise up against You?
22   I hate them with the utmost hatred;
     They have become my enemies.

23   Search me, O God, and know my heart;
     Try me and know my anxious thoughts;
24   And see if there be any hurtful way in me,
     And lead me in the everlasting way.

from **PSALM 139**

NOTE: This was my favorite psalm as a teenager. I prayed the last two verses a lot.

Lord, You know everything about me -- everything. You know everything I do and everywhere I go. You even know why I went there and why I did that -- though half the time I don't know why I do things.

You know every thought I think. I can't come close to keeping track of all the stuff going on in my head. But You know it all. What's better and maybe more amazing, You understand me. I'm misunderstood all the time, but You always understand me. You know where I'm coming from.

You watch me. You're interested in everything I do. You come to all my games. You even like to watch me sleep.

You know everything I say, before I even say it. And with my mouth, that's kinda scary.

And, Lord, You surround me. You're always looking out for me. You've placed Your hand on me to guide me, to encourage me, to calm me, to protect me . . . .

All this is too wonderful for me. I cannot take it in. I can not begin to comprehend it. It is too extreme, too high over my head, I'll never be able to get a grip on it. You are too awesome to me, Lord.

You are always with me.

You are always with me. Even when I want to do my own thing without You and I run away from You, You stick with me. You stick with me even when I feel like ditching You. You never let go of me. You always lead me with Your strong, gentle hand. That's how patient You are with me. That's how much You love me.

And when things get dark, so dark I can't see any hope, so dark I can't see any light, and I think my life will always be night -- You're there for me. No matter how dark the night is, you see. And you know where to lead me. With Your vision and Your hand, You lead me to the light.

Before I was, You knew me. Then You made me in detail inside my mom. You made me just the way You wanted me to be.

I know I can be picky about things like zits and my hair. If I look in the mirror long enough, and I often do, I can find some-

thing I don't like. But it is cool the way You made me. The way the whole human body works is amazing when I think about it; my body, too. My mom sure was amazed when I grew out of the shoes she bought me in one month.

You know me so well, far better than anyone else, even me. After all, You made me -- You detailed me. Nothing is hidden from You. I couldn't hide anything from You if I tried. And there's been a couple of times I've tried. You know everything about every day of my life. You knew it before I ever lived a day.

And You think about me now. You think about me always. You, O God, think about me! Lord, your thoughts toward me mean so much to me. All your thoughts are so valuable, vast, and infinite.

Some nights, I go to bed thinking about You, and how You're everywhere and know everything. I think about what You must be like, and what Your thoughts must be like. I drift off to sleep that way. And it's like You're there with me.

When I wake up, You're still with me. Because You are, I can go through the day and through life with confidence.

Lord, I'm glad You know me and are with me, because I need You. I need You to help me live this life right.

So search me and know me deep inside. Check me out as much as You want. Know the things I worry about, the things I dread inside. Where You can take those things away, do it. Where I just need to trust in You anyway, help me and give me Your peace.

And see if there's any way I think or live that will end up hurting me or others. Help me to ditch it and leave it behind. And lead me in living life Your way, which is the best and lasts forever.

Thanks.

BONUS

I still can't get over how awesome God is after I read Psalm 139.

This is as good a place as any to tell you of a free bonus you get as the proud owner of this book: a special section of my web site. The url for this section is:

www.godknows99.com/bookowner.htm.

I won't mess with passwords and such, but I'm not going to make this available to anyone but those who get my book.

The section may start out small, but I'm going to put in stuff like full color versions of my pieces with photos, opportunities for you to have input into my writing, and no telling what else. So check it out.

Psalm 140

For the choir director. A Psalm of David.

1   Rescue me, O LORD, from evil men;
Preserve me from violent men
2   Who devise evil things in their hearts; They continually stir up wars.
3   They sharpen their tongues as a serpent;
Poison of a viper is under their lips.   Selah.

4   Keep me, O LORD, from the hands of the wicked;
Preserve me from violent men
Who have purposed to trip up my feet.
5   The proud have hidden a trap for me, and cords;
They have spread a net by the wayside;
They have set snares for me.   Selah.

6   I said to the LORD, "You are my God;
Give ear, O LORD, to the voice of my supplications.
7   "O GOD the Lord, the strength of my salvation,
You have covered my head in the day of battle.
8   "Do not grant, O LORD, the desires of the wicked;
Do not promote his evil device, that they not be exalted.   Selah.

9   "As for the head of those who surround me,
May the mischief of their lips cover them.
10   "May burning coals fall upon them; May they be cast into the fire,
Into deep pits from which they cannot rise.
11   "May a slanderer not be established in the earth;
May evil hunt the violent man speedily."

12   I know that the LORD will maintain the cause of the afflicted
And justice for the poor.
13   Surely the righteous will give thanks to Your name;
The upright will dwell in Your presence.

from PSALM 140

There's evil men all around me, Lord. I need Your protection. Some think everyone is good deep inside. Yeah, right.

At times, I feel surrounded by evil people. And I can see their violence all too well. Other times, I can't see them or what they're doing. But I know doing wrong is all they can think about. They are always plotting to hurt someone. And I don't know when or where that someone could be me.

Whether in the open or in secret, their evil makes me nervous. For I don't know when these snakes might strike. And I can't withstand them alone. It's not so much that they're strong or brave. They're not. They are cowards. But their cowardice makes them dangerous. For they attack by outnumbering the innocent and by fighting dirty. They're not man enough to fight clean, one-on-one, face-to-face. Or they use concealment, trapping people so they can't defend themselves. One of their favorite traps is using hidden words. They speak their poison in secret, but spread it everywhere. What defense is there against secret slander?

I don't know where, when, how, or even from whom their evil will strike. So how can I defend myself? How can I live without fear?

You are my defense, Lord. You are the one who saved me. You are the One who has guarded me. And now I need you again. You are my God. Please listen to my prayers. Do not let evil against me succeed. Do not let evil men have their way. Keep me from their hands. Guard me from their words.

Instead, cause their lies and wrong to fall back on them so their plotting against me and others will fail and be no more.

Lord, thanks that You will make things right in the end. I know You are the God of justice. You take up for people who are put down -- like me!

Thanks. I need you.

Psalm 141
A Psalm of David.

1   O LORD, I call upon You; hasten to me!
Give ear to my voice when I call to You!
2   May my prayer be counted as incense before You;
The lifting up of my hands as the evening offering.
3   Set a guard, O LORD, over my mouth;
Keep watch over the door of my lips.
4   Do not incline my heart to any evil thing,
To practice deeds of wickedness
With men who do iniquity;
And do not let me eat of their delicacies.

5   Let the righteous smite me in kindness and reprove me;
It is oil upon the head; Do not let my head refuse it,
For still my prayer is against their wicked deeds.
6   Their judges are thrown down by the sides of the rock,
And they hear my words, for they are pleasant.
7   As when one plows and breaks open the earth,
Our bones have been scattered at the mouth of Sheol.

8   For my eyes are toward You, O GOD, the Lord;
In You I take refuge; do not leave me defenseless.
9   Keep me from the jaws of the trap which they have set for me,
And from the snares of those who do iniquity.
10   Let the wicked fall into their own nets,
While I pass by safely.

Living right definitely isn't easy.

from PSALM 141

Oh Lord, I'm praying! I need Your help. Please listen when I call. And help me to pray so my prayers will be good and pleasing to You. It's hard for me a lot of times to know what to say. I mean, what do I say to God? I sure don't want to say something stupid.

Speaking of saying stupid things, that's one of the things I need help with. All the time, I say stuff that's dumb, because I embarrass myself, or hurt a friend, or . . . because it's just dumb! It's like I have this wild tongue in my mouth that needs to be tamed in the worst way, but I don't know how, and I can't control it. Lord, help me! Keep watch over this tongue of mine before it hurts someone else or embarrasses me even more. I've found out the hard way that words can be dangerous. So guard my big mouth and help me to guard it and keep it under control.

My thoughts and desires can be pretty hard to control, too. I'm not going into detail because if it doesn't make me feel too guilty, it will make me too embarrassed. You know the struggles I have with my mind and my self-control. I need Your help. Help me with the thoughts and decisions I face every day.

Lord I want to live right. I don't want to do or say things I'll regret. So help me. And give me good friends to run with. Because if I hang with friends who are trying to live right, that will help me live right. If I have friends who care enough to smack me when I need it, that will help, too.

And when someone is straight with me and tells me where I'm off, help me to listen, take it well, and not get defensive. It's not fun, but it's a lot better than staying on the wrong road. Being told straight by someone who cares is a lot better than being sweet-talked anyway.

Help me to be a friend to those friends who really don't want to do the right thing. But help me resist their peer pressure. A lot of the stupid stuff I've done happened because my friends were doing stupid stuff, and I wanted to do whatever my friends were doing and be cool with them. But it's more important to me now to be cool with You. So if they want me to do wrong with them, especially stuff like drugs, give me the courage to say no and even walk away if have to.

Oh God, I'm looking to You for help. For You are the One I trust. And I need You. Life isn't easy. Living right definitely isn't easy.

Jesus, when I first trusted in You, I know that must have ticked off Satan. Now, he would probably do anything to trip me up and trap me. There are all sorts of traps he sets for teenagers, like drug addiction, alcohol, teen pregnancy, AIDS and other STDs, shootings, and gangs, just for starters.

But You're far stronger and smarter than him. And You defend me and guide me. It's a good thing, 'cause without You I would be defenseless.

So help me to keep my eyes on You, to follow You and Your ways. May Satan and his allies fall into their own traps, while I follow You close, while You lead me safely through.

Psalm 142

Maskil of David, when he was in the cave. A Prayer.

1   I cry aloud with my voice to the LORD;
  I make supplication with my voice to the LORD.
2   I pour out my complaint before Him;
  I declare my trouble before Him.
3   When my spirit was overwhelmed within me,
  You knew my path.
  In the way where I walk
  They have hidden a trap for me.
4   Look to the right and see;
  For there is no one who regards me;
  There is no escape for me;
  No one cares for my soul.

5   I cried out to You, O LORD;
  I said, "You are my refuge,
  My portion in the land of the living.
6   "Give heed to my cry,
  For I am brought very low;
  Deliver me from my persecutors,
  For they are too strong for me.
7   "Bring my soul out of prison,
  So that I may give thanks to Your name;
  The righteous will surround me,
  For You will deal bountifully with me."

Life is more than I can handle.

from PSALM 142

Lord, I'm praying to You straight. I'm going to be honest and tell You how I feel about life.

How I feel is overwhelmed and hopeless. Life is more than I can handle. And I can hardly see how it can ever be any good for me. I feel trapped in this so-called life.

And nobody cares. Nobody ever cares about me.

I think You care. You know what I'm going through. And You know what I should do, though I don't. You know the path I should walk. You see the way out, though I'm losing hope a good way exists. But maybe You have already prepared it.

So show me the way. I'm so down. I feel like I'm in prison in my life and inside, trapped in darkness. And I can see no escape. Oh Lord, hear my cries and lead me out so I can be free and happy again. Surround me with light and friends instead of darkness and uncaring faces.

I'd much rather thank You than be the downer I am now. But life is too much for me. I need You to help me, before I give up. You're all I've got left.

Psalm 143
A Psalm of David.

1   Hear my prayer, O LORD,
Give ear to my supplications!
Answer me in Your faithfulness, in Your righteousness!
2   And do not enter into judgment with Your servant,
For in Your sight no man living is righteous.
3   For the enemy has persecuted my soul;
He has crushed my life to the ground;
He has made me dwell in dark places, like those who have long been dead.
4   Therefore my spirit is overwhelmed within me;
My heart is appalled within me.

5   I remember the days of old;
I meditate on all Your doings;
I muse on the work of Your hands.
6   I stretch out my hands to You;
My soul longs for You, as a parched land.   Selah.

7   Answer me quickly, O LORD, my spirit fails;
Do not hide Your face from me,
Or I will become like those who go down to the pit.
8   Let me hear Your lovingkindness in the morning;
For I trust in You;
Teach me the way in which I should walk;
For to You I lift up my soul.
9   Deliver me, O LORD, from my enemies;
I take refuge in You.

10   Teach me to do Your will,
For You are my God;
Let Your good Spirit lead me on level ground.
11   For the sake of Your name, O LORD, revive me.
In Your righteousness bring my soul out of trouble.
12   And in Your lovingkindness, cut off my enemies
And destroy all those who afflict my soul,
For I am Your servant.

will the constant simply dissolve
or will i find myself here in this place
searching for something that tells me
screaming out loud my name
i feel i'm being summoned by this
calling out of the darkness
i've found myself returning
to the place i left behind
so long ago to toy with simple things
joshua stevens, from "only for a short while"

from PSALM 143

Oh Lord, listen to my prayer and answer me out of Your right-eousness and faithfulness. I'm not asking You to answer be-cause of my righteousness, because that's part of the problem. No one lives up to Your perfect standards, especially not me. So I pray You'll forgive me instead of judging me, because if You judge me I'm in even deeper trouble than I am already.

And I am in trouble and more. Satan and others who want the worst for me have crushed me down to the ground. My life is dark. Lately, there are times I feel like those who die too young.

I'd hear about guys who die young because of getting in-volved with drugs, gangs, crime, or driving drunk and other stuff. And I'd wonder how anyone could be that stupid. Well, now I know -- because I'm the stupid one. I've never been so ashamed of myself and so mad at myself.

I've been led into messing my life up big time. I'm not making excuses. I wanted to be led. Yet I didn't want to follow Your lead. I was more interested in having "fun" than I was in what was best. I was more interested in fun than I was in You.

I try to keep cool about it all on the outside. But inside, I can't handle it. I look at how stupid I've been and how far down I've gone, and I can't believe it. I'm overwhelmed with what my life has become.

I look back to how things used to be. I was a lot happier when I walked with You -- before I started running from You. I saw a lot more of You in creation and in You working in my life. It was cool. I want things to be that way again. I want to be close to

You again bad. I am so thirsty for You.

Answer me quick, Lord. I can't hold on much longer. I know I tried to run and hide from You more than once, but please don't hide from me. Because if you do, I'll really go down.

The night's dark now, but You can make my morning light. Let me experience Your light and love again. For I trust in You. I'm through with trusting in the wrong people and the wrong things.

And teach me to walk right, Your way. You're my God. Teach me to live like it. Bring me out of my trouble and give me a real life again. Instead of living for myself, I want to live for You. So let Your kind Spirit lead me.

Thank you, though living through now isn't easy, You give my life meaning and purpose. To serve You, to glorify You, to enjoy You -- what greater purpose is there? What can have more meaning?

And if You have a purpose for me, Your servant, You'll give me the guidance, the protection, and the power to fulfill it.

WHEN YOU'RE DOWN

Since 143 is the last of the "Bad Day" psalms, this is a good place to list some things the Psalms show us on how to handle down times:

1. Keep your focus on God and how great He is.
2. Don't focus only on your problems, but look past them at the big picture and focus on what's good. A big part of that is . . .
3. Get into God's word.
4. Pray
5. Read some Bad Day psalms. I'm serious. They'll help you see God knows where you're at and will help you pray.
6. Cry. There's plenty of crying in the psalms, so it's O.K., for guys, too.
7. Let yourself be down a while. The psalmists had to let themselves be down a while to write some of the psalms. And we sometimes need to let ourselves work through our feelings. This is especially important for grieving.
8. Pray for wisdom -- wisdom to understand your situation and to see the big picture (See #2) and wisdom on what to do. (James 1:5)
9. Remember things you can be thankful for and thank Him. (Philippians 4:4, 6-8)
10. Remember God is faithful. You can trust Him no matter what.

11. So trust Him. (See "Trusting God" after Psalm 37. Also check out Psalm 105.)

12. Trust God more than your own understanding and abilities. (Psalm 60: 11-12; Proverbs 3: 5, 6)

13. Don't worry. Worry doesn't help anyway.

14. Instead, pray. (Philippians 4: 6-7)

15. Music -- both listening to it and creating it. A lot of teens have told me music helps them when they're down. For me, down music helps me work through my feelings, and up music at the right time helps cheer me up. And, hey, the Psalms were songs. So the psalmists definitely used music when they were down.

16. Writing. Being a writer, this may be a bit biased, but I actually got this idea from others.

17. Be creative. This goes with the above two. Incidentally, being down isn't all bad. It can help creativity. There's a lot I have written I wouldn't have been able to without some serious down times.

18. Remember times in the past when God was good to you in a bad situation or brought good out of a bad situation. (Psalm 13:6; Romans 8:28)

19. When God helps you out this time, remember it so you can be encouraged next time. (I suggest keeping a journal.)

20. Be honest with God about how you feel.

21. Be honest with yourself, too. Some find making a list of what has them down helps as a starting point in eliminating that list.

22. Know God hasn't changed. He still cares about you.

23. Know God is in control of both the present and the future.

24. Remember God has a great future prepared for those who trust in Him, including you. (Psalm 37: 3-6, 34; Psalm 84:11-12; Proverbs 29:25 and elsewhere)

25. Pray.

26. Have some time alone with yourself and God. Go for a long walk.

27. But don't isolate yourself too much. When you're down, you might feel like just going to your room and being by yourself. And some time alone can be good. Still, we also need others, especially Christian brothers and sisters to encourage us. (Psalm 133)

28. Do things for others. I'm one of those who finds that ministering and being good to others helps get your mind off your problems and lifts your mood. More than once, I've

been in the dumps before, say, teaching kids the Bible on Sunday morning but afterwards was O.K. God using You in others' lives puts things in perspective and can make you feel better about yourself and life.

29. Get some good sleep. Sleep deprivation can weaken you mentally and make depression worse. And God "gives to His beloved even in his sleep." (Psalm 127:2)
30. Remember God answers prayer.
31. Pray.
32. Wait patiently for God to answer your prayers, knowing He'll answer out of His love and that His timing is the best. (Psalm 25)
33. Don't assume you're suffering because you did something wrong.
34. But if you know you've done wrong, confess it and ask God's forgiveness. (Psalm 51 for starters.)
35. Remember God loves you.
36. Pray.

Psalm 144
A Psalm of David.

1   Blessed be the LORD, my rock,
Who trains my hands for war,
And my fingers for battle;
2   My lovingkindness and my fortress,
My stronghold and my deliverer,
My shield and He in whom I take refuge,
Who subdues my people under me.
3   O LORD, what is man, that You take knowledge of him?
Or the son of man, that You think of him?
4   Man is like a mere breath;
His days are like a passing shadow.

5   Bow Your heavens, O LORD, and come down;
Touch the mountains, that they may smoke.
6   Flash forth lightning and scatter them;
Send out Your arrows and confuse them.
7   Stretch forth Your hand from on high;
Rescue me and deliver me out of great waters,
Out of the hand of aliens
8   Whose mouths speak deceit,
And whose right hand is a right hand of falsehood.
9   I will sing a new song to You, O God;

Upon a harp of ten strings I will sing praises to You,
10   Who gives salvation to kings,
Who rescues David His servant from the evil sword.
11   Rescue me and deliver me out of the hand of aliens,
Whose mouth speaks deceit
And whose right hand is a right hand of falsehood.

12   Let our sons in their youth be as grown-up plants,
And our daughters as corner pillars fashioned as for a palace;
13   Let our garners be full, furnishing every kind of produce,
And our flocks bring forth thousands and ten thousands in our fields;
14   Let our cattle bear
Without mishap and without loss,
Let there be no outcry in our streets!
15   How blessed are the people who are so situated;
How blessed are the people whose God is the LORD!

Who am I?

from PSALM 144

O Lord, who is man that You pay any attention to him? Who am I that You give me a thought? I'm just one of billions of people on Earth. And Earth is less than a speck compared to the rest of the universe. I feel and act like I'm something and am going to live forever, but really my life on this planet is just a breath in eternity.

Yet I'm significant to You. You love me and are faithful to me -- more than faithful! You protect me. You're like a shield and fortress to me. Anything that gets to me has to get through You first. You train me, strengthen me, and prepare me for life ahead. And when I am in over my head, You rescue me. Lord Jesus, You've already rescued me from hell.

You provide for me. And it's a good thing, because the way I'm growing and with everything I get into, I go through food and clothing pretty fast.

As if that isn't more than enough, You make me a part of Your plan.

You're at war against Satan and his evil. And You're gonna win! I get to be a part of it. You've enlisted me in Your army and are training me for the war. You're teaching me and strengthening me for battle. You're going to use me to combat Satan and his darkness on Earth, in people's lives. You're going to use me to free people from his oppression. By spreading Your word and meeting needs, I get to be in the front lines of Your liberating people out of Satan's doomed dominion.

Then, in the end, I get to take part in Your total annihilation of evil!

When the final battle is won, I'll be psyched out of my mind to march in Your victory parade. Then I get to experience Your peace forever.

It is awesome to have You, Lord, as my God!

Psalm 145
A Psalm of Praise, of David.

1   I will extol You, my God, O King,
    And I will bless Your name forever and ever.
2   Every day I will bless You,
    And I will praise Your name forever and ever.
3   Great is the LORD, and highly to be praised,
    And His greatness is unsearchable.
4   One generation shall praise Your works to another,
    And shall declare Your mighty acts.
5   On the glorious splendor of Your majesty
    And on Your wonderful works, I will meditate.
6   Men shall speak of the power of Your awesome acts,
    And I will tell of Your greatness.
7   They shall eagerly utter the memory of Your abundant goodness
    And will shout joyfully of Your righteousness.

8   The LORD is gracious and merciful;
    Slow to anger and great in lovingkindness.
9   The LORD is good to all,
    And His mercies are over all His works.
10   All Your works shall give thanks to You, O LORD,
    And Your godly ones shall bless You.
11   They shall speak of the glory of Your kingdom
    And talk of Your power;
12   To make known to the sons of men Your mighty acts
    And the glory of the majesty of Your kingdom.
13   Your kingdom is an everlasting kingdom,
    And Your dominion endures throughout all generations.

14   The LORD sustains all who fall
    And raises up all who are bowed down.
15   The eyes of all look to You,
    And You give them their food in due time.
16   You open Your hand
    And satisfy the desire of every living thing.
17   The LORD is righteous in all His ways

And kind in all His deeds.
18   The LORD is near to all who call upon Him,
    To all who call upon Him in truth.
19   He will fulfill the desire of those who fear Him;
    He will also hear their cry and will save them.
20   The LORD keeps all who love Him,
    But all the wicked He will destroy.
21   My mouth will speak the praise of the LORD,
    And all flesh will bless His holy name forever and ever.

I can't keep it to myself.

from PSALM 145

Oh Lord, I am too glad You rule. I'm going to thank You for who You are, every day. You are King of the universe. Yet You also are my God.

And You are so great. I could spend a lifetime, an eternity even, searching for everything cool about You, and what I'd find would blow me away. Yet after a million years of searching, I would have only started.

So I better get started now.

There's all Your powerful acts, in history and in people's lives. And Your power is infinite. There's all Your wonderful works, like creation just to begin with.

Creation can be so beautiful. How much more beautiful You, the Creator, must be. Your majesty has got to be incredibly glorious.

But You're not just up there being majestic. You are good and kind to us down here. And You're righteous, yet You are merciful to us down here who are not righteous -- all of us. You are very slow to get angry with us. I'm especially glad about that. Not only that, You love us -- You love me.

You rule. And Your rule is awesome and will be forever.

Yet You pay attention to people others overlook or ignore. You care about those who are down and raise them up. You are kind and generous to all who look up to You. You meet their needs. Though high and exalted, You are near to all who sincerely call out to You, especially those who pray for You to save them. You hear and answer their prayer. You give them Yourself and life forever.

And You never forget them. You never forget anyone who loves You. You keep them as Your sons and daughters and friends forever.

Lord, You are so great. You are so cool in everything You do. I can't keep it to myself, and I don't want to. I'm going to tell others about You, to my generation and the next. I'm going to tell about You until I die.

Then I'm going to enjoy You and praise You forever and then some.

But I'm not going to wait. I'm going to get started -- now.

Psalm 146

1   Praise the LORD!
Praise the LORD, O my soul!
2   I will praise the LORD while I live;
I will sing praises to my God while I have my being.
3   Do not trust in princes,
In mortal man, in whom there is no salvation.
4   His spirit departs, he returns to the earth;
In that very day his thoughts perish.
5   How blessed is he whose help is the God of Jacob,
Whose hope is in the LORD his God,
6   Who made heaven and earth,
The sea and all that is in them;
Who keeps faith forever;
7   Who executes justice for the oppressed;
Who gives food to the hungry.
The LORD sets the prisoners free.

8   The LORD opens the eyes of the blind;
The LORD raises up those who are bowed down;
The LORD loves the righteous;
9   The LORD protects the strangers;
He supports the fatherless and the widow,
But He thwarts the way of the wicked.
10   The LORD will reign forever,
Your God, O Zion, to all generations.
Praise the LORD!

They guarantee our freedom, but freedom isn't real.
Unless you know Christ, you won't know how I feel.
MxPx "False Fiction"
from *Teenage Politics*

from PSALM 146

I'm going to praise God as long as I live.

Most people praise and trust the people and things of this world instead of the God who made this world. That is off.

Especially do not trust in politicians. They can't save you or meet your real needs. But they try to create needs to take advantage of people. Then they try to get votes by promising to meet those so-called needs. But they can't keep their promises. And if they can, they probably won't. I've noticed on TV there's a lot of idealistic, and pushy, people who think if their people and their policies get in power, then everything will be all right. It won't. Political leaders mess the world up, then die, just like they always have.

Get it right and trust in God. He's got all the real power. He's the one who created the earth, the oceans, and the universe while He was at it. Sounds like power to me.

He keeps His word. Everything He does is right. He is perfectly just -- and not only for rich people with high-priced lawyers. He carries out justice for those who are put down. He meets peoples' deepest needs. He looks out for the new kid at school and is a Father to those without a dad. He frees people instead of oppressing them or taxing them to death.

Instead of sticking it to good people and letting criminals get away with everything like sorry judges do, God helps out the righteous and thwarts the plans of evil scum.

The more I read about what this world's governments, politicians and judges do, the more I want Jesus to come back and take over. That will be the best. And He will rule forever. Praise the Lord!

Psalm 147

1   Praise the LORD!
For it is good to sing praises to our God;
For it is pleasant and praise is becoming.
2   The LORD builds up Jerusalem;
He gathers the outcasts of Israel.
3   He heals the brokenhearted
And binds up their wounds.
4   He counts the number of the stars;
He gives names to all of them.
5   Great is our Lord and abundant in strength;
His understanding is infinite.

6   The LORD supports the afflicted;
     He brings down the wicked to the ground.

7   Sing to the LORD with thanksgiving;
     Sing praises to our God on the lyre,
8   Who covers the heavens with clouds,
     Who provides rain for the earth,
     Who makes grass to grow on the mountains.
9   He gives to the beast its food,
     And to the young ravens which cry.
10   He does not delight in the strength of the horse;
     He does not take pleasure in the legs of a man.
11   The LORD favors those who fear Him,
     Those who wait for His lovingkindness.

12   Praise the LORD, O Jerusalem!
     Praise your God, O Zion!
13   For He has strengthened the bars of your gates;
     He has blessed your sons within you.
14   He makes peace in your borders;
     He satisfies you with the finest of the wheat.
15   He sends forth His command to the earth;
     His word runs very swiftly.
16   He gives snow like wool;
     He scatters the frost like ashes.
17   He casts forth His ice as fragments;
     Who can stand before His cold?
18   He sends forth His word and melts them;
     He causes His wind to blow and the waters to flow.
19   He declares His words to Jacob,
     His statutes and His ordinances to Israel.
20   He has not dealt thus with any nation;
     And as for His ordinances, they have not known them.
     Praise the LORD!

from PSALM 147

It is good to praise God. 'Cause there is so much to praise Him about. My God is great! And He is strong.

His mind is strong. He knows everything. He knows exactly how many stars and planets there are in the universe, and He knows which one is which, every one of them. Now if only He'd do my math and science homework! God's understanding is infinite. Hey, He even understands me.

I told you His understanding is infinite.

He not only understands me, He appreciates me. At school, the ones who are popular and get all the attention are the good athletes and those who look like they could be on a magazine cover. That stuff doesn't impress God. He doesn't play favorites that way. He favors those who try to put Him first and who rely on Him. And He helps them with their down times. It doesn't matter if they're not with the "in" crowd. It doesn't matter if they're outcasts others reject. Instead of being all caught up with clothes, looks, and superficial stuff like people at school, He cares about who I am on the inside.

God is good to His people.

I especially like it when He decides to make it snow big. Who can stand before His cold? Not the school district. So I get school off. Praise the Lord!

What's even better is He's given us His word. God has spoken to us. When I dig into the word, there are a lot of times it's like He's talking straight to me. The Lord of the universe likes to say stuff to me. Can anything beat that?

God is the best.

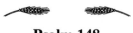

Psalm 148

1   Praise the LORD!
Praise the LORD from the heavens;
Praise Him in the heights!
2   Praise Him, all His angels;
Praise Him, all His hosts!
3   Praise Him, sun and moon;
Praise Him, all stars of light!
4   Praise Him, highest heavens,
And the waters that are above the heavens!
5   Let them praise the name of the LORD,
For He commanded and they were created.
6   He has also established them forever and ever;
He has made a decree which will not pass away.

7   Praise the LORD from the earth,
Sea monsters and all deeps;
8   Fire and hail, snow and clouds;
Stormy wind, fulfilling His word;
9   Mountains and all hills;
Fruit trees and all cedars;
10   Beasts and all cattle;
Creeping things and winged fowl;
11   Kings of the earth and all peoples;
Princes and all judges of the earth;
12   Both young men and virgins;
Old men and children.

13   Let them praise the name of the LORD,
For His name alone is exalted;
His glory is above earth and heaven.
14   And He has lifted up a horn for His people,
Praise for all His godly ones;
Even for the sons of Israel, a people near to Him.
Praise the LORD!

from PSALM 148

Creation praises God.

The stars and moon shining at night, the height of mountains, the flight of a bird, the underwater songs of the blue whale, all the different colors of wildflowers --all creation praises God and His strength, creativity, and beauty.

All creation should praise God. After all, He created it all. Black holes, galaxies, planets, moons, space dust, and the spaced-out, whales, elephant seals, sea cucumbers, and all kinds of fish, from big-mouth bass to catfish to mudcats to all those weird fish at the bottom of the ocean, lightning and hail, snow and fog, winds, hurricanes, tornadoes, and all sorts of weather, every mountain and hill, trees, from crabapple trees and hackberries to soapberries to redwoods, beasts, even the ones on the football team, kangaroos, orangutans and all cattle, centipedes, beetles -- especially VWs -- worms, yellow-bellied sapsuckers, tree ducks, and chickens, and all people, gerber-spitters, rug-rats, ankle-biters, yard-monsters, kids, teenagers, and old people, and even politicians and judges -- **all** should praise the Lord. Because no one comes close to being as awesome as God. His excellence and glory is way high over our heads.

And He cares about us. He is good to His people. He gives us life to beat a teenage pizza riot.

I want to be close to Him and tell Him how much I appreciate Him. — Because God is awesome!

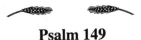

Psalm 149

1   Praise the LORD!
Sing to the LORD a new song,
And His praise in the congregation of the godly ones.
2   Let Israel be glad in his Maker;
Let the sons of Zion rejoice in their King.
3   Let them praise His name with dancing;

Let them sing praises to Him with timbrel and lyre.
4   For the LORD takes pleasure in His people;
    He will beautify the afflicted ones with salvation.

5   Let the godly ones exult in glory;
    Let them sing for joy on their beds.
6   Let the high praises of God be in their mouth,
    And a two-edged sword in their hand,
7   To execute vengeance on the nations
    And punishment on the peoples,
8   To bind their kings with chains
    And their nobles with fetters of iron,
9   To execute on them the judgment written;
    This is an honor for all His godly ones.
    Praise the LORD!

I'm so hyped about Him.

from PSALM 149

Praise God! He is excellent. I'm so hyped about Him and the life He's given me, the old songs aren't enough to praise Him. I want some new music to play and sing for God.

The usual times, like at church and youth group, are cool and I'm there, but they aren't enough to tell Him how much I appreciate Him. Heck, even the daytime isn't enough. I like to pray and just talk to Him in bed as I go to sleep at night and when I wake up in the morning. And it's not just because I want an excuse to stay in bed longer. I'm that glad God is my Creator. I am beyond glad He's my God. I am psyched He rules. He makes me feel like cranking up the volume and dancing. He makes me want to jam on my guitar and bounce off the walls.

And it's so cool He loves me like He does. Not only does He love me, He enjoys having me around.

He likes me.

I know life has its downers. I know there will be times when I'll suffer and when life will wear me down. I will even get old. But the Lord loves me and has saved me. I'm His. And He'll make everything perfect in the end. He'll even make me perfect.

Until then, my voice will honor God and praise Him. My hands will hold on to His word -- and it slices up evil like a double-edged sword. And the Lord will use me in His war against evil. What an honor it is and will be to be part of God's defeat of Satan.

There is too much I can thank and praise God about. So -- praise God!

Psalm 150

1   Praise the LORD!
Praise God in His sanctuary;
Praise Him in His mighty expanse.
2   Praise Him for His mighty deeds;
Praise Him according to His excellent greatness.

3   Praise Him with trumpet sound;
Praise Him with harp and lyre.
4   Praise Him with timbrel and dancing;
Praise Him with stringed instruments and pipe.
5   Praise Him with loud cymbals;
Praise Him with resounding cymbals.
6   Let everything that has breath praise the LORD.
Praise the LORD!

from PSALM 150

Praise the Lord!
Praise the Lord at church.
Praise Him outside enjoying His creation. Praise Him looking up at the stars at night.
Praise Him for all the awesome things He has done and will do.
Praise Him for who He is. He is majestic. He is Almighty. He is holy. He is truth. He is love. He is the greatest. He is God. He deserves all our praise. He deserves everything we've got.

So don't hold back. Get loud!
Bring out the brass. God's angels will one day. So make those horns wail!
Praise Him with every kind of guitar -- bass, electric, steel, twelve-string, you name it, with distortion pedals and huge amps, of course. Play loud enough to raise the dead. 'Cause when Jesus comes back, that's what He's gonna do.
Praise Him with a massive drum set. Drum out a monster beat like the power of God beating evil.
Break out and dance at how awesome He is. Mosh before Him. Crowd surf until you drop.
For there's no praise too strong for Jesus. No matter how much we give it up for Him, He's given far more. He is the best.
And He's coming back. Jesus is coming back to rule and make everything perfect. He is the end of all war and hunger and crying and pain. Jesus is the end of history. Jesus is the

end that's perfect, the end that's eternal, the end that's infinite.

So praise the Lord Jesus, the Messiah, as long as you're breathing. Never stop!

Praise God forever!

**Jesus is
the end that's perfect,
the end that's eternal,
the end that's infinite.**

PSALM INDEX

Although there are a lot of them, these categories are for starters. You might want to make up your own groups of psalms that mean a lot to you.

There's a lot of categories about when you're glad or happy about something. Most of these are good for when you want to be glad about the same thing, too. The other way around works most of the time, too.

Does that make sense? Good. Anyway, I hope these categories make sense and are helpful in all sorts of times and in life in general.

And remember the numbers refer to psalms, not to page numbers.

THINKING ABOUT GOD

On knowing God
Psalms 9 16 17 23 25 27 29 40 41 46 54 56 57 59 62 63 68 73 76 84 91 92 97 111 138 143 145 149

On being known by God
Ps. 87 113 134 139 149

On not knowing God
Ps. 77 95

Thinking about how high above us God is
Ps. 77 92 97 99 108 113 144

Thinking about how God created the earth and the universe
Ps. 8 19 29 33 65 104 124 135 136 148

When you're watching a serious storm
Ps. 29 77 93

Thinking about God's thoughts
Ps. 40 92 113 139

To know God appreciates you
Ps. 134 147 149

When you want to be closer to God
Ps. 42 61 63 70 84 99 119 131 143

To think about Jesus dying on the cross.
Ps. 22 85 98

When you want to tell people about God (or have problems telling people about God)
Ps. 9 40 71 67 92 96 105 145 149

ABOUT LIFE

When you want to put God first
Psalms 40 84 86 95 97 103 115 127 132 135

About idolatry
Ps. 16 97 106 115 135

About money and possessions
Ps. 39 49 52 135

About remembering the poor and needy
Ps. 41

When you want to make the most of your life
Ps. 1 18 40 67 71 81 86 90 95 108 127 128 144 149

Wanting to live right
Ps. 5 14 15 17 19 25 32 40 51 53 86 90 101 119 141 143

When you're glad God helps you live right
Ps. 1 26 32 81 108 111 122 127 128 144

When you wonder if living right is worth it
Ps. 1 15 24 37 39 73 75 109 112 126 128

When you need encouragement to do the right thing
Ps. 1 101

Needing help to know the right things to do
Ps. 5 16 19 25 32 81 86 119 141 143

Wanting to be clean and right deep inside
Ps. 51 86

If you think you can live up to God's standards and earn your way to heaven
Ps. 14 53

About being saved and received into heaven by God
Ps. 49 85 87

Having a really bad day
Ps. 88 102

When life gets too complicated or difficult
Ps. 11 25 46 61 124 131 142

When you're sick bad
Ps. 6 41

When you realize you're not going to be a teenager (or even live) forever
Ps. 71 90 103

When you're thinking about what you'll be like when you're an adult
Ps. 71

When you wonder if (or how) your life will be good
Ps. 1 25 37 39 60 75 80 90 102 124 125 126 128 138 142 143

When you think your life will never be good
Ps. 4 13 25 74 77 107

When you know you need God to help you get things right
Ps. 5 14 19 48 53 60 81 90 101 108 115 127 139 141 143

GUILT AND FORGIVENESS

When you feel really guilty
Psalms 14 32 38 51 53 103 143

When you've sinned and tried to cover it up
Ps. 32 51

When you need to confess your sin
Ps. 32 38 51

When you're suffering because of your sin
Ps. 38 41 51 89 107 143

Needing forgiveness
Ps. 19 22 25 32 39 51 85 99 103 106 130 143

When you've had it with your sin and it's consequences
Ps. 5 14 53 78 79 81 101 106 107 141 143

When you're bothered by your unintentional sins
Ps. 19 39

When you're glad God forgives you
Ps. 32 41 65 86 99 103 106 107 130

When you're affected by your family's sin
Ps. 79 106

When you need help with your mouth
Ps. 141

When you need help with your thoughts and desires
Ps. 19 141

ABOUT FRIENDS

When people are leading you wrong
Psalms 5 101 143

When friends betray you
Ps. 35 41 55

Feeling like you can't trust anyone
Ps. 12 55

Wanting faithful friends
Ps. 26 101 141

When you're glad you have your friends
Ps. 122 133

GOD AND YOU

When you're glad (or want to be glad) God is your God
Psalms 16 20 37 48 67 84 92 95 99 104 113 135 144 145 147 14

When you're glad you belong to God
Ps. 40 65 87 95 100 114 149

Happy to be His child
Ps. 68 87 131

To be glad God is with you
Ps. 16 18 21 23 34 37 41 46 68 73 91 108 121 125 138 139 144 145

To be hyped God is for you
Ps. 9 17 21 27 56 68 89 91 92 103 109 114 115 118 124 138 147

Thankful that God watches you
Ps. 34 56 91 113 121 139

When you appreciate God knowing what you're going through
Ps. 31 34

When you're glad God wants you to spend time with Him
Ps. 27 105 116

When you want to be close to God
Ps. 25 27

Thankful that God answers prayer
Ps. 3 4 9 17 18 20 21 28 31 34 40 54 65 66 81 86 91 99 102 107 116 118 120 138 145

To ask God to hear and answer your prayer
Ps. 4 5 17 27 28 39 54 55 61 69 86 102 119 123 130 141 142 143

To pray for others
Ps. 69

To ask God to take up for you (or for friends)
Ps. 9 10 35 44 59 60 64 109 120 123

When you're thankful God listens to you
Ps. 27 31 34 55 61 99 116

When you're glad God showed you in your life how awesome He is
Ps. 17 18 20 21 28 66 106 111 126 138

WHEN STUFF TICKS YOU OFF

When you're hyped God takes vengeance
    (or when YOU feel like taking vengeance)
Psalms 45 58 59 94 109

Ticked at liars
Ps. 4 5 10 12 31 35 50 52 58 63 64 109 120

Ticked at hypocrites
Ps. 26 50

About anger
Ps. 4

When you've had it with being a hypocrite
Ps. 101

When you've had it with religion
Ps. 40 50

Ticked at injustice
Ps. 10 14 45 53 76 82 94

When you've been cheated
Ps. 41

When you're angry at evil governments and politicians
Ps. 2 45 76 82 146

About cliques and racism
Ps. 117 118

About anti-Semitism
Ps. 83 129

Wondering why good people suffer and bad people don't
Ps. 10 73

When you're frustrated with evil people getting away with their evil
Ps. 10 36 37 50 52 58 59 94 146

On envy
Ps. 37 73

CONFIDENCE AND HUMILITY

When you think nothing can touch you
Psalms 30 66 91 108 125

If you brag too much
Ps. 20 52 53 75

If you want something to brag about
Ps. 20 108 135

If you worry about what people think about you
Ps. 20

When you need some humility
Ps. 14 30 39 53 107 108 127

When you're humble
Ps. 39 60 76 106 108 131 132 134

When you need security
Ps. 4 16 27 46 56 91 121 125 139

When you're not confident in yourself
Ps. 14 25 39 53 60 108 125 127 130 131 141 143

When you need confidence
Ps. 20 71 112 138

When you need strength
Ps. 84

About fear and courage
Ps. 3 27 46 56 57 91 112 118

When you're afraid to go to school
Ps. 49 55 120

TOUGH TIMES AND GOD'S PROTECTION

When people twist your words
Psalm 56

When people are trashing your reputation
Ps. 4 7 27 31 35 41 44 62 64 109 119 140

When people are cutting you down
Ps. 57 69 80 102 123

Being punished or threatened for something you didn't do
Ps. 7 27 35 59 69 120

When you're put down for being a Christian
Ps. 44 69 83 119 129

When you're put down for being Jewish
Ps. 83 114 119 120 123 129

When a gang is after you
Ps. 3 11 17 27 35 56 59 83 118 120 129 140

When the "cool" crowd is on you
Ps. 49

When you need protection
Ps. 3 5 17 23 25 40 44 55 59 61 120 140 143

When you need protection and only have time for a short Bible study
Ps. 70

When you're glad God protects you
Ps. 3 23 27 36 46 57 62 66 71 91 115 118 121 125 129 144

When you're thankful God protected you and brought you out of a bad situation
Ps. 18 34 56 66 103 107 116 124

When you're glad God takes up for the weak (or for you)
Ps. 9 12 17 31 35 45 59 64 72 76 83 94 107 109 113 116 118 129 140 146

GOD RULES

God is strong
Psalms 18 21 24 29 33 35 46 54 57 59 62 65 68 76 89 93 97 99 108 114 125 135 147

God is loving
Ps. 21 23 33 36 59 68 86 89 100 103 106 116 118 130 136 138 145 146

God is righteous
Ps. 36 45 65 89 92 96 98 99

God is just
Ps. 9 10 17 52 72 75 82 99 109

When you're hyped (or want to be hyped) God rules
Ps. 2 9 21 24 33 45 46 47 48 62 72 75 76 82 87 93 96 97 99 103 108 113 123 125 135 145 146

God doesn't change or get weak
Ps. 135

God's in control of the future
Ps. 33 46 102 110 125

God knows the way to go
Ps. 16 19 32 81 108 111 142

To ask God to show you the way to go
Ps. 5 25 43 61 86 139 141 142 143

When you've been waiting a llllong time for God to act
Ps. 37 126

Looking forward to Judgment Day
Ps. 2 50 75 76 82 87 96 98

When you're glad Jesus is coming back
Ps. 2 24 45 47 72 76 82 96 98 110 146 150

When you're glad Jesus came
Ps. 85 98

DOWN TIMES

When you're down
Psalms 6 9 13 25 42 69 70 88 89 102 107 113 116 126 142

When you feel nobody cares about you
Ps. 88 134 142

When you feel God's forgotten you
Ps. 13 42 44 74 102 134 138

When you feel God's rejected you
Ps. 43 60 74 77 80 88 108

When you need God, but He seems far away
Ps. 10 42 61 63 70 77 143

When you've been crying
Ps. 6 30 31 42 43 56 69 80 88 107 116 126

When your heart's broken
Ps. 34

When you're lonely
Ps. 25

When you feel like being by yourself
Ps. 11 55

When you think you don't belong
Ps. 118 120 137 142 146 147

After moving (when you wish you didn't)
Ps. 120 137

When you feel trapped
Ps. 66 142

When you're feeling small
Ps. 8 39 90 108 113 131 134 138

Feeling like a loser
Ps. 14 53 60

TRUST AND LOVE

About trusting God
Psalms 9 12 33 37 49 65 66 78 81 84 85 91 95 108 112 115 119
121 125 127

To trust and hope in God when you're down
Ps. 9 13 25 42 43 60 86 102 112 113 126 130

Trusting God in a difficult situation
Ps. 4 11 13 23 25 27 28 31 34 46 54 55 56 57 59 61 62 89 91 94
102 105 107 123 138 143

To be hopeful in tough situations
Ps. 42 43 54 57 138

When you love His word
Ps. 1 12 19 33 111 119 147

To thank God for doing His word
Ps. 12 56 111 138 147

To thank God for being good to you
Ps. 16 18 21 23 36 65 66 67 84 86 92 100 103 113 116 126 138
145 147

To tell God you love Him
Ps. 18 116 145

To cut loose and praise God
Ps. 92 98 113 135 145 148 149 150

When you want (or don't want) to go to church
Ps. 100 122

When you're glad God is good to You in this life, not just in heaven
Ps. 27 36 103 138

Thinking about how God takes bad things and uses them for good
Ps. 66 105 112 126

OTHER STUFF

For oily hair days
Psalms 23 133

For really long road trips
Ps. 119

When you only have time for a short Bible study
Ps. 100 117 123 131 134

History lessons!
Ps. 78 106

ABOUT THE AUTHOR

Mark Marshall once was a teenager.

Thirteen was both the worst and the best for him. First, his mom died unexpectedly. Later, just before he turned fourteen, he trusted Jesus and started a new life.

That didn't make his teen years easy. But he got through them somewhat sane with God's help. A lot of that help came through the Psalms.

At Duke University, his "In His Right Mind" student newspaper column both delighted and infuriated many -- and turned Mark on to writing. After graduating from Duke with a political science degree, then burning out on politics, he focused on his writing.

After a first novel (which he is now tempted to burn), then a post-modern American West novel (to be published in the future), and also having defeated world communism, he wrote God Knows What It's Like to be a Teenager, his first published book.

Mark is the director of GK Ministries. His web site is www.godknows99.com.

Mark is available for speaking and youth ministry. He may be contacted through his web site.

GROUP SALES

Discounts are available for group or bulk sales of 10 books or more. Contact Mark through his web site -- www.godknows99.com.

Or contact 139 Press; P.O. Box 2689; Denton, Texas 76202-2689